FROM OPPRESSION TO GRACE

FROM OPPRESSION

TO GRACE

Women of Color and
Their Dilemmas in the Academy

Edited by

Theodorea Regina Berry
and Nathalie D. Mizelle

STERLING, VIRGINIA

Published by Stylus Publishing, LLC
22883 Quicksilver Drive
Sterling, Virginia 20166–2102

Library of Congress Cataloging-in-Publication-Data
From oppression to grace : women of color and their
dilemmas in the academy / edited by Theodorea Regina
Berry and Nathalie D. Mizelle.—1st ed.
    p.   cm.
ISBN 1-57922-110-6 (hard cover : alk. paper)
ISBN 1-57922-111-4 (pbk. : alk. paper)
1. Sex discrimination in higher education—United
States. 2. Women in higher education—United States.
3. Feminism and education—United States. I. Berry,
Theodorea Regina, 1963– II. Mizelle, Nathalie D.

LC212.82.F76 2005
379.1'9822—dc22

                                        2005015760

ISBN: 1-57922-110-6 (cloth) /
13-digit ISBN: 978-1-57922-110-2
ISBN: 1-57922-111-4 (paper) /
13-digit ISBN: 978-1-57922-111-9

Printed in the United States of America

All first editions printed on acid-free paper
that meets the American National Standards Institute
Z39-48 Standard.

First Edition, 2006

10   9   8   7   6   5   4   3   2   1

CONTENTS

ACKNOWLEDGMENTS

Theodorea Regina Berry, Ed.D. On this road along the journey, there are many who have made the travel possible. But, first, there is the power of the Holy Trinity, who makes all things possible, for which I am deeply grateful.

It is with sincere appreciation that I acknowledge my family. It is the memory of my father, the late Richard Berry (April 24, 1934–February 3, 1998), that often encourages me when I just don't feel like pushing forward. And the special love of my mother, Verlene Catheryn Conway Berry (February 12, 1932–November 29, 2005), and my siblings, Kevin, Kimberlee, and Andre, that has kept me strong. Special gratitude is extended to Henry L. McDonald for his continuous support: Thank you for everything.

To my beloved sorority, Delta Sigma Theta Sorority, Inc., you have added new meaning to love and excellence in my life. Sorors Alissa Bonner, Vivian Norton, Crystal Brown, Georgia Edwards, Bonita Benn, Mildred Trent, and so many others have expressed immeasurable care and compassion while supporting important and worthwhile endeavors. Special Delta love to the sorors of 48 Destined to Deliver.

Colleagues such as Drs. James Anderson, Darrell Cleveland, Dionne Danns, Kimberly Gomez, Annette Henry, Marvin Lynn, Tayari kwa Salaam, David Stovall, Steve Tozer, William Trent, and William Watkins have generously expended their time and, frequently, their energy working with and/or listening to this Philly girl as she embeds her Germantown ways into her ivory-tower scholarship. I am grateful for your generosity. Special gratitude is extended to my AERA-IES postdoctoral colleagues and Dr. Felice Levine for her continuous support.

I am grateful for the loving prayers and support of my parish family at Saint Phillip Neri Catholic Church. You were always with me, even on those (numerous) days I was absent from your company, as I traveled on professional endeavors. Peace and blessings always!

To all of those who have touched my life in so many valuable ways, I thank you. The fingerprints you have placed upon my heart will remain forever.

Nathalie D. Mizelle, Ph.D.   To my beloved family: my mother and father, Dr. Richard and Julye Mizelle; my brother, Richard Mizelle; my sister, Dezmona Mizelle Howard; my brother-in-law, John Howard; and my nephews, John and David, whose continued love and support have been my inspiration. I cannot fail to thank my grandparents, Joseph and Mary Roberts, whose unconditional love has made me who I am.

Drs. Berry and Mizelle both wish to thank Dr. Christine Sleeter, California State University Monterey Bay, for her mentorship and guidance. Without you, this project would not have come to fruition. Your direction and support have truly been valuable. We sincerely appreciate your willingness to share with us.

We also sincerely appreciate the wonderfully fulfilling relationship with John Von Knorring, publisher and owner of Stylus Publishing. The process of developing and implementing a project like this can be challenging. We are grateful for your wisdom and guidance. Many, many blessings to you always!

Most important, we wish to thank all of the contributors of this volume. With your stories, many lessons can be found sprinkled throughout the pages. Your words, your tremendously powerful, spiritual, thought-provoking words, are now accessible for all the world to see! Thank you for sharing.

WHAT THE FUCK, NOW WHAT?

The Social and Psychological Dilemmas of Multidimensional Being as a Woman of Color in the Academy

Theodorea Regina Berry

Philadelphia, 2003. I walk into the living room of a longtime family friend and godmother to my younger brother. "Come on in, Dr. Berry," she warmly greets after giving me a snug hug. Little has changed about this room in the 30-plus years that I have known this woman and her family. Just past the multipaned white door of the vestibule, there is a large wall to the left filled with photographs of family members and friends: wedding photos, graduation photos, baby photos. To the right across the room is a fireplace with a mantel full of additional photos. On the side of the fireplace closest to the front doorway is a large bay window completely occupied with plants and tropical potted trees, some about 20 years old. On the other side of the fireplace is a staircase leading to the second floor of the house. Across from the staircase and along the same wall with the collage of photographs is a long and large sofa that extends to one side of the arched doorway to the dining room. On the other side of the doorway by the staircase is a large wingback chair.

"Oh, don't call me Dr. Berry, Miss Mattie. My students don't call me Dr. Berry," I gently protest. Miss Mattie proceeds to scold me for protesting, as if I weren't proud of my accomplishment. "You're the only one from the neighborhood to get an advanced degree, to go so far with your education. You should be proud of that, girl. You stayed out of trouble, studied hard, and got a good job. And you still come home. I'm proud of you. Be glad."

After I concede, we sit—Miss Mattie on the sofa and I in my favorite spot in the house, near the bottom of the staircase directly across from her. We continue our conversation, with Miss Mattie giving me the latest news about all of the people I grew up with in the neighborhood. New home purchases. Illnesses. New jobs. Deaths. New cars. New babies.

"Oh, wait. Let me get the baby photo album," she inserts as she gets up from the sofa and moves quickly into the dining room. Seconds later, she emerges with a small but thick photo album. "I keep a photo album with pictures of all the babies of kids from the neighborhood," she states, as she opens the photo album. I move to the sofa and together we look through the album. At the end, Miss Mattie turns to me with a look of disappointment and says, "You're the only one of the kids from the neighborhood who doesn't have any kids. When are you gonna have some babies?"

◆ ►☼◄※►☼◄ ◆

A longtime male friend called me earlier in the day and, during our conversation, expressed his guilt for not spending enough time with me while complaining about being tired and working too hard. So, we agreed to get together at my home just to hang out. We spent the evening relaxing in front of the television—just chillin'. In fact, he was so tired he fell asleep in the middle of the movie.

Just as he was about to leave, we went into the kitchen and began a conversation. There we were, both divorced and, to the best of my knowledge, both single, unattached, and alone. As in many homes of people I know, my kitchen is the hub of activity. So, it was not strange that we would end up standing and sitting in this brightly lit, well-decorated space. I sat at my kitchen table, a counter-level maple set with a stainless steel tabletop and matching stool-height chairs, on one side of the room. He stood in one corner of the room, leaning against the ivory countertop adorned with red and white appliances and canisters. Somewhere in the conversation, he started complaining about the number of African American women he had encountered who he felt had questionable virtues—women he believed to be manipulating, selfish, or gold diggers. "They find out I'm a lawyer and they think I have all kinds of money to spend on them. They always want something *from* me but aren't willing to do anything *for* me," he ranted. I listened patiently. Then I tried to explain that he should not put all African American women in a box, as if we were all the same. As he continued, he noted, "There are few women like you. You're not a single mother; you're not on welfare; you have a good job and a good education.

You're gonna go far and do great things . . . but any dude who wants to be with you has to live with riding on *your* coattails. He will have to understand that *he* will be second to your career. You know, just like Oprah and Stedman. And nobody wants to be Stedman."

◆▸▣◂※▸◌◂◆

Another conference. Different town, same cast of significant characters. But, I realize it's part of being in the academy—an important part. My conference roommate and I go out to what appears to be a very trendy restaurant for dinner that, subsequently, has a very trendy wait time for a table: nearly an hour. And we decide to wait. While we wait, we engage in a conversation about the challenges of being in a dual-scholar household. Mostly, as a graduate student in the midst of writing my dissertation and longing for the day I'll have a "real" life, I listen and take mental notes. You see, she and her husband attended graduate school together and then graduated together. This tall, slender, attractive, nearly 40 mother of two seems to me very secure in her goals and her relationship. I perceive the possibility of a mentoring relationship. However, as we continue our conversation, she reveals her dislike for male academic professionals who stray from their marital relationship to pursue female students. "I would never allow my husband to work so closely with a single female," she states, to make her point. "You mean to tell me that if your husband and I had similar research interests and I wanted to work on a project with him, you wouldn't trust that nothing would happen?" I ask. She responds, "Absolutely not. Too many hours working together alone. And things can happen."

◆▸▣◂※▸◌◂◆

It's always something (what the fuck?). As a woman of color, some facet of my multidimensional being is always a problem, a dilemma for someone. My social status in my personal, community, cultural, and professional spheres is causing fatigue to my psyche. But I can't change who I am. I won't change who I am.

I am an African American female teacher-educator, researcher, scholar, and community activist who is also a daughter, sister, cousin, niece, and aunt. I am single, divorced, and childless. I am also well educated, socially conscious, multilingual, and well traveled. I was born and raised in a large, urban, Northeastern locale, socially and politically tied to the African American community. I could go on and on because, you see, as a woman of color, there are multiple layers and sides to who I am. And one, if not more, of those sides is involved in sociological and psychological collisions with societal and cultural norms, ideas, and realities.

Raised in a community that is now largely African American I find that my trips home often remind me of the expectations of that community culture for an African American woman. Go to school. Stay out of trouble. Find a husband. Buy a house. Have some kids. In her own way, Miss Mattie reminded me that getting all the education you can is a good thing as long as you find a husband, buy a house, and have some kids. Clearly, no matter how many degrees I had earned, how much money I made, or how many other things I did, I was being measured by the one thing only women can do. Being Dr. Berry at home really didn't matter much on that terrain. For me, being Dr. Berry at home should mean that I can talk to friends and family about what I do and why I do it, integrating the cultural with the cerebral, while still kickin' it with the brothas and sistahs from around the way. It's not that I don't desire a home, a husband, and little ones to hug and love, but I don't see myself in such singular ways. Being a wife and mother are only two of the many ways I want to be in this life. And, I realize that when that transition happens, those two identities will need to be balanced with the others I currently possess. The effects of the coexistence of cultural and societal influences on the identities of women of color are many and variable. Chapters in this book address the sociological and psychological balancing of such identities.

My lawyer friend reminded me that many view it as unacceptable to be a single mother. Now here is a well-educated African American man who, in my mind, should be an ally to women of color. But he, like many others, views single African American mothers in limited ways: on welfare, having poor or limited education, with low-paying jobs. Yet, being with a successful, well-educated, hard-working African American woman would to him mean the man taking a backseat to the woman. Instead of seeing someone like Stedman Graham as a supportive partner, lover, and friend whom he should model after, he sees a man living in the shadow of an African American woman. In what ways can a woman of color in the academy challenge the very notion of such subservience, remain true to her work, and be loyal and supportive in her relationships? Chapters in this book address the multiple social positionalities of woman of color as scholar and spouse.

As a woman of color growing up in the academy, learning to stand on my own, taking first steps, mastering the language, walking, running, falling, and getting up to run again, I know that mentorship is important. It is important to have someone who is willing to guide and direct you (and, sometimes hold your hand) through the growing stages. It is important to have someone help you stand, hold your hands when you are learning to walk, and pick you up when you fall. But, as a single woman in the academy, I suffered the shock of learning that there are barriers to getting mentored, especially when there is the desire to be mentored by someone who looks like you. This book addresses the negative and positive psychological effects of being (or not being) mentored.

Now what? The women of color highlighted in this volume are from various walks of life and have endured differing and numerous trials and tribulations, joys and celebrations in American society in relationship to the multidimensionality of being a woman of color. The academy, a microcosm of this society, bears no exception to the existence of these dilemmas and rewards. Issues of race and gender have complicated our lives because "those identified as 'people of color' have been changed according to political circumstance" (Castenell & Pinar, 1993, p. 3) by those identified as "White" in American society. This was an attempt to place people of color "into monolithic, racialized categories" (p. 3) to perpetuate oppression, subdue and suppress conflict, and silence voices. The same holds true regarding the identity of womanhood. The White supremacist patriarchal thinking (hooks, 1994, 2001) often promoted in the United States leads both men and women to consider "tending to the house and home, to the needs of children, as woman's work" (hooks, 2001, p. 129), "leads men to be 'emotionally unavailable'" (p. 129), and "still encourages women and men to believe that paternal contribution to parenting is never as important as that of mothers" (p. 141). Identity that is placed upon us tends to be static. However, identity is a gendered, racialized, and historical construct. It is construed from what we know and what we don't know. It is construed from our experiences through and in place and time. For women of color, these experiences construct differences that we negotiate within the dominant culture that usually places us on the periphery of society.

Critical Race Feminism (CRF) places women of color in the center, rather than the margins, of the discussion, debate, contemplation, reflection, theorization, research, and praxis of our lives as we coexist in dominant culture. With its historical, philosophical, and developmental roots in law, CRF examines the intersections of race and gender in relationship to power (Wing, 1997). It has its origins in Critical Legal Studies (CLS), a movement that attracted White women and people of color because it challenged mainstream legal ideas that oppressed White women and people of color for years (Delgado, 1995; Wing, 1997).

From the CLS movement evolved the Critical Race Theory (CRT) genre, of which CRF is a part. CRF was developed based on the need to voice a distinction in the experiences between men of color and White women. The feminist movement appeared to exclude race as a domination factor in women's experiences (Davis, 1983; Delgado, 1995; hooks, 1984, 1990; Wing, 1997). Additionally, CRT perspectives "assumed that women of color's experiences were the same as that of men" (Wing, 1997, p. 3).

Three of the four characteristics of CRF are especially important to this particular work. First, CRF is supportive of and concerned with theory and practice. Adherents of the CRF movement believe abstract theorizing must be supported with actual concerns of the community. This book addresses issues concerning the academic community, home, and family in the personal narratives contributed. Second, CRF supports a discourse of resistance. This is to avoid the acceptance of the status quo, the dominant discourse regarding women of color as women and scholars, and to assist women of color toward overcoming the "double bind" (Wing, 1997, p. 5) of race and gender while providing different voices as multirepresentations of the counterstories. Including the personal narratives of women of color from various ethnic, social, and cultural backgrounds seeks to accomplish this goal. Third, CRF adherents utilize narrative or storytelling as counterstories to the narrative(s) of the dominant culture. This is done to emphasize critical race feminists as "anti-essentialists who call for a deeper understanding of the lives of women of color based on the multiple nature of their identities" (Romeo & Stewart, 1999, p. 4).

From Oppression to Grace: Women of Color and Their Dilemmas in the Academy highlights the experiences of women of color (women of African, Native American, Latina, East Indian, Korean, and Japanese descent) as students in pursuit of terminal degrees and as faculty members across the United States continuing to navigate the academy while facing the dilemmas embedded for others regarding the intersections of our work and our identities. This book focuses on the theoretical and philosophical viewpoints and understandings regarding the complexities and entanglements involved in coexisting within multiple identities embedded in race and gender within the academy with CRF as a central perspective. This book also explores various sociological, political, and ideological forces (and the histories embedded therein) that shape the experiences within this place.

Part One, Move on Up a Little Higher: Completing the Terminal Degree, provides works from scholars Amanda C. Bryant-Friedrich, Menthia P. Clark, Aki Murata, M. Francyne Huckaby, Tiffany S. Lee, Tinaya Webb, Ming Fang He, Kiran Katira, and Beatrice Bridglall. Their works, collectively, address issues of participating in the process toward a terminal degree, sociological and psychological struggles they encountered in the process, and the lessons they learned along the way. In each of their narratives, growth and guidance are central themes that permeate the multiplicity of their lives as emerging women-of-color scholars.

Part Two, Pride and Prejudice: Finding Your Place after the Degree (scholars Danielle Conway-Jones, Amanda Kim, Cassandra Sligh DeWalt, Cheryl Thompkins Horton, KaaVonia Hinton-Johnson, LaVada Taylor Brandon, Denise Taliaferro Baszile, Maria V. Balderrama, Mary T. Texeira, and Elsa Valdez) addresses the lives of these women with multiple identities as scholars with family, with friends, at home, and at work. Central to these narratives is the complicatedness of being all they are without being everything to everyone.

Scholars Adrian K. Wing and Sonia Nieto provide us with experienced guidance in Part Three, Words of Womanhood Wisdom: Voices of Senior Faculty Who Are Women of Color. Each scholar shares her journey with us and, in doing so, provides us with valuable lessons learned, foregrounded in the knowledge and revelation of their continual growth.

Although the focus of this text involves life in the academy for women of color through the central theoretical lenses of CRF, this text also includes diverse scholarship relating to the intersections of race and gender and the complicatedness therein. Menthia Clark utilizes Smith's (2003) "dis-dancing" as a means of viewing the complexities and, sometimes, discomfort in the moving to and fro between her intellectual and Southern identities as a Christian, African American emerging scholar. Ming Fang He develops a theoretical framework of in-betweenness, resisting the assumed movement from oppression to grace in her personal identity as Chinese woman-of-color intercontinental scholar. Amanda Kim focuses on Berry's (2001) use of intercultural space to identify her place as Korean American woman of color, scholar, and family member. Both KaaVonia Hinton-Johnson and Denise Taliaferro Baszile address the work of Patricia Hill Collins (1990, 1994, 2000) to place forward and center their issues of Black motherhood and belongingness, respectively, as women of color in the academy. Additionally, Baszile centers womanist ideology from the work of Alice Walker. As an advocate of CRF, I do not see these lenses working in opposition to CRF as a framework for this text. Rather, I view them as upholding some of the very tenets of this theoretical framework. All of these lenses center the identities of women of color. Additionally, each of them permits, encourages, and incorporates story/counterstory as a means of defying stereotypes/master narratives regarding women of color. Most important, each of these lenses puts forward a discourse of resistance, upholding the very significance of the presence of women of color in the academy. It is the multidimensionality of our lives within the community at large that makes our presence valid and viable.

This book emphasizes that women of color in the academy face dilemmas as emerging and existing scholars that profoundly shape our ways of being and living in the world. Likewise, it illuminates for readers various ways in which our work is shaped by our individual experiences, opportunities, and consciousnesses. This book highlights, through the lenses of CRF and other theoretical frameworks intersecting race and gender, the significance of the multidimensional nature of the lives of women of color scholars as we navigate through oppression and conflict in concert with issues of identity and self-definition.

References

Berry, J. W. (2001). A psychology of immigration. *Journal of Social Issues, 57*(3), 615–631.

Castenell, L. A., Jr., & Pinar, W. F. (1993). Introduction. In L. A. Castenell, Jr., & W. F. Pinar (Eds.), *Understanding curriculum as racial text: Representations of identity and difference in education* (pp. 1–30). Albany, NY: State University of New York Press.

Collins, P. H. (1994). Shifting the center: Race, class, and feminist theorizing about motherhood. In E. N. Glenn, G. Chang, & L. R. Focey (Eds.), *Mothering: Ideology, experience, and agency* (pp. 45–65). New York: Routledge.

Collins, P. H. (1990/2000). *Black feminist thought: Knowledge, consciousness, and the politics of empowerment.* New York: Routledge.

Davis, A. Y. (1983). *Women, race, and class.* New York: Vintage Books.

Delgado, R., & Stefancic, J. (Eds.). (1995). *Critical race theory: The cutting edge.* Philadelphia: Temple University Press.

hooks, b. (1984). *Feminist theory: From margin to center.* Boston: South End Press.

hooks, b. (1990). *Yearning: Race, gender, and cultural politics.* Boston: South End Press.

hooks, b. (1994). *Teaching to transgress: Education as the practice of freedom.* New York: Routledge.

hooks, b. (2001). *Salvation: Black people and love.* New York: William Morrow.

Smith, D. (2003). Foreword. In G. G. Generett & R. B. Jeffries (Eds.), *Black women in the field: Experiences understanding ourselves and others through qualitative research* (pp. x–xii). Creskill, NJ: Hampton Press.

Wing, A. K. (Ed.). (1997). *Critical race feminism: A reader.* New York: New York University Press.

PART ONE

MOVE ON UP A LITTLE HIGHER: COMPLETING THE TERMINAL DEGREE

THE JOURNEY OF AN AFRICAN AMERICAN FEMALE CHEMIST-SCHOLAR

Amanda C. Bryant-Friedrich

The Author

Born in Enfield, North Carolina, Dr. Amanda Bryant-Friedrich attended the public schools of Halifax County. The daughter of a farmer, she spent most of her time working on the family farm or taking care of the home when she was not in school. As she got older, she worked on other farms in the community. After graduating from high school as valedictorian of her class, she decided to attend college at North Carolina Central University in Durham. From the day she stepped foot on campus, she knew that chemistry was her major. She jumped immediately into the chemistry curriculum and during her second year started doing laboratory research under the mentorship of Professor John Meyer as a Minority Biomedical Research Support (MBRS) student. Finding that the laboratory setting was a perfect match for her, she became involved in laboratory research. For several summers, she spent time as an industrial intern at both Dow Chemical Company in Midland, Michigan, and Merck Sharpe and Dohme Research Laboratories in Lansdale, Pennsylvania. Even though these experiences were very enjoyable and challenging, she knew that she wanted to be a researcher in an academic setting.

Amanda dreamed of attending Duke University. After graduating from high school, she was offered a full academic scholarship to attend this university but was strongly advised by her guidance counselors not to attend. Even after completing four years of undergraduate education, the idea of attending Duke remained very important to her. In the fall of 1990, she enrolled as a first-year graduate student in the Department of Chemistry at Duke University with the intention of obtaining a Ph.D. in chemistry. After two very long and difficult years of struggling to prove to the department that she was worthy of being given the opportunity to pursue a Ph.D. in the department, Amanda was awarded a Master of Science in chemistry and allowed to begin her doctoral research. About six months into the doctoral program, she was informed that her research director had been denied tenure and was told that she would have to switch to another research group and another project.

At this point Amanda decided to pursue her Ph.D. in Germany. German universities accepted her M.S. degree as the first two years of graduate study, which was not the case for American institutions. In 1993, after attending several weeks of German-language classes, Amanda began her doctoral studies under the direction of Prof. Richard Neidlein at the Universität Heidelberg in Heidelberg, Germany, where she was able to pursue her area of interest in the field of organic chemistry. Professor Neidlein was in a pharmaceutical chemistry department, which allowed her to learn a great deal about not only the synthetic preparation of organic compounds as drugs, but also the technology and biology involved in the development of medications. In 1997, Amanda Bryant-Friedrich was awarded a Dr. rer. nat. in pharmaceutical chemistry.

Dr. Bryant-Friedrich acquired a postdoctoral fellowship at the University of Basel in Switzerland in 1997 immediately following the completion of her degree. It was at this time that she was introduced to the use of organic chemistry as a tool for the investigation of biological mechanisms, her current area of research. It was in the laboratories of Prof. Bernd Giese that she learned how to perform research in a multidisciplinary fashion. After spending two years in his laboratories, she decided that it was time for her to return to her home country and try her hand at independent academic research.

Dr. Bryant-Friedrich is currently an assistant professor of chemistry at Oakland University in Rochester, Michigan. In her current position, she has directed the research of several undergraduate and graduate students and has presented work at regional, national, and international conferences. She is the recipient of several research grants, with the National Science Foundation's Early Career Development Award (CAREER) the most prestigious. Her research combines the areas of synthetic organic and physical organic chemistry with bioorganic and biophysical methods to investigate several biological processes that involve nucleic acids. Her primary focus is to understand the mechanism by which cancer develops in the human body and to find ways to prevent these events from occurring.

Arriving at the point in your journey where you turn to look at how you actually arrived at your destination is always a defining moment. If you like what you see, you can actually sit and rest for some time to enjoy the view. If your journey was a wonderful experience, you can keep going to find out what other new things you can discover. If you don't like what you see or you want to forget the trip, you can run as fast as you can until you arrive at a new point and start the process again. My trip to academia involved a lot of running and very little enjoying of the view. I performed well in school, always mastering the materials presented to me and always thirsty for more. I was taught from very early in my life that mediocre was not acceptable and that school was to be my top priority. This resounding message came from my parents, my aunts and uncles, my many cousins, and even the sweet little old White lady for whom my mother made clothes. This attitude, along with the work ethic that my parents instilled in me and the idea that hard work came in many different forms, some clean and enjoyable and others dirty and unpleasant, made it possible for me to graduate at the top of my high school class and later magna cum laude from North Carolina Central University (NCCU) with a bachelor's degree in chemistry.

Gaining admittance to a graduate program in chemistry was not difficult. The low numbers of minorities and women in the physical sciences was then—and still remains—a point of national concern. Efforts to recruit individuals like me into the science and engineering fields were intense, and offers of admittance with beautifully accommodating financial aid packages were easy to come by. I actually applied to and subsequently gained admittance to only two universities, The Ohio State University and Duke University. The dream of going to Duke had been with me for many years as the result of a seed that was planted in me by that same sweet little old White lady for whom my mother made clothes. She always spoke fondly of her experiences at the university and extolled the high quality of her academic experience. Directly after graduating from high school, I was offered a full academic scholarship to attend Duke. However, because of the discouragement of school counselors and a basic "gut" feeling, I decided that this was most likely not the best place for me at that time in my life. This decision completely directed the rest of my journey.

I would never have imagined that admittance to the Ph.D. program at Duke was just the beginning of a rite of passage that would take me years of hard knocks to complete. The academic training that I gained at NCCU was excellent in that it taught me how to learn. However, I was not exposed to the materials required for success in the graduate program of which I was a part, at least not at the same level of intensity as the other students who entered with me. This made the initial course work very difficult and gave me a sense of fear and self-doubt that I had never experienced before. During that phase of my academic training, there was no time to contemplate why or how I had come to this point in my journey, because all of my energies were focused on continuing the trip. I can attribute my success in this graduate program to many different elements, but one of the most important would be my friends. When I started this program, I met and befriended a wonderful group of graduate students and postdoctoral researchers who came from a variety of socioeconomic backgrounds, ethnicities, and nationalities. No matter our differences, we all had a general love of humanity and an overwhelming desire to become excellent scientists in common. My weaknesses in physical chemistry were corrected by a wonderful classmate, who happened to come from China and who not only provided me with explanations of concepts that I had never seen before, but also performed this task with the compassion and patience required to make sure that learning the material was neither painful nor demeaning. My grip on organic chemistry was strengthened by a cohort of three students also interested in organic chemistry, two of whom happened to be of African descent, African American and Afro-Caribbean, and the other a "nontraditional student" who returned to graduate school after a period of time working in the real world. Organic chemistry, my strongest subject and the area in which I had decided to concentrate my academic studies, was exciting for all of us and a common thread that made our friendships unique and our commitment to the success of the whole very strong. These are only two of many examples that taught me that becoming a part of a group and not a bystander was my only means of obtaining my goal. Belonging was not difficult when I realized that outwardly we had many differences but inwardly we had commonalities that would allow us to surmount any barriers that language or culture could build.

The support of friends can, however, only go so far. All of the fear and self-doubt that were precipitated by my difficulties in the initial course work affected one of the most important decisions that a graduate student makes, choosing a research mentor. This choice dictates the overall tone of one's graduate experience in the sciences to a large extent. The relationship between a graduate student and his or her research advisor is one characterized by codependency and a need to please on the part of the mentored. When this relationship is dysfunctional, it has the same impact on the student as being a member of a dysfunctional family has on a child. The other members of the research group share this experience with you, and this group truly takes on the appearance of a dysfunctional unit. During the first semester of my graduate program, I was required to choose a research advisor. I knew that the mentor whom I ultimately chose was a treasure of knowledge from which I could obtain a great deal. However, I also knew from the experiences of other graduate students in his group that he was not the easiest person to work with and that the day-to-day laboratory atmosphere was a difficult one. Owing to my lack of confidence in my abilities and my diminished self-image, I decided it would be best for me to choose someone who was desperate for students to work in his or her laboratory but in whom other students would not be interested. After making this decision and becoming a part of the family, I made some very startling discoveries. The female members of the laboratory felt a significant amount of gender bias. We attempted to support each other as much as we could. At some point during my time there, we had all emerged in tears from meetings with our research advisor as the result of comments he made attacking our abilities and our desire to become good scientists.

After the course work was successfully completed and the department decided that I still had something to prove, it was announced to me that I would have to go through the preparation and defense of a master's thesis in order to enter the Ph.D. program formally. The fulfillment of such a requirement was not usually necessary for progression through the doctoral program. This was definitely a point where looking back was not an option because the trip leading to that point had been bitterly difficult and I wanted the trip ahead to be over as soon as possible. The fact that I had to prepare a thesis and defend it immediately made me different from the rest of my classmates and put an incredible dent in my already shattered ego. Again, my newly made friends came to my rescue. How? By not making me feel different through treating my preparation for the master's exam just as they treated their own preparation for the preliminary exams that were a requirement to become a Ph.D. candidate. They also provided me with academic and emotional support as well as the type of encouragement that friends provide in hard times. One of these friends, who provided me with the crucial coaching and support that resulted in the very successful defense of my thesis, is now my husband.

My research advisor was denied tenure several months after I received my master's degree. At this point, I realized that the entire experience had brought me to a point where I should make some serious decisions about my pursuit of happiness. The loss of my research mentor, as the result of a negative tenure decision, meant that I would have to find a new mentor either at Duke or at another university. It would also mean beginning a new research project with a new chemical direction. Having invested more than two years in obtaining my master's degree and having already started the research for my dissertation, I was devastated. This devastation resulted in the most life-changing decision I have ever made: to leave the country and pursue my Ph.D. in Europe.

Besides the academic challenge, the cultural challenge related to pursuing a graduate degree in a top-ranked university was quite daunting. Circumventing one's own cultural norms and expectations can be difficult. Being thrown unexpectedly into a new culture is like getting on the wrong plane and landing in a foreign country whose language and culture you know only superficially. Climbing the academic ladder has had some of the same hallmarks for me. Because many African Americans of my generation are still the first in the family to attend graduate school, the nuances of the academic world at this level are still foreign to us, and we have few guides, mentors, or family accounts that can teach us how to avoid the pits in the road from our own cultural perspective. African American culture for me has always been one full of nurturing, where hard work is merited and you are never beaten when you are down. Many of those who have gone through the very difficult experience of obtaining a Ph.D. and the additional trials and tribulations related to becoming a faculty member have decided that the experience should be just as difficult for those who follow them. This type of initiation-through-hazing mentality is most likely not something that most people would expect to find in an academic environment. This stress, compounded with the lack of preparation that many African Americans enter graduate programs with, especially in the sciences, makes the experience for many al-most unbearable. The feeling of isolation based on race and/or ethnicity, and the realization that the same prejudices that we encounter on a regular basis in the grocery store or the mall department store are also found within the ivy-covered towers, can be earth shattering. It is extremely difficult to make someone of another ethnic background truly understand that a fear of "the man" that was instilled in you at an early age for your own safety affects your interactions with non–African American faculty and students. That the feelings of discomfort you felt as a child when entering a restaurant filled with mostly White patrons may come back to you when you enter a class-room of the same description is difficult to explain to someone who has not experienced such discomfort. These feelings made it very difficult for me to seek help when help was needed or to make demands that would have been in my better interest instead of taking what was given to me.

Many African Americans throughout history have abandoned the United States to pursue knowledge and understanding without the restraints of racial bias. It is true that European countries also have their own issues with racial and ethnic oppression. However, without the historical baggage that the United States carries when it comes to the treatment of people of color in higher education, some of the factors that I have mentioned that make the graduate experience so difficult for many of us fall away in Europe. In Germany, where I received my Dr. rer. nat in pharmaceutical chemistry, I never felt that failure was expected of me because of my skin color. I was given the opportunity to prove myself to my teachers and schoolmates with-out battling preconceived bias. After completing my degree, I moved on to Switzerland, where I performed postdoctoral research. Again, the same was true. I believed my intellect was allowed to flourish under these conditions.

There was, however, one drawback to my decision to leave the country. I knew from very early on in my academic career that I wanted to become a faculty member at a research-oriented university. Having left the United States after obtaining my master's degree, I had not established the type of professional connections needed to obtain a faculty position. I contacted American professors who came to visit my university when I was a postdoc-toral researcher, but most of them offered only superficial support or none at all. In attempts to gain some type of footing in the academic arena, I accepted a position as a lecturer at a large urban research-intensive university.

My graduate and postdoctoral research experiences encompassed a span of approximately six years. These years coincided with an age range in which most young adults develop many of the social and political viewpoints that shape them as individuals for the rest of their lives. As it would be, I developed into a strong-willed "womanist" who always looks for the good in every individual and believes that the future should be better than the past. A naïve and optimistic individual, I thought that academia in the United States would have the same attitude, at least to some extent, as I did. It was the most painful experience in my life to find that this was not true.

When the company for which my husband worked decided to transfer him from Germany to the United States, I started to look for positions in the same geographical area as his new location. We had spent the two years of my postdoctoral fellowship at different addresses, and we knew that we did not want to do this again. I sent an application to a university for a lecturer position through the wife of a professional acquaintance of my husband's who also held a lecturer position at the university. The department chair seemed very excited about the prospect of having someone of my description become a part of the faculty. He expressed to me that he saw a need for more diversity in the department and that the position could very likely turn into a tenure track appointment. This urban university, which boasts one of the highest enrollments of minority students without the classification of a historically Black college and university, has an excellent reputation both in research and in the quality of education that it offers. It was also 30 minutes away from our new place of residence, so, of course, when I was offered the position, I jumped at the opportunity. Very shortly after my arrival I began to teach several courses and became a quite popular instructor. My teaching evaluations were outstanding, and my interactions with the students were very positive. I was generously given $1,000 to perform research in a small space provided by the department chair. Things were starting off well. However, it took only a short amount of time for me to realize that even though several of my colleagues were very supportive of me becoming an assistant professor on the faculty, several members of the faculty had no interest in my receiving a tenure track appointment. This resulted in discussions that attacked my reputation as a scientist and included references to my being considered for hiring only because of my race and gender. After making the realization that I was in hostile territory, I presented the department with an ultimatum—either tenure track or I would leave and start looking for other academic positions. The department ultimately decided not even to give me the chance to present myself as a serious faculty candidate through an interview. Having me around in a subordinate position as an instructor who could assist the vast number of students thirsty for mentoring or to give the appearance of increased diversity was fine, but considering me as the well-rounded scientist that I am was out of the question.

Even though the desire to diversify academic departments across the country is a genuine objective, the success rate is dismal, to say the least. One of the reasons for this can be derived from my experience. Well-meaning individuals who have the power to make change try diligently to force others to get on the bandwagon that preaches inclusion of all individuals in all academic arenas. This tactic is very hurtful for the new person who is brought in, especially if he or she has no idea as to the real motivations for the hire. The promotion of diversity through faculty hiring should be based on choosing quality individuals, those who have a strong desire to perform well and a true understanding of the need for the representation of all groups in all aspects of society. It should not be done to enhance the image of an individual, a department, or a university by creating the appearance of social progressiveness. Just having one of "those" is not enough to truly create a race-, ethnic-, and gender-unbiased atmosphere. There must be a general feeling of cohesiveness among the whole that the success of the entire country is based on the success of each individual, each race, and both men and women.

All of my experiences prepared me for my current position as an assistant professor of chemistry at Oakland University in Rochester, Michigan. The university is a progressive suburban institution that offers high-quality instruction and the infrastructure and commitment required to perform cutting-edge research. The most difficult part of being a minority at such a progressive institution is that you are very frequently called to the plate to participate in all aspects of university life because of the institution's strong desire to establish full inclusion of all individuals in every aspect of the academic process. Owing to the still low numbers of minority faculty at Oakland and most other institutions, achieving this goal requires that a few serve in many different capacities. This requirement combined with the normal responsibilities of an assistant professor can be a bit overwhelming.

On a final note, I would just like to muse a few moments about some of the things that still surprise me about the attitudes of students and faculty both minority and majority. I have had so many students come to me and say in a hushed whisper that I am the first African American teacher that they have ever had since they started kindergarten. Those who are socially aware speak to me about the struggles that I must have overcome to get to the point in my career where I am today. I often remind them that we all have our struggles. Whether they are created by the constructs of an ailing society or by the shortcomings of an unhealthy family situation, they are still struggles, and the same tactics can be used to overcome their difficulties and obtain their dreams.

As far as faculty members are concerned, I have made a very important decision. Those who have no interest in my continued success are of no interest to me. Through conference attendance and participation in several professional organizations and committees, I have established a very supportive network of world-renowned scientists who are committed not only to my success but the success of others like me. They accept me not only as a minority female but also, more important, as a scientist who is committed to the advancement of my discipline and improvement of the quality of life of all individuals through science. How did I create this network? I used my work as my business card. When the scientific community recognized the significance and quality of my work, the gender and the race of the individual behind the work became much less important.

2

MY SKIN IS BROWN AND I DO NOT WEAR A TIE

Exploring My *Selves* as a Southern, Black, Educated, Christian Woman

Menthia P. Clark

The Author

Menthia P. Clark's educational career has always been centered on activism, so much so that prior to entering the doctoral program, she did not even know the differences between the big "qs"—qualitative and quantitative research. After earning her master's degree in educational administration, she decided to work and travel before pursuing her life's dream of teaching middle school English. These travels sent her to Malawi, Central Africa, where she worked with the International Foundation for Education and Self-Help as a member of the Teachers for Africa program. The cohort was assigned to develop special education programs in this newly democratic state. Though Menthia did not meet the minimum three-year teaching requirement, a sign language course she had taken out of curiosity became her ticket to Africa. The only applicant from the pool with such knowledge, she became the "Sign Language Expert," with the daunting job assignment of developing a sign language for the country of Malawi.

Menthia accepted the challenge, admittedly a bit fearful, but excited about the task she faced. While in Malawi, she taught teacher trainees who were working with hearing-impaired children. One day, while observing the children, she noticed the trainees' fascination with the American Sign Language book she carried everywhere. They had never seen a documentation of sign language, and they were amazed to see it in print. This was her motivation to produce a book to "legitimize" their language. Instead of teaching the American Sign Language, she worked with the teacher trainees and the hearing-impaired children to publish the first and only sign language book in the country, *Children's Sign Language at Maryview School for the Deaf in Malawi.* Menthia took the teacher trainees into the schools to observe and document their language, using the hearing-impaired students as experts and a local artist to complete the work for this publication. This was her first major research project.

Upon completing her tenure in Malawi, Menthia returned to the United States with the intent to complete more research and enroll in a graduate program. She applied and was accepted at a prestigious Midwestern university and found that the "culture shock" was more profound at this school than what she had experienced when she moved to Malawi! After one semester, she transferred to Louisiana State University (LSU), where she is currently a doctoral candidate in the Department of Educational Leadership.

Menthia makes the most of her graduate program, maximizing opportunities to present at conferences, attend symposiums, and encourage other graduate students to do the same. Though she has not attended any football games at LSU, she is still recognized as an outstanding student, earning the Huel Perkins Doctoral Fellowship, and she is the founder and president of the ELRC Graduate Student Association. She has presented papers at American Educational Research Association, Southwest Educational Research Association, and Louisiana Educational Research Association conferences. In addition, she serves the Baton Rouge community, as a board member for a nonprofit agency that assists former women inmates, Connections for Life, Inc., and as a cell leader at Bethany World Prayer Center. This year, the Baton Rouge chapter of the American Association for University Women awarded Menthia a scholarship to support her dissertation research, which is an ethnography focusing on academic achievement and racial identity among high-achieving Black female middle school students. She looks forward to completing her dissertation, graduating, and engaging in the next exciting challenge.

One day in a graduate-level course at a large Midwestern university, the White male professor jokingly claimed he felt powerless because his normal style of delivering the lecture was thwarted by the stimulating conversations of the students. Instead of stopping the discussions in which we were so passionately involved, he allowed the talk to continue and joined the debate. When commenting on the professor's "lack of power" this particular night, a male graduate student who noticed his uncommonly casual attire jokingly warned, "Next week wear a tie; then you will get your power back." Immediately my mind began to wander as I processed that statement, and I came to the jarring conclusion that the tie is a piece of clothing that indicates power, but I do not wear a tie. I frankly asked my fellow classmate, "Well, what do I wear when I want to exude power?" He paused, looked me over, and rudely retorted, "Wear a power suit."

While everyone else in the class laughed, I searched for the face of someone—anyone—who did not find humor in such a sexist comment. I found no one. As class continued, I thought about the meanings of these images and the connection between a typically male piece of clothing and power. Questions came to my mind, such as, Why is it that when a woman in a position of authority wears a suit, it is not simply a suit, but it is known as a "power suit"? This widely held belief suggests that without that clothing, she cannot exude authority. Why is a tie, a Westernized masculine clothing accessory, considered the ultimate expression of power? As I thought even deeper, I came to a painful, yet startlingly true, realization: not only is the professor the "right" gender, and thus able to wear comfortably the authentic symbol of power, he is also the "right" race, and thus able to assume a position of authority comfortably (Meyers, 2002). When I, a Black female, wish to exude authority, should I wear a "power suit" (skirt or pants?) since I do not wear a tie? That is only a small piece of the puzzle; what can I do about my race? Is there anything I can wear that displays power despite the fact that not only am I a woman, but I am a Black woman?

Prior to attending that university, I taught sign language for one year in Malawi, Central Africa, and traveled extensively throughout the United States. However, coming back to America and subsequent experiences at that institution constituted the biggest "culture shock" I had ever faced. This was my first year facing the rigors of the academy; I had been sheltered at my historically Black undergraduate institution and nurtured by a Black female mentor at the institution where I received my master's degree.[1] This place, however, was quite different, for other Black female graduate students also expressed a lack of shelter, nurture, and protection in their respective departments in conversations about our experiences. After one semester, I decided that my emotional health and sense of belonging were too important to sacrifice, so I transferred without any regrets. That seemingly minute "power suit" incident was only one example of a series of disappointments and hostilities I endured. However, it became the foundation of my investigation of the intricacies of being a Black, educated, Christian woman from the South.

My search for understanding of identity led me to Lorde (1990; in Wing, 2000), who claims there are many coexisting selves that constitute an individual, though women are often forced to choose which *self* to portray: "I find I am constantly encouraged to pluck out some aspect of myself and present this as a meaningful whole, eclipsing or denying the other parts of myself. But this is a destructive and fragmented way to live" (p. 85). So I began to consider myself juxtaposed against my *selves*. My self as a Southerner. My self as a Black woman. My self as an educated woman. My self as a Christian. My future self. Utilizing the lens of Critical Race Feminism (Wing, 2000), which explores the lives of women facing multiple discrimination framed in the belief that "identity is not additive. Black women are not White women plus color, or Black men plus gender" (p. 7), this essay deconstructs and reconstructs my *selves* through personal narrative, philosophical musings, and counterstories (Delgado, 1995).

Allow Me to Introduce My *Selves*: Shall We Dance?

Historically, Black women have been unjustly slapped by the gargantuan hands of media and societal misrepresentations that depict us as too loud, brassy, flashy, dominant, sexualized, and overbearing (hooks, 1981; Jones &

Shorter-Gooden, 2003). The great tragedy is the entrance and permeation of these stereotypes in higher education, where these images take residence and are expressed in inequitable hiring practices and discriminatory attitudes (Gregory, 1999; Meyers, 2002). Black women in the academy who contend with such stereotypes often unconsciously disengage from themselves and create or emerge into new women, women who are disenfranchised and racked with conflict over the need to express who they really are (Fordham, 1993; Jones & Shorter-Gooden, 2003). The turmoil between changing, altering, suppressing, or forgetting the former self and re-creating and emerging as a new academic self disconnected from the past leaves women scholars with a fragmented, unauthentic identity. Women of color in the academy often express difficulty in merging their different selves into a whole when the institution does not value or validate the uniqueness of their race, class, gender, or background (Fordham, 1993; Gregory, 1999; Jones & Shorter-Gooden, 2003; Smith, 2003; Snearl, 1997). As Smith (2003) explains:

> As a Black woman who has been educated in some rather elite White institutions, I struggled, and still struggle, to "prove" myself worthy of such a "privilege." I work hard at staying in my mind and not allowing spirit to visit me as I speak about critical education theory, womanist/feminist theory and pedagogy, or qualitative/ethnographic research. It is the dis-dancing with myself that creates a kind of distancing from the southern Black girl/woman who enjoys spirit-filled conversations that push the boundaries of a different kind of intellectual life. (p. vii)

Smith's (2003) very accurate description of "dis-dancing" captures my life in the academy as I evaluate my experiences in the classroom, attending conferences, and during scholarly presentations. Like Smith (2003), I also grew up in the South, and I find myself dancing between my intellectual and Southern identities. I dance between my native, Southern tongue and the academic tongue that I continuously refine (Lanehart, 2002). When I get too excited in intellectual/academic circles, I find myself reverting to a Southern twang that I try to subvert in such arenas. So I switch back to my educated self, calm down, and begin speaking again. It is a never-ending "dis-dancing," not a tango, because that takes two, but more of a lindy hop, which is a constantly evolving, ever-flowing rhythmic dance movement that is re-created and refined as it is produced.

When women in the academy dance between identities, it creates a hierarchy between selves, and the Black/Southern/working class/ethnic self is often relegated to a lower position than the academic self. Fortunately, I am now at a place in my academic endeavors where I feel a relative sense of success in merging, collaborating, and infusing my *selves* into my scholarly work. In fact, this dance has brought me to my dissertation topic on Black high-achieving middle school girls who are proud of their academic accomplishments, and also proud to be Black, a topic of great concern, because, unfortunately, I did not have the liberty to enjoy my academic success and Black identity as an adolescent.

Though I dance between identities, I am keenly aware that my academic status is more advantageous than my Southern identity in some respects and affords me the opportunity to enter into circles and arenas in which my race/class does not. As Wing (2000) states, women of color, though subject to multiple forms of discrimination, have some identities that relatively privilege them. I wrestle with this statement, painful as it is to someone who tries to "keep it real," because it is the stark realization that some people view me in higher regard than other Black women because I am educated. Reluctantly, I accept this privilege with the ultimate humility and innate knowledge that although I have chosen the less-traveled road of intellectualism, I do not believe that I am better than people who are not educated. Smith's (2003) identity as a member of the academy and my identity as a doctoral candidate preclude our shared Southern heritage and allow us privileges that many of our other sisters of color with similar backgrounds are not privy to (Wing, 2000), thus bringing into question the possession of such privilege, and causing concern with the necessity to prove our worth.

"Dis-dancing" (Smith, 2003) oneself and engaging in fragmenting of identities (Lorde, 1990) is a common activity among high-achieving Black women, and these dilemmas do not begin upon entrance into the academy. However, they are evidenced from childhood and extend into adulthood (Fordham, 1993; Grantham & Ford, 1998; Hemmings, 1998; Horvat & Antonio, 1999; Schultz, 1999). Female members of the academy contend with pressure to alter their behaviors and appearances to fit into this male-dominated arena and are involved in strategies such as gender passing (Fordham, 1993), silencing (Davidson, 1996; Evans, 1988; Fordham, 1993; Harrison, 1997; Irvine, 1990), cultural code switching (Horvat & Antonio, 1999; Lei, 2003; Schultz, 1999), and shifting (Jones & Shorter-Gooden, 2003) to detract from negative stereotypes of women. Unfortunately, a high-achieving woman of color must often work tirelessly to prove she is educated, articulate, and well spoken, and she often counteracts negative images through an equally disturbing means of silence (Davidson, 1996; Evans, 1988; Fordham, 1993; Lei, 2003).

As Evans (1988) explains in her landmark article about loud Black girls, schools often fail to acknowledge the existence of high-achieving Black female students, and, therefore, despite her academic achievement she was invisible, ignored, and unrecognized at school. Fordham (1993) elaborated on the concept of silence and gender passing, noting that "for African American women in the Academy, being taken seriously also means disassociating oneself from the image of loud Black girls" (p. 22) because high-achieving women "are compelled to pass as the male dominant other if they desire to achieve a modicum of academic success" (p. 3). Similarly, Jones and Shorter-Gooden (2003) describe the constant struggle that Black women undergo as they alter their identities by "shifting." This strategy of changing from Black to White, to corporate to cool, is developed to cope with the many demands. However, these constant inner and outer changes diminish the joys of authentic lives and leave Black women depressed, conflicted, weary, and isolated.

My intellectualism has evolved through many phases. Phases of silencing. Phases of invisibility. Phases of unrecognition. As a Black female growing up in the South, I had mixed feelings about the meaning of being a Black female and the meaning of being smart. I did understand that I was a Black person, and I and other Black people I knew certainly participated in similar activities. Yes, I lived a very stereotypical Southern Black girl life. I grew up in an all-Black community and attended an all-Black church. I watched *Soul Train* and *Good Times* with my cousins, ate cornbread and greens with my grandmother, and endured getting my hair braided by my older sister. I visited my extended family in Mississippi and snubbed my city-girl nose at their "country" lifestyle. Also, I did understand that I was smart. I made good grades in school, completed my homework every day, and even perfected my handwriting skills so the teacher would choose me to write on the board. I did, however, misunderstand the reasons my smartness remained unacknowledged at school. Though my parents supported my efforts, at school I passed along with either good or mediocre grades, never caused problems, never stepped out of line, but was still never encouraged to higher levels of achievement (Evans, 1988). The year I was bold enough to enter the spelling bee, I defeated the White female incumbent, only to find my success undermined as her family and the school authorities questioned my eligibility, by bringing me into the counselor's office to inquire about my grades to ensure that I met the requirements for participating.

Fast-forward fifteen years. I have now completed my bachelor's degree, master's degree, and a year abroad teaching, efforts I chose of my own volition. When I decided to pursue a doctoral degree instead of coming back to my hometown of Memphis, Tennessee, to teach English, many of my extended family members were confused about that decision. In their minds, my choice to continue in school was irrational—I already had two degrees, so it was time to get a real job and a husband. I did not blame my well-meaning family members for their lack of knowledge on women who aspire for higher education, because I am the first family member, male or female, to pursue a Ph.D. My grandmother's house in the "country" is not the place to invoke discussions on feminism, gender equality, or women's rights, and I often silence my reactions to their comments, fully realizing my silence as an adherence to patriarchy (hooks, 1994, 2001). My comments would be interpreted as rude, so I listen to their philosophies on women, sports, media, and religion and call my first-generation Ph.D. friend who has similar experiences to critique our shared silences in the company of our families.[2]

As I continue to dance, this lindy hop through my identities is ever expanding and evolving, as new aspects of my *self* emerge. Two years ago, I went through a major life transformation, and I rededicated my life to Jesus Christ, with the firm commitment to be guided by Him in every area. Because religious affiliation is an important aspect of identity (Wing, 2000), my premier concern was how a Black woman with strong views on race, politics, women's rights, and equality would properly merge newfound Christian beliefs with academic scholarship. Though my faith is the guiding force of all that I accomplish, I had worries that I would have to subvert this identity. One day as I was in the library gathering books related to my dissertation, I found a very comforting and affirming message in Kunjufu's (1988) introduction of *To Be Popular or Smart: The Black Peer Group* that spoke directly to my concerns: "I am a Christian, my Lord and Savior is Jesus Christ. I want everyone to know, because some people assume if you have an African name, believe in self-determination, don't eat meat, and believe in God, you must be from another religious persuasion" (p. v). This bold, outright affirmation of his faith made me feel more relaxed in the world of the academy, where I often feel isolated in expressing my beliefs. Though I know there are "out" Christian scholars, I truly treasure the candor of his stance. Kunjufu's (1988) expression of his Christian identity, and his further explanation of how these beliefs lead him throughout his research, assured me that I could still maintain both my academic and my Christian identities without compromise.

My Future Self

Being a Black, female Ph.D. candidate can be lonesome, and it has isolated me from people I love who do not understand my struggles and my need for solitude, or who question my motives for remaining in school for such an extensive period (hooks, 1991). My friends who completed their bachelor's degree and did not pursue graduate work are confused about my financial sacrifices because they went to school for a shorter period of time yet are already receiving a higher salary than that of a first-year professor. My Southern family continually asks when I will graduate, and they believe I fear entering the real world of work because they view the intangible tasks of reading, writing, and thinking as procrastination and overindulgence in "free time." My Christian friends and personal beliefs remind me to remain humble though my academic identity is privileging (Wing, 2000), for there are so few Black females who have earned Ph.D. degrees.

As I persevere through my graduate program and learn more about the struggles, triumphs, and successes of Black women, I realize I was taught very little about myself as a Black person and as a woman in this society. Jones and Shorter-Gooden (2003) describe our successes despite the persistent misrepresentations that we have endured:

> Black women in America . . . have risen over years of oppression so that, today, after years of dealing with society's racist and sexist misconceptions, with its brutal hostilities and unthinkable mistreatment, not only are they supporting families, they're leading corporations, major media organizations, the military, our state and federal governments. (p. 1)

Reflecting upon my educational experiences, I am aware that this drain in my exposure to successful Black women has been consistent, because of the exclusion of Black people's contributions in the curriculum (Kincheloe, 1993). Essentially, I was taught that as a Black female in America, I have no existence, and that which is, is not worthy of being taught. With the omission of Black women's contributions in academic arenas, negative media images, low societal expectations, and the denigration of women in society as a whole, women of all races in the academy have the charge to deconstruct these images.

As I become closer to being yet another statistic because there are so few Black women faculty at predominantly White institutions (Carteledge, Gardner, & Tillman, 1995), the misrepresentations, omissions, and invalidations in the academy cause me to question my future career moves. Though the Black intellectuals who nurture me at conferences encourage me to pursue the academic life, I often wonder if I will be among the Black women doctoral recipients who do not seek such employment (Gregory, 1999). If I do choose higher education, will I work in the "safer" environment of the historically Black college? Or will I pursue my first love and original intention before earning a Ph.D. was even a consideration—to teach English to middle school students? Though I am unsure of my next challenge, I am confident that I will succeed—even though my skin is brown and I do not wear a tie.

References

Carteledge, G., Gardner, R., III, & Tillman, L. (1995). African-Americans in higher education special education: Issues in recruitment and retention. *TESE, 18*(3), 166–178.

Davidson, A. (1996). *Making and molding identities in schools: Student narratives on race, gender, and academic engagement.* Albany, NY: State University of New York Press.

Delgado, R. (1995). Storytelling for oppositionists and others: A plea for narrative. In R. Delgado (Ed.), *Critical race theory: The cutting edge* (pp. 60–70). Philadelphia: Temple University Press.

Evans, G. (1988). Those loud Black girls. In *Learning to lose: Sexism and education* (pp. 17–32). London, England: The Women's Press.

Fordham, S. (1993). "Those loud Black girls": (Black) women, silence, and gender "passing" in the academy. *Anthropology & Education Quarterly, 24*(3), 3–32.

Grantham, T., & Ford, D. (1998). A case study of the social needs of Danisha: An underachieving gifted African-American female. *Roeper Review, 21*(2), 96–101.

Gregory, S. T. (1999). *Black women in the Academy: The secrets to success and achievement.* Lanham, MD: University Press of America.

Harrison, J. (1997). Lisa's quiet fight: School structure and African-American adolescent females. In K. Lomotey (Ed.), *Sailing against the wind: African-Americans and women in U.S. education* (pp. 45–54). New York: State University of New York Press.

Hemmings, A. (1998). The self-transformations of African American achievers. *Youth & Society, 29*(3), 330–368.

hooks, b. (1981). *Ain't I a woman: Black women and feminism.* Cambridge, MA: South End Press.

hooks, b. (1991). Black women intellectuals. In b. hooks & C. West (Eds.), *Breaking bread: Insurgent Black intellectual life* (pp. 147–174). Boston: South End Press.

hooks, b. (1994). *Teaching to transgress: Education as the practice of freedom.* New York: Routledge.

Horvat, E. M., & Antonio, A. L. (1999). "Hey those shoes are out of uniform": African-American girls in an elite high school and the importance of habitus. *Anthropology & Education Quarterly, 30*(3), 317–342.

Irvine, J. (1990). *Black students and school failure: Policies, practices, and prescriptions.* New York: Greenwood Press.

Jones, C., & Shorter-Gooden, K. (2003). *Shifting: The double lives of Black women in America.* New York: Harper Collins.

Kincheloe, J. (1993). *Toward a critical politics of teacher thinking: Mapping the post-modern.* Westport, CO: Bergin & Garvey.

Kunjufu, J. (1988). *To be popular or smart: The Black peer group.* Chicago, IL: African-American Images.

Lanehart, S. L. (2002). *Sista, speak! Black women kinfolk talk about language and literacy.* Austin: University of Texas Press.

Lei, J. L. (2003). (Un)necessary toughness? Those "loud Black girls" and those "quiet Asian boys." *Anthropology & Education Quarterly, 34*(2), 158–181.

Meyers, L. W. (2002). *A broken silence: Voices of African-American women in the academy.* Westport, CO: Bergin & Garvey.

Schultz, K. (1999). Identity narratives: Stories from the lives of urban adolescent females. *The Urban Review, 31*(1), 79–105.

Smith, D. (2003). Foreword. In G. G. Generett & R. B. Jeffries (Eds.), *Black women in the field: Experiences understanding ourselves and others through qualitative research* (pp. x–xii). Creskill, NJ: Hampton Press.

Snearl, G. E. (1997). Sailing against the wind: African American women, higher education, and power. In K. Lomotey (Ed.), *Sailing against the wind: African-Americans and women in U.S. education* (pp. 125–132). New York: State University of New York Press.

Wing, A. K. (2000). *Global critical race feminism: An international reader.* New York: New York University Press.

Endnotes

1. Dr. Linda Tillman was my advisor and mentor at the University of New Orleans, and she continues to provide support and encouragement.

2. Tameka Cage, another Southern, Black, educated, Christian woman from Shreveport, Louisiana, is a graduate student in the English department at Louisiana State University.

3

BRIDGING IDENTITIES
Making Sense of Who We Are Becoming to Be

Aki Murata

The Author

Aki Murata is a research associate in the education department of Mills College, Oakland, California. Under an AERA/IES postdoctoral grant, she is currently studying teacher and student learning while teachers engage in lesson study (a professional development process for teachers originated in Japan, based on peer collaboration). She works closely with elementary school teachers to investigate how their thinking about teaching, student learning, and mathematics changes. Contextual and social factors that motivate and support the learning and change are examined, as well as their impact on student learning. Her work in this area has been presented at several international research conferences.

Born and raised in Japan, Aki came to the United States as a student in the mid-1980s. After completing her bachelor's degree in elementary education at The Ohio State University, Aki taught elementary school in the United States for a few years prior to commencing her doctoral work at Northwestern University. Her doctoral research studied how Japanese students in the first grade developed their understanding of quantities in a culturally relevant way over time, and how individual understanding and classroom taken-as-shared understanding interacted in the process. She worked with teachers and students at the Chicago Japanese School for this study. Her dissertation work has been presented at several international research conferences and will also be included in the forthcoming volume of *National Council of Teachers of Mathematics Yearbook 2004* and in *Cognition and Instruction*.

Aki is fluent in both Japanese and English and knowledgeable about education in both cultures. Her expertise in the area comes not only from her scholarly research work but also from her personal experiences living in the two cultures with her two children, teaching school in a culture that is not her own, and working with teachers and students cross-culturally. Aki supports meaningful teacher and student learning through the adaptation of lesson study to the United States.

(Immigrant women are) dealing with the tedious-
ness of having to constantly weigh their desire
to belong to one place against the possible consequences of betraying the other, all the while
negotiating the undefined space in-between the
two.

—Danquah (2000, p. ix)

W hen we experience something new, we bridge who we are and
who we are becoming to be to fit better with the new context.
For some, it is a fairly easy and painless transition when two identities are close to each other. For others, the experience can be extremely
difficult when the identities are so far apart. As I started my doctoral journey,
my case was the latter.

Cultural Orientations toward Ways of Knowing

I was born and grew up in Japan. It was not until I was in my mid-twenties
that I came to the United States as an undergraduate student. I spent more
than a decade in the U.S. culture prior to going into the doctoral program,
yet my orientation toward knowing and learning was still very much Japanese. Unlike the Western tradition, in Japanese schools, emotional and social
aspects of the learning process are largely valued (Lewis, 1995). Subject matters are often taught in a very personal manner. Compared to the Western
dry and impersonal approach of teaching facts, Japanese students are sup-

ported in making connections between abstract ideas and their own experiences and identities. They are encouraged to construct their understanding inside out (from their personal intuitions to more generalized and shared concepts) in the classroom. Knowledge is most valued when expressed through people's experiences to benefit others (Suzuki, 2002), and students are expected to share their subjective insights with one another. Through sharing of multiple personal ideas, the intersubjective and shared meaning are created and owned by the people who are in the learning context. With the relational cultural orientation (Kim, 1994; Schneider, Hieshima, Lee, & Plank, 1994), learning is not an activity of individuals—it is a collective effort through which individuals make meanings.

This mode of knowing through personal experiences and relationships was also found when Belenky, Clinchy, Goldberger, and Tarule (1997) interviewed American women of different life paths to examine their ways of knowing. Their study describes five different perspectives from which the women viewed their realities and drew conclusions about truth, knowledge, and authority. Among the categories of perspectives identified, the authors found a small number of women who knew and thought about their worlds in a personally connected way, and called them "connected knowers." These women considered that the most valuable knowledge came from their personal experiences and understood others through empathy. They were highly reflective and intelligent individuals who were also deeply in touch with who they were. Ironically, few of these women existed in a higher-education context, because this personal way of knowing conflicts with the culture of the academy. Methods of critical thinking and objectivity are the academic norm, and people are taught and expected to separate their personal sides of selves in order to survive. Belenky and colleagues (1997) identified a group of women in the academy who successfully adapted this orientation toward knowing as "separate knowers." Connected knowers, on the other hand, remain connected to their inner voice and value personal experiences and intuition. The authors hypothesized that compared to the connected knowers, the separate knowers would experience alienation between their expanding academic knowledge and personal intuition, making it more difficult to integrate their knowledge later on in their development. However, the authors' analysis did not go beyond this stage because the number of connected knowers was very limited in the study. In the Western academic culture, it is challenging for connected knowers to survive: they are not given the opportunities and support necessary to develop. The academy is not a friendly place for connected knowers.

I am a connected knower. I have always been one. As already described, I grew up in a culture where knowledge is more valued when it is expressed through people's own experiences, and I am a large part of what I know. I am also a woman, and my life experiences, enveloped by various biological and social factors, directed me toward the connected orientation for knowing with emphasis on empathy and feelings. In the academy, however, facts and knowledge are considered to exist outside of ourselves. We are required to look at the reality objectively and discuss it without making reference to who we are. It is as if there is this ultimate truth for which all of us should be able to observe and understand in the same way, away from our personal experiences and identities. When we do not share the same perception, we become unworthy to be in the intellectual environment. It is not what we know that is important; it is how we know it and how we communicate it that are important. This certainly gives privilege to the few in the hierarchy who share this positivist view, while alienating those with different backgrounds and orientations toward knowing.

When people talk about different parts of who they are in Western cultures, they often make distinctions between their thinking function in their mind and feelings in their heart. In this framework, the mind is an exclusive place for higher thinking and intellectual functions, whereas the heart is for feelings and emotions. Academic work requires separation of the two, and we only use the intellectual side of us, disregarding the emotional side altogether. In Japan, mind and heart are considered to be one, residing in our bodies together. Our brain, which is located in our head, is a machine-like organ that processes information while Kokoro, "心" (mind and heart), makes sense and knows things. Thinking and feeling are an integrated function for knowing in Japanese culture. When I experience something in my life, I feel the phenomenon first, taking in the parts of the experience with all my senses, then understand and know it in my Kokoro. More detailed and careful articulation of how and why that particular experience means certain things to who I am may not come until later, after the information is processed in my brain. Knowing is a process in which feeling and thinking work together, and feeling plays a rather large part at the beginning of the process.

Entering the Unknown

The doctoral program I attended was at a major Research One Institution in a Midwestern state of the United States. I did not choose the institution for its name and reputation, though most of my colleagues did. As with most major decisions I have made in my life, it was a personal connection that led me there: I wanted to work with a professor whom I admired professionally and personally. I had a vague understanding of the doctoral program from the information obtained on the institution's Web site and from people I had met when I went there for interviews. All appeared good from outside.

I experienced a strange gap as soon as the fall quarter started. During that first quarter of the program, I was walking in a heavy cloud. People did not seem to be able to hear my thoughts or see my ideas. The more I tried to communicate, the worse the situation became, it seemed. In traditional seminars, students competed to be on center stage, and they seemed to enjoy the competition to the greatest degree. Each of us, individually, tried diligently to get the recognition of the professors, and the atmosphere changed dramatically by the minute, depending on who was getting the attention of the perceived authority. I never imagined that, at that stage of my personal development, I would play the please-the-teacher game. But I found myself standing in the middle of the battleground with the others. The most ironic thing is that we were in the field of education. Whereas we enthusiastically discussed the importance of allowing students to express their own ideas in the classroom and how we valued a learning community in which students could safely take risks, what went on in our seminars was an unsafe and cruel competition in which we strived to say what professors wanted to hear and act in the manner they expected of us. The race was orchestrated tactfully by the professors, who enjoyed their authority, and we rose and sank with each comment they made. This was my introduction to the academy.

I knew I was not doing well, and I did not understand why. The professors and their colleagues often cut off my contributions to the discussions with comments such as, "We don't have time for this now, Aki," and "What you are saying does not make sense here." My competitors enjoyed this, of course, and they brutally argued against my ideas whenever they were given a chance. Because it is my nature to reach out and try to understand others' different points of view, I found their behavior difficult to accept. I had known myself as a good communicator up to that point in my life, but I needed to change the perception of who I was. I experienced the identity gap.

One of the first difficult lessons I needed to learn in the program was to be silent and not get in the others' way, or I would receive 10 oppositions for every small comment I made. I often thought that the ideas expressed by me and by the others in the seminars were quite similar. We were talking about the same idea, just in different ways. So why were my ideas attacked whereas theirs were accepted? There definitely seemed to be a communication gap there. It reminded me of the time I had first come to the United States, unable to speak the language well. This time, however, I knew the language, but I still could not communicate. I became more and more silenced as the quarter progressed.

Understanding the Gap

There was a huge gap between these two identities: the person I was as a connected knower who entered the world with feelings, and the person I was expected to be as a separate knower who analyzed the facts objectively outside of my skin to communicate. As a newcomer in this context, I was expected to become someone different. Of course, at the time, I did not experience and see this as a gap between two identities. It was experienced as a brutal denial of who I was as a person. I was not good enough to be where I was placed. I was a disappointment to the others and the program of which I was a part. I was considered not capable of high-level academic talk.

While I struggled to make sense of what went on, I also saw many women students of color dropping out of the program and/or transferring to other institutions. They attributed the changes to the lack of support and social connections. Although these were true and well-founded reasons, I also had to wonder why some colleagues were supported and socially connected more readily than others. It seemed that some came equipped with identities that were well suited for that context, whereas others, including myself, were placed far behind the starting line. There was no guidance or support to help us understand why such a condition existed and/or how to go about making progress. We were left alone to figure out and solve the mystery.

As I mentioned earlier, I came to the doctoral program to work with a professor I had known earlier. Because I am a connected knower, relationships with others are very critical for my learning and development, and I value personal knowledge of others. At the same time, I need to feel okay to be myself before moving forward to shift my identity. Colleen (a pseudonym for the professor) played a critical role for me. First, she listened. Really listened. She took in my ideas and accepted me as a knower. She did not deny what I was feeling, and she empathized. Second, she carefully analyzed with me the context in which I was feeling challenged and my place in it. While she warmly accepted my feelings, she also made many constructive suggestions for me in nonthreatening ways. She did not make me feel that there was something wrong with me that I needed to change. Instead, she helped me understand certain expectations people had for me and a possible process to meet those expectations without changing the core of who I was.

One of the issues that together we understood needed change was my communication style, which was different from the academic norm. When I communicate, my preferred mode is still to set up a lengthy background first, before making an important point in the context. The backgrounds often include my personal experiences. I use a narrative style, one that is also known to be used, expected, and valued in many U.S. subcultures, such as Asian, Latino, and Native American. I learned that academic argument usually takes the opposite approach: one makes the point first, then supports the argument. Colleen and I analyzed different examples together and saw that in academic settings people might think I had no point to make after listening to the background for a full minute. My style of communication is effective in different contexts, and I should not lose it; however, within the academic context, I needed to change the way I presented my ideas.

Another important issue was objectivity and subjectivity. Objectivity and separation in the academy are expected, but they did not come naturally to me. While Colleen and I talked, she often pointed out the parts of my talk where I presented the facts objectively and effectively, while also recognizing the personal value I placed on supporting the development of those ideas. I felt content to present my ideas in a dry and artificial way as long as Colleen was there to share the real meanings, which were largely personal and subjective, that I placed on the ideas.

Colleen attended all of my practices for public talks through the years and took careful notes on my methods of presentation. Her comments were not always positive, and I often found them rather harsh. Still, they were very helpful, for I knew they came from her genuine desire to support me. She understood the process I was going through and guided me to be successful in the academy from the point of view of a senior colleague. Also, as I changed my speech style from giving a lengthy background first to making the point first, people started hearing my ideas without being distracted by my supporting argument, which could still be rather personal. I realized that people did not necessarily listen to all I had to say. For separate knowers, listening requires time and energy to empathize. They tend to hear the initial points others make and tune out the rest.

Bridging the Gap

Understanding the identity gap as well as the reasons for its existence and finding ways to communicate differently all were helpful to me, but they did not bridge the internal gap within me. After finishing my dissertation and having a "Ph.D." after my name, I am still working on bridging that gap. This is a process that requires constant reflection on who I am as a whole person and who I am in a particular context. Living across multiple cultures—Japanese and U.S. cultures, connection and separation cultures, academy and nonacademy cultures (these might seem to be different names for the same categories, but they are slightly different and overlap)—means continuously shifting identities at multiple levels at a time. Maintaining a meaningful balance among different identities to meet the expectations of the particular context is a challenge to me. The process is not always a conscious one; it is often done naturally, unintentionally, and intuitively. Reflecting on the ways in which I shift my identities is a process of self-discovery, and it helps me understand who I am and the person I am becoming to be.

Others may skillfully adopt the approach of separating their different identities to use in different contexts, but my identities are still closely connected with one another, and one cannot function without support from the other. Different parts of who I am need to work in harmony for me to feel "whole" and be truly myself. Although one identity may play a stronger role in a particular setting, denying any other will lead to denying my whole self in the long run. If we push ourselves to take a new identity too quickly, we lose sight of who we really are. In time, that can catch up with us and make us realize that we are becoming a stranger to ourselves. The constant reflection on this balancing act and how I may be feeling as I shift my identities is a process of self-awareness. After all, feeling is a large part of my way of knowing.

Roles That Mentors Play

Colleen played a significant role in my professional and personal development during the doctoral journey and continues to be my best friend. She lived through my social storms, emotional earthquakes, and intellectual blizzards right next to me. I believe it is helpful to mention that she is not Japanese. She is White. Although she had had experiences working with Asian scholars before, there is no doubt that she needed to stretch her thinking to understand my situation and give me guidance. It is also helpful to state that at the time I was separated from my husband, taking care of my two school-age children on my own, and proceeding with a divorce. Colleen not only supported me in my intellectual growth but also took care of me emotionally and socially. She gave me the strength to continue when nothing seemed to make sense. I felt accepted and respected for my ideas and as an individual.

For women scholars of color who come into the academy with a connected and relational orientation toward knowing and learning, it is critical to find mentors with whom they can feel connected. While the culture of the academy requires us to be objective and impersonal, we can attain a degree of connectedness through personal relationships with others within and outside the academy. Because we, as connected knowers, value knowledge that comes from personal experiences and intuition, a critical part of our growth comes from empathizing with others' experiences/ideas and sharing their insights. Working with mentors with whom we can share the personal sides of each other's knowledge is a powerful experience as we learn about the new culture and what it means to be in this new place. When learning is considered a collaborative activity in which people create shared meanings, mentors and mentees learn together. It is a mutually beneficial learning process, and we develop new understanding as we interact.

Bridging Identities

There is no doubt that some of us have a bigger gap to bridge as we enter the academy. It is also true that the academy is thought to be a place for the exclusive few, and one that alienates people who try to introduce different ways. What is important to communicate to newcomers with different backgrounds is that they do not and should not have to lose their present identities to assimilate into the culture of the academy, although the pressure to do so may feel rather strong at times. We should recognize and embrace the value of the ways of knowing that may be different from what is traditionally considered scientific and positive. The knowledge that comes from personal reflections and deep analysis of firsthand experiences may be just as powerful. All of us need to find a good balance among different identities to fit in the new context, whenever we experience something new, and the academy is not an exception to the rule. It is also important to note that the culture of the academy also changes and becomes stronger as it incorporates the new and different styles and perspectives brought in by new people. Cultures and people interact constantly and change; thus, although it is a challenge to be a change agent, our contribution to the culture enriches the experiences of all involved and beyond.

Our personal growth and development can be supported by carefully examining who we are as changing people and by embracing ourselves as a whole. We are always in in-between places, constantly shifting identities, constantly learning, and to bridge the gap is to understand the meanings of being in the in-between places. Through the process, we understand the changes, us, the people we are becoming to be, and create new meanings of the world around us.

References

Belenky, M. F., Clinchy, B. M., Goldberger, N. R., & Tarule, J. M. (1997). *Women's ways of knowing*. New York: Basic Books.

Danquah, M. N.-A. (2000). Introduction. In M. N.-A. Danquah (Ed.), *Becoming American: Personal essays by first generation immigrant women*. New York: Hyperion.

Kim, U., & Choi, S.-H. (1994). Individualism, collectivism, and child development: A Korean perspective. In P. Greenfield & R. Cocking (Eds.), *Cross-cultural roots of minority child development*. Hillsdale, NJ: Erlbaum.

Lewis, C. C. (1995). *Educating hearts and minds: Reflections on Japanese preschool and elementary education*. Cambridge, MA: Cambridge University Press.

Schneider, B., Hieshima, J. A., Lee, S., & Plank, S. (1994). East-Asian academic success in the United States: Family, school, and community explanations. In P. Greenfield & R. Cocking (Eds.), *Cross-cultural roots of minority child development*. Hillsdale, NJ: Erlbaum.

Suzuki, M. J. (2002). *Facilitating "Intellectual mind" (2)—Hazard from kindergarten classrooms*. Paper presented at annual meeting of American Educational Research Association, New Orleans, LA.

4

WATCHING, MY OTHER EDUCATION

Vicarious Learning about Gender and Race in the Professorate

M. Francyne Huckaby

The Author

M. Francyne Huckaby is currently a doctoral candidate at Texas A&M University, focusing on higher education and educational administration. She intends for her scholarship to encourage scholars, teachers, and institutions to explore critically the processes, products, and effects of research on education. This academic year (2003–2004) she is completing her dissertation, "Challenging the Hegemony in Educational Research: Interpretive Analytics of Power/Knowledge as It Intersects with Faculty Scholars Who Address Racism, Sexism, and Oppression in Their Research." This study asks how philosophical positions and approaches to research have emerged for researchers who challenge hegemony. It studies the strategies and tactics by which scholars produce nonoppressive research discourses within academic traditions that produce knowledge that benefits those in dominant positions.

This dissertation stems from Fran's recent research in the area of researchers and research paradigms. These works describe how researchers approach their work, judge other research and researchers, view research paradigms, and change as researchers and scholars. It also explores how researchers are situated in social/cultural contexts; bodies that are affected by critical issues such as race, gender, privilege, and inequality; and discourses that influence thought, knowledge, and policy (C. Gordon, 1980).

While in the U.S. Peace Corps in Papua New Guinea (1997–1999), Fran helped six rural villages develop primary schools. Through this experience she developed an interest in decolonization and has written about the colonial influence on education and ideals about education in Papua New Guinea. Prior to entering the Peace Corps, Fran received a master's in educational research from Texas Christian University. Her bachelor's of arts in psychology, sociology, and art is from Austin College in Sherman, Texas.

Even though she is a nascent teacher, Fran's graduate-level students have described her teaching as refreshing, thought provoking, passionate, and innovative. Fran is the recipient of a Regents Graduate Fellowship from Texas A&M (2000–2001), an Academic Excellence Award (2002–2003), a Gender Issues Educational Enhancement Grant (Spring 2003), and a Race and Ethnic Studies Institute Graduate Student Mini-Grant (Summer and Fall 2003).

Before I was admitted into my doctoral program, I had to present a statement on the issues facing education to a small group of faculty. While editing my draft comments, my spouse asked if I really wanted to focus so much on social divisions of race, gender, and class given the reputation of my prospective university. This was a reasonable concern. After all, students outside the phenotypic or ideological mainstream are called "two percenters" in this institution. I boldly commented that if they did not want me because of my concern for critical issues in education, then I did not need to be there. I practiced and perfected my statement, paying attention to where I wanted to pause, change my tone of voice, and make eye contact for emphasis. I arrived on campus for my interview, parked, and found my way to the building. I was rather early, so I walked around the campus.

I noticed by the education building a bronze sculpture depicting children climbing on a partially opened book. A girl at the apex held a feather toward the sky; other children of various ages reached and climbed around her; and a teacher extended her hand, as if supporting or encouraging them. Close by, a bronze statue on a five-foot-high granite base outside the sociology building caught my attention. I assumed this figure of a man had been there for years, but the only signs of weathering were in the patina creases. He was recently polished, and coins were stacked at his feet. In relief on the back of the base, he was described as a "Soldier Statesman and Knightly Gentleman" on the first line, a "Brigadier General U.S.A. Governor of Texas" on the second line, and the "President" of the college on the final line. Had I seen the first line of text on a statue in Britain, the term *knightly* would have had a very different connotation. But because this university is in the South, and he was president of the university in the late 1800s, only one type of knight came to mind. I wondered and continue to question why the last line that connected him to the university was not the first. In conversations with faculty, staff, and students on campus, I later learned that he was indeed believed to be a Klansman, and that the coins are placed at his feet by students who wish for luck on their exams.

I found my way to the interview room and was enthusiastically welcomed by a recently tenured member of the faculty. I was pleasantly surprised that she was Black, like me. Soon another professor joined us. This senior White professor was quite pleasant, and there was nothing intimidating about his presence, yet I viscerally judged him through the reputation of the university. My heart raced as I began to worry about how he might be offended by my presentation. I tried to remember which sentences and phrases I had been cautioned to take out, if I wanted to play it safe. I do not remember what questions were asked of me or how I responded. During the interview, I worried about my statement. With much disappointment in my nervousness, I only read it as it was written. My eyes stayed on the paper. I did not alter my voice. I stumbled over some words. Afterward, I was asked more questions, but the older professor sat quietly in a reflective posture. I knew that he did not appreciate my statement and that I had just challenged this institution. Eventually a third member of the faculty joined us. She apologized for being late, and we were introduced. Then the quiet professor began to talk. He updated the professor who had just joined us and told her how they needed more students like me who were willing to look at such important issues in education. After this experience, I understood that I would have to consider each individual independently, and not make sweeping judgments about people. I also knew that I was prepared to be a student at this university even if other professors and students lived up to the school's reputation. It was observing the academic lives of Black, White, and Latina women professors that took me by surprise.

Watching

I watch, listen, and try to make sense of what I notice and how it relates to my life. My grandmother taught me this. Persistently, she would ask me to paint her pictures with words of what I observed in school and in my world. I went to her house most days after school, and I knew the questions would be waiting for me. "Nothing" or "it was nice" were not acceptable answers and only led to more questions. One year my descriptions of elementary school days included details of the lives of a group of girls I befriended. Their families were wealthier than my family, and I was intrigued by their homes, toys, and after-school entertainment. Through a series of questions, my grandmother encouraged me to pay close attention to what I enjoyed with them and what I enjoyed with my other friends. What was it I liked about them besides the video games, scooters, pools, and shopping? How were these relationships different from my other ones? These questions continued into my first year in college. The topics changed as my surroundings and interests changed, but she always asked me to observe closely and ask questions about social relations. My mother still reminds me of these lessons on occasion by asking me to paint her a picture. Lorde (in Collins, 2000) reminds us that those of us who are oppressed in America have had to become watchers. Through watching, we have been able to develop a dual consciousness that offers us familiarity with "the language and manners of the oppressor" (p. 97). So, I watch. Sometimes, when I know a place or circumstances well, I am passive in my observations. Other times, when in unfamiliar surroundings, I pay close attention and challenge my assumptions with questions, as my grandmother taught me.

I paid attention in my new academic environment. Every now and again, a male professor would make a comment to me or in class that expressed disrespect for a female professor or administrator on campus. I did not witness these professors doing this to other male faculty. I noticed stress hidden behind pleasant greetings and smiles in many of the women professors. I began to hear other students and women faculty recount events of intimidation, and later I personally observed events that shocked me. It took about a semester for me to realize that I was in what Gordon (1999) described as a 'hood: "The 'hood metaphor works because you, rather we—those of us that live in this "academic 'hood"—are as vulnerable as our urban counterparts. The only difference is that the danger is very subtle and the blood and bloodletting is invisible to the naked eye" (p. 407). Although the environment offered difficulties to students, as students we were able to insulate ourselves fairly well. To some degree, we could choose whose classes we took and who sat on our committees. The real conflict was among the faculty, and I believe the women faculty were targets.

I first hung onto the myth that what I heard and saw were only isolated experiences and random incidents. There had to be some explanation other than systematic mistreatment. I maintained my disbelief through justifications for why these things were happening in the twenty-first century. Like most places in the United States, this college town was divided racially and economically. Newcomers were told what areas they should avoid and where they should not live. When I heard these comments, I excused them as not being so much racist as insensitive to how a person of color would feel when told not to live with her people. But as I heard comments about the "white," well-lit halls getting "dark," other interpretations became more difficult. I had to stop denying that there was a pattern. What I found most interesting and difficult was the experience of seeing the professors who were most like me being mistreated. I also realized that I was entering a profession that could potentially be the most charged in terms of race and gender that I had ever experienced—and that I would be the target. These vicarious experiences influenced my vision of what academic life might be for me.

Being There

One thing that I appreciated from the women faculty is that they would check in with me and ask how I was doing, how my classes were going, and what I thought of my professors. When I felt comfortable enough to share my misgivings and concerns, they listened. It was not until I shared my interpretation of events that I began to hear about their experiences. I listened and asked questions, because I knew I could be in their position one day. I noticed myself doing a similar thing when a classmate from South Africa was enrolled. I worried that her experiences at this institution might not be much better than in South Africa. I did not say anything at first. I waited until she noticed it for herself, and then we talked. I was saddened and embarrassed that she had traveled so far to find herself in the same situation.

My first year, I noticed the strategies used against women professors and the impact on their work. They seemed to be working harder and maintaining busier schedules. More of them were untenured and working to ensure that their tenure files would be ready. In my second and third years, I noticed more blatant and obvious tactics. I was asked to serve as a student representative on a faculty search committee and was very honored and excited about seeing what the search process was like from the inside. The committee had decided on a point system. The candidates' applications were discussed, and we each gave our points in various areas for each person. These were marked on a grid on the blackboard. Somehow, the meeting deteriorated in what seemed like an instant to me. One male faculty member began shouting at two of the female faculty members (one Black and one White) on the committee. He was arguing for a candidate who was not in the top three of the group average but still focused his vehemence on only two members of the committee. I sat there silent, worrying about what could happen if this escalated further. Eventually, everyone gave up presenting their arguments for candidates, and the meeting was ended. I reproduced the grid from the blackboard on a computer and passed copies out to each faculty member. Even though I was not given a reason, I was relieved when I was told I did not have to attend the next meeting.

I witnessed other instances of verbal and even physical intimidation, but one was particularly disturbing because my emotional reaction was fear. Our evening class had taken a break, and I stayed in the room to talk with classmates. Just before the break was over, I went to the second floor vending machines to get a snack. As I was getting off the elevator, I noticed my professor on the balcony. The professor who had yelled during the meeting had cornered her outside the building. The glass door to the balcony was on her left, the cement ledge on her right, and this tall male professor was blocking her path out of the corner. He was yelling, although I could not hear what he was saying. I pretended to be perusing the vending machines, looking out of the corner of my eye to make sure. To make sure of exactly what, I did not know, but I had to make sure, and my mind was racing. Should I stay and be a witness? What might I witness if I stay? Is she in physical danger? Is he just yelling or will he hit her? He wouldn't push her, would he?

I also did not know how my professor would feel if she knew I was there. She might feel grateful or possibly embarrassed. I took my time walking in front of the machines, digging in my bag for change, lingering, and looking out of the corner of my eye. I was afraid to leave but also worried that the antagonism could be redirected toward me. Not knowing what else to do to stall, I went back upstairs to my classmates, telling myself that if she was not back soon I would go back downstairs. Luckily, my professor did return to the class a few long minutes after I did. She resumed teaching and showed no sign that she had just been physically intimidated. After class, I walked her to her office and told her about my discomfort with what I saw. After I explained to her that I did not know what to do, we decided to walk together to her car after class each night, and she would then drive me to my apartment. We also talked about getting pepper spray. I thought about that moment all night and for the days and weeks that followed. I told my family about it and gave them the name and description of the intimidating professor. I also talked to fellow students whom I trusted and eventually found out that I was not the only one who had observed the incident. I was no longer able to ignore the systematic sexism and racism.

Awakening

I sat in classes in which professors presented arguments for the logic of salary discrepancies (past and future) by race and gender based on a history of the workforce, discredited feminist scholarship, predicted that the university's major donors would successfully foil plans to increase campus diversity, and advocated for not negatively judging slave owners. This was an academic environment in which a few of my male professors discursively maintained the values of an institution that had historically been predominantly White, male, and hostile to women and people of color. However, there were other professors of the same gender and ethnicity who did not maintain these values. Unfortunately, all these other male professors I had contact with except the professor in my interview and one other did not offer an alternative discourse. Most were silent, and because of their silence, the voices of the few intolerant ones still echo in my thoughts as the voice of this institution.

I am no longer surprised that the academy is a place where power strategies are used to suppress us. After all, knowledge is an essential apparatus of power (Foucault, 1980a), and the presence of women of color in the academy, the producer and transmitter of knowledge, is a threat to the established truth. We reveal other knowledge, truths, and power in our scholarship and teaching. Making the academy a hostile environment for female faculty not only affects faculty; it also influences students. At the time, I was feeling increasingly less comfortable and more uncertain about my academic career choice. I knew that a scholarly career was ideal for me, but I doubted my ability to survive in situations with these subtle and blatant forms of domination and oppression.

In my last few semesters of coursework, I began reading literature in critical theory, decolonization, ethnic relations, postmodernism, poststructuralism, social and political philosophy, embodiment, and power. I found Foucault's work particularly insightful in that it helped me to consider the comments and intimidation I had observed as discursive strategies intended to maintain power (Dreyfus & Rabinow, 1983; Foucault, 1983). Obtaining tenure was related to the role of desire in power. It was a desire where the threat of not becoming realized was directed toward more women than men because of the history of the professor labor market at this institution. Foucault (1980b) also reminded me that the exercise of power is "more material, physical, corporal" than anything else (p. 57) and is directed at the body. With this theoretical framework, the physical threat used to establish or maintain power was not as surprising. What was particularly useful was that these readings offered me an opportunity to look past my shock and fear, and to watch women faculty work.

Claiming

Instead of leaving when I noticed women faculty members gathering in some proximity to me around the lunch table or in a professor's office, I stayed put. At times, I felt I should leave—after all I was only a graduate student. But I stayed, and they did not send me away. I watched. I heard them tell each other their experiences, and I saw them listening to each other. They slowly began to gather around a table in one office for lunch instead of in the floor's lunchroom. At first, there were two and occasionally three; eventually there were five or six. This became a space for them to present their grievances and to be heard. Once they were heard, they talked about what they could do. It was a somewhat safe realm, which Collins (2000) identifies as a necessary condition for Black women's resistance, although this group was Black, White, and Latina. Of course, I sometimes worried about who might be listening on the other side of the wall, but as the numbers grew and the voices got louder, I worried less. My attention shifted from possible retaliation to how these professors were claiming their positions and seeking changes in their professional world.

I noticed the strategies that were used against them *along with* their work to counter these strategies and was then able to imagine how I might respond in similar situations. They stood their ground and allied with each other. They shared letters they were writing to administrators expressing their concerns, and they planned what they would bring up in meetings. They brought pieces of their tenure files and papers they were writing to share and received feedback. I went from believing "I cannot do this" to "This is going to be more difficult than I thought" to "I am going to make this work." It would take work and tenacity. It would require my finding support and a community. More important, it would require knowing that my work is deserving of my making and maintaining a space and vehicle for it.

Although I wish that my graduate study could have been less transparent around faculty interactions, I feel privileged to have had three years of insight into this discursive environment. I shudder to think what my life as a professor might be if I ended up in a similar institution as an unsuspecting assistant professor. I am hoping for a less confrontational environment and will be observing and asking about the subtle interactions when I interview. I will look for what is said and done, and what is not. I have known how to watch since I was a child. Now I know what to watch.

I am not going to be another career tragedy of the 'hood—the empty desk still warm when the new occupant arrives, as Gordon (1999) describes. I am also not content with the academy being the 'hood. It should not be a place of harassment. It should be a place where ideas and even ideology are discussed and challenged. I will think of my grandmother as I paint pictures of what happens at school with words, and I will encourage others to watch and create images with words, while I listen to and support them, because I know there will be others watching.

References

Collins, P. H. (2000). *Black feminist thought: Knowledge, consciousness, and the politics of empowerment* (2nd ed.). New York: Routledge.

Dreyfus, H. L., & Rabinow, P. (1983). *Michel Foucault: Beyond structuralism and hermeneutics.* Chicago: The University of Chicago Press.

Foucault, M. (1980a). Body/power. In C. Gordon (Ed.), *Power/knowledge: Selected interviews and other writings 1972–1977* (pp. 55–62). New York: Pantheon Books.

Foucault, M. (1980b). Truth and power. In C. Gordon (Ed.), *Power/knowledge: Selected interviews and other writings 1972–1977* (pp. 109–133). New York: Pantheon Books.

Foucault, M. (1983). The subject and power. In H. L. Dreyfus & P. Rabinow, *Michel Foucault: Beyond structuralism and hermeneutics* (pp. 208–228). Chicago: The University of Chicago Press.

Gordon, B. M. (1999). Who do you believe—Me or your eyes? Perceptions and issues in educational research: Reviews and the journals that validate them. *Review of Educational Research, 69*(4), 407–410.

Gordon, C. (Ed.). (1980). *Power/knowledge: Selected interviews and other writings 1972–1977.* New York: Pantheon Books.

5

BALANCING THE MARGIN IS MY CENTER

A Navajo Woman's Navigations through
the Academy and Her Community

Tiffany S. Lee

The Author

Dr. Tiffany Lee is from Crystal, New Mexico, a small community in northeast New Mexico located within the Navajo Nation. She received her B.A. in psychology from Pomona College in Claremont, California, in 1990. After taking a year to work on a research project in a Navajo elementary school and do substitute teaching, she then went on to Stanford University to earn a master's degree in sociology and a Ph.D. in sociology of education. When she began her graduate work at Stanford in the early 1990s, she felt she needed additional teaching experience in order to conduct more meaningful research in Native American education. She returned to Arizona in 1992, where she earned a secondary social studies teaching certificate from Northern Arizona University in Flagstaff. After completion of the program, she taught U.S., Arizona, and Navajo history and government at Greyhills Academy High School in Tuba City, Arizona, on the Navajo Nation. An avid volleyball fan and player, she thoroughly enjoyed coaching volleyball at Greyhills and supporting Stanford's outstanding women's volleyball team throughout the 1990s.

Dr. Lee returned to Stanford in 1997 to complete her dissertation work, which involved examining socialization influences on Navajo adolescent language attitudes and language use. She then returned to New Mexico, because it was important for her and her husband, as new parents, to raise their children near their cultural roots and family. They moved to Cochiti Pueblo, a small Native American tribe from which her children and spouse are descended. Living within Cochiti and being in close proximity to the Navajo Nation are important factors for her family's quality of life. Dr. Lee began teaching high school again at the Santa Fe Indian School in a unique experiential educational program called the Community-Based Education Model (CBEM). In this program, she taught tribal government and communications. However, the heart of the program entailed weekly travel with her students to neighboring Pueblo (Native American) villages to work with community members on tribal government and environmental science issues relevant to the tribe. Her experience teaching in this program profoundly influenced her thinking about the importance of community-based, relevant education for Native American students.

In 2001, Dr. Lee left the Santa Fe Indian School to pursue work in another community-based program called the Tribal Resource Institute in Business, Engineering, and Science (TRIBES). Her personal experiences throughout college and graduate school developed her interest in the academic preparation and social transition of Native American students pursuing higher education. TRIBES is a program created by several tribes throughout the nation, and its goal is to instill tribal values and promote service to Native communities, while preparing students to become academically competent and successful in college.

It was through her work at Greyhills and with the CBEM and TRIBES programs that Dr. Lee wanted to be able to research and document the important impact of these types of unique programs. She is now pursuing research examining educational influences on Native identity and on commitment to community through her AERA/IES fellowship. Her latest publication is an article about the TRIBES program in *InterActions: UCLA Journal of Education and Information Studies,* entitled "'I Came Here to Learn How to Be a Leader': An Intersection of Critical Pedagogy and Indigenous Education." In addition, she has contributed a chapter, entitled "Reversing Navajo Language Shift, Revisited," to Joshua Fishman's (editor) book *Can Threatened Languages Be Saved? Reversing Language Shift Revisited,* published in 2000.

For most challenging events in my life as a young child, my mother told me, "You have to be strong." But this event was particularly difficult. She was preparing me for her death. I was 13, and she had cancer. Telling me to be strong in the face of losing her was her way of telling me that life would go on, to hold my head up, and to live on without her. Those words took on extraordinary meaning for me at that time and have continued to carry me through other challenging times in my life, particularly as I pursue an academic career.

A Mother's Legacy

Even though I only knew my mother for such a short time, she laid the foundation of my identity, my roots, and my values. My mother was full Navajo from New Mexico. She came from a large family and was the third oldest of 11 children. She and her other siblings pursued higher education during a time when that was not very common among Navajo people. After receiving a bachelor's degree, she returned to the reservation, her home, and became a teacher. She met my father, a Lakota Indian[1] from Pine Ridge, South Dakota, while teaching in a small Navajo community in Arizona. When she and my father divorced when I was five, she raised me alone. She had a very successful career in Indian education, working her way up the ranks in the Bureau of Indian Affairs (BIA).[2] We moved to Santa Fe, where she became a superintendent of BIA schools in northern New Mexico. She became sick when I was about eight years old and struggled for the next five years with her illness. Yet, she maintained a demanding career while raising a child. Her importance in my life is immeasurable. She taught me who I am through her role modeling, through her strength and dignity, and through her love for her family and me. The fact that she was more concerned with how her death would impact me, rather than her own loss of life at age 47, I found unbelievably altruistic and selfless.

This short history of my mother is important for understanding how I came to know myself. My mother's influence and the strong family ties she created for me with my aunts, uncles, and cousins helped me to understand myself as a strong Navajo woman. I also have Lakota, French, Irish, and German lineage. But I grew up Navajo, and that is how I identify myself. I feel centered in Navajo culture because I know my family, the land we come from, my clan, and my feelings of belonging. However, growing up on and off the reservation has taken me through several experiences in which people have challenged my identity and have constantly placed me on the margin of their group. When I decided to pursue an academic career, I never imagined this sort of marginalization would occur there as well, but it did. Although the academy has challenged me, I do not think it has changed me. I have remained strong in my values. But I continue to pursue an academic line of work because I am hoping to change the academy and its role in working with Native people.

Layers of Life Experiences

On the reservation, as I grew up during high school and later when I was a teacher, I often would hear people referring to Native people's abilities to live in two worlds, their traditional Native world and the mainstream world. Many have critiqued this idea (Deyhle, 1998; Henze & Vanett, 1993) as a misrepresentation of Native people's acculturation processes. I also do not subscribe to the two-world notion because I am the same person in my Indian world that I am in the mainstream world. It is my interactions in these settings that differ. I think the idea behind the two-world metaphor is the recognition of the differences between mainstream and American Indian cultures, and how Native people are able to function in these very different settings. However, I have visualized my experiences more within a circle in which I place myself at the center. The Native or mainstream community can be layered in closer or farther away from one's center regarding one's sense of self in these two settings. For myself, the people I interact with generally fall into these two layers. The inner layer is filled with family, friends, and a few acquaintances. They are positioned closest to me because these are people who accept me. They are people with whom I am most comfortable.

Together our shared space is relaxed, secure, and safe. I can be myself in this space. The other layer is the outer, which is most distant from me. I approach people in this layer much more cautiously but with an open mind. People in this layer do not know me, nor do I know them. Thus, I am particularly careful in my interaction with them because of my past experiences in how people have perceived and treated me.

The distinction between these two layers is important because of the divergent experiences I have shared with each group throughout my life with regard to my identity. Furthermore, the issue of identity is extremely sensitive among Native Americans. It extends back to historical transformations of the definition of membership. Prior to the federal government's involvement, Native nations had control over distinguishing their own membership and did so along cultural lines. When the federal government imposed its own definitions based on racial categories, it disempowered Native people in determining membership of their own tribes (Churchill, 2001; Lawrence, 2003). The federal government imposed blood quantum criteria, at one-fourth Indian blood for most tribes, to determine membership status. Over time, tribal governments and Native people have internalized this European conception of membership so that most federally recognized tribes continue to use blood quantum as a determiner in enrollment. On a less formal level, other indicators of membership include appearance, place of residence (on or off reservation), family, and participation in cultural practices. Thus, any one or a combination of these factors, having more or less of one factor, is used to judge how much an individual belongs to the group with which he or she lays claim.

Because I come from a mixed background, people (Native and non-Native alike) on the outer layer of my life experiences continually question the authenticity of my claim as a Native American. Thus, my life experiences within my community and outside my community have always placed me on the margin. My involvement in the academy only complicates matters further because of the negative history of research in Native communities. Anya Dozier Enos (2001), a scholar from Santa Clara Pueblo,[3] writes of similar experiences and the personal ambiguity she feels in these places on the margin, but, like her, I never felt "uncentered" or "misplaced" as a result of other people's perceptions of me. Instead, she describes these experiences as "times of comfort and times of discomfort." She says she is never out of the center of power in either arena, as a Pueblo member and as an academic. Likewise, the identity I learned in the academy as a researcher and the identity constructed for me by my mother as a Navajo person are unwavering. My Navajo identity is demonstrated in the work I do, the way I live, and the values I hold. I try to live my life in balance. Navajo people have lived their lives according to the Navajo philosophy of *Sa'ą Naagháí Bik'e Hózhó*, which means to live one's life in balance involving four elements in life. It is connected to the way Navajo people think, speak, and act in their lifetime. The four elements are *Nitsáhákees* (thinking), *Nahat'á* (planning), *'Iiná* (living), and *Sihasin* (reflecting). These elements that make up *Sa'ą Naagháí Bik'e Hózhó* reflect a "foundational value that embodies the way Diné people are supposed to live their lives" (Lee, 2004).[4] To live by this philosophy, Navajo people learn how to live a complete, healthy, and satisfying life, even amid the challenges or struggles life may bring them. My mother lived her life according to this Navajo philosophy. Even in times of stress and illness, she maintained herself and did not ever seem out of step. She tried to balance the struggles in her life by focusing on her work and her family, which brought her happiness.

My mother was a typical Navajo woman, however. Navajo women are known for their strength and perseverance. They are revered in Navajo society as the holders of clans, home, and nurture. They are also known for economic contributions to their families and historical contributions to Navajo society (Denetdale, 2001). It was a female Navajo deity called Changing Woman who created Navajo people and Navajo clans in our creation story. With European and American invasion and influence, Navajo society has adapted and changed in order to survive. Navajo society has become complicated by the inclusion of Western, patriarchal methods of governance, yet, because of historical matrilineal roles and influence, Navajo women still hold much power and authority in the household and among extended family. In our family, my grandmother was the matriarch. After she passed away, my mother was an influential figure. My uncle once told me how she often delegated family responsibilities to her siblings without asking, but they did not question her because her authority was understood and accepted within the family. I always looked up to her as an incredibly powerful woman. I sense this type of empowerment now among my female relatives and within myself. I believe it is Navajo culture and the example of my mother as an empowered Navajo woman that have given me confidence and strengthened my position and identity when I come to intersections between my roles as a researcher, a community member, and a Native woman.

On the Margins in the Academy

My life on the margin began as I was growing up both on and off the Navajo reservation. When I was off the reservation, I was the light-skinned, light-haired Navajo child trying to fit in with my other non-Indian, mostly Chicano and Chicana classmates. When I moved back to the reservation, I was the light-skinned, light-haired Navajo trying to fit in with my Navajo-speaking, dark-skinned, dark-haired classmates. But I did fit in. Once my classmates began to know me beyond the superficial appearance, they realized I was like them. They became part of my inner circle. It was always interesting to me how much easier it was for me to satisfy Indians regarding my identity than non-Indians. Native people could see my identity in the way I presented myself, the family I come from, the place I live, and the work I do. Appearance played only a superficial role. Paula Gunn Allen, a Laguna Pueblo literary scholar, writes about how Native identity is defined by the individual's family, the mother in particular, because they and she determine the individual's place in Laguna society. Not knowing one's family is the same as being lost, isolated, abandoned, self-estranged, and alienated (Allen, 1988). This definition of identity is very similar to that of the Navajo. Navajo is a matrilineal society, so the individual knows his or her point of origin is where his or her mother is from. The individual's clan, which is the basis of Navajo identity, is the mother's clan.

It was not until I reached college that I noticed large differences between myself and my classmates, who were largely middle- to upper-class White students. But I acculturated and learned how to navigate the system. People, mostly in the outer layers of my experiences in college, were not sure what to make of my Native identity, but I think they regarded it as a trendy accessory. I have come across many non-Indians who feel they have no culture, and, therefore, they might see having a Native culture as more a reflection of artifact or appearance, rather than as a sense of being. By the time I went to graduate school, I was adept in the culture of the academy, but I also felt much resistance toward continuing in the same environment, because my Navajo culture was considered to be exotic, unique, and a separate part of myself. In other words, it was an environment that could not see how my identity, values, and sense of self were shaped by my culture. I resisted blending in with my non-Indian classmates. I was tired of explaining myself, of educating them, and of being treated like my culture was a nice ornament. I also found I could not relate to my fellow graduate students. The social functions, and even the academic ones, seemed highly superficial. Invariably the topic of my heritage would come up, and I was put on center stage as a representative of all Native American people, cultures, beliefs, and trends. I can understand people's interest, given that the average American's general knowledge of Native Americans is quite minimal. But it was hard to be enthusiastic about continually addressing America's ignorance to the influence, contributions, and just plain presence of Native Americans in our country.

I spent my first two years in graduate school isolating myself from my cohort in the school of education and, conversely, befriending the Native students enrolled at the university, most of whom were undergraduates. Although I had very positive experiences with my graduate advisor, I was afraid of how the academy might blind me and allow me to begin viewing myself from an outsider's perspective. In other words, I was worried about judging myself from a White person's eyes. The nature of the academy, which I feel includes a great deal of competitiveness, a hierarchical worldview, and aggressiveness, scared me, and I did not want to take on those values. The culture of higher education and its impact on learning and identity at the student and faculty levels is a significant issue among many scholars (Clark, 1987; Meck, Goedegebuure, Kivinen, & Rinne, 1996; Tierney & Rhoads, 1993; Valimaa, 1998). It is a topic I may want to pursue at some point. However, I am still trying to reconcile my place in the academy, which is why I think I feel most comfortable where I am now, in Native American Studies. This department at the university where I work now encompasses people who understand this struggle for Native scholars. There are many Indigenous scholars across international lines who struggle with blending their Western academic training with their roles in their communities and their values as Indigenous people (Enos, 2001; Mihesuah, 1998; Smith, 2000). My motivation for pursuing a Ph.D. was for both personal and community-level benefits. My mother had started work on a Ph.D. but was unable to complete it when she became ill. My personal motivation to complete the degree came from her educational drive. It was important for me to complete what she had started. At the community level, I felt it was important for more Native people to earn doctorates, to create positive change in education for Native students. I was interested in doing something good for my community, be that my Navajo community or my larger Native American community.

Has the academy changed me? I have tried not to let it. For example, the pressure to write and speak in educational jargon in my field makes me uncomfortable. This type of language is so far removed and unimportant to the people in my community. Yet, there are links between academia and Native people in that many current paradigms that scholars write about echo the practices of Native communities. For example, many Native communities have traditionally engaged in community-based learning practices for language acquisition and cultural knowledge. Many scholars now write about this approach to learning as place-based, action, or activist research (Corson, 1999; McCarty & Watahomigie, 1998; Stringer, 2004). Yet, that connection of this conceptualization of learning is not clear between academics and nonacademics. According to Enos (2001), who also discussed this issue in an essay, community people feel distanced from the world of the academy and "researchers do not see the connection either, because they have made themselves inaccessible, in part, through their language" (p. 83). She discussed the similarity of paradigms of thought between scholars and Native people, but there is also a disconnect between the two groups. I have felt that disconnect while attending college and graduate school. I have had to reconcile how my values and how I carry myself (the way I speak and the way I interact with people, all culturally learned) could be interwoven with Western research practices. In college and graduate school, I learned and accepted Western or positivist traditions of research as the only way to conduct research. This made me question much more carefully my own conduct in the research process when designing my dissertation study. I had viewed my own perspectives and positionality as "limitations" to my research because they lessened the objectivity of the research approach. It was not until I returned home, back to the Southwest, and re-immersed myself among Native people and other Native scholars that I had a revelation and came to understand how my perspective and positionality enrich my research. My positionality is influenced by my culture, my gender, and my life experience. I can take a stronger stance in my research by acknowledging these influences and, I hope, create more positive change. I realize that to try to take a neutral stance by viewing my influence in the research process as a limitation does nothing to help me in creating change, and creating change was the main reason I entered an academic career. I wish to be able to say in all my research projects, "This is my passion, this is how it shapes my research approach, and this is the impact I hope to make."

I have benefited a great deal from the academy in the sense that I am a better critical thinker. In fact, I have learned how to be critical, if not skeptical, of current research on or about Native Americans and its benefits to our communities. I tend to agree with Deloria (1991), who points out that research enables scholars to study Native people as an objective science, and these scholars can reap many rewards for what little knowledge they gain. On the other hand, the Native person, with so much more knowledge, who provides that knowledge, receives no compensation, no awards, and continues to perform work with considerably less prestige. I do believe, however, that research is a valuable tool for Native people to continue to use as long as it is conducted in ways that are culturally appropriate, sensitive, and respectful. It is my goal to perform research that is meaningful and accessible to Native people, and my position as a Native woman enriches the perspective I can bring to the research. There is a new movement among Native and non-Native scholars who are trying to conduct research in the same way (for example, see Brayboy & Deyhle, 2000; Holm & Holm, 1995; Lomawaima & McCarty, 2002; May, 1999; Smith, 1999, 2000; Stringer, 2004). I have learned from these scholars how research can include a wider set of activities, thought processes, and rules of engagement. Since I returned home, and especially as I pursue academic work along with several other Native scholars at this university, I find I am learning more about how to blend my training and my values for my Native communities in order to conduct meaningful research that can create positive change. My graduate work taught me the skills, but it was when I came home that I was reminded of my values. Now, I am learning more how to interweave my sensibilities with my research.

Indigenous research and methodologies are emerging for many other Native scholars as well as a type of research that respects community, accesses indigenous knowledge, and appropriately involves Native people in the research process (see Romero, 1994; Smith, 1999). Indigenous research and methodologies incorporate community-based approaches. Community-based research helps reduce cynicism on the part of the practitioners and the people in the community participating in the research because they are involved from the start. Research in this setting is meaningful and, most important, community driven. The results are practical and accessible because they can be applied directly to the site of study. I am pursuing this type of research as a way of contributing something back to my Native American community.

On the Margins at Home

Soon after completing my Ph.D., I decided to move back to New Mexico. I did not seek an academic position through the national job pipeline, because, as a new mother, it was more important for me to return home to raise my children near their family and cultural roots. In addition, there is an expectation among many Native communities that one should return home after completing educational goals in order to apply one's expertise toward community interests and needs.

However, several choices I have made complicated my role in the community and placed me on the margins at home as well, to some extent. I moved to a Pueblo village, where my husband is from, for various reasons. My children are Navajo and Pueblo, and it was important to us that they be raised in one of these communities. The proximity of the Pueblo to two cities, Albuquerque and Santa Fe, allowed more job opportunities for both my husband and myself. Being Navajo and living in a Pueblo village has somewhat positioned me simultaneously as an outsider and an insider. I am a woman who is not from the Pueblo, who looks non-Indian to many people, and who does not speak the Pueblo language. These characteristics position me more on the outside. However, I am simultaneously a Native American, a mother, and a spouse and have Pueblo family and community ties, which positions me more on the inside. My first job when we returned to New Mexico was as a teacher at a federal grant school for Indian students located in Santa Fe. I began to meet people from the Pueblo where I live on a professional level before we moved to the Pueblo and before I began to know them on a personal level. This helped with my acceptance into the Pueblo because I knew people from there on these two different levels.

In other ways, having a Ph.D. further positioned me on the margin, because it is uncommon, and in many respects, I found that it was rather unimpressive or less important than other characteristics. My participation in the Pueblo, such as when I danced in the annual Feast Day,[4] was recognized as more worthy and valuable, because it contributes something directly back to the community. Having a Ph.D. is considered of no use unless one uses it to benefit the community. Thus, I am still not quite sure how my choice to leave teaching at the Santa Fe school to work at the university in first an administrative position and now an academic one has been viewed. People in the Pueblo have been supportive, and my sense is that they are probably waiting to see whether the good I can do with this position will be greater than what I did with my teaching position, which directly contributed to the education of students from the Pueblo.

The issue of conducting research in Native American communities is a sensitive subject and is confounded by my role as a community member. Smith (1999) referred to the problems Native researchers have with their roles as insiders and outsiders when engaging in research in their communities. Research has a negative history in Native communities and can be considered an intrusive exercise, because it has resulted in sharing of information or knowledge that is not open to noncommunity members. The idea of Native persons engaging in this activity may confuse or make one question the commitment of Native researchers to their community's best interests. Furthermore, Native researchers often have other confounding variables that come into play during the research process. Their family background and history may be used to judge them. Their own personal reputation in their community, which may have nothing to do with their research, will certainly influence prospective participants' views of them and possibly affect the nature of their relationship and the outcomes of the research itself. My graduate training did not prepare me for how to address these issues. It simply could not prepare me because these are issues particular to Native researchers. Traditionally, Western research practices are of a completely different mind-set, in that they objectify and distance the subjects of the research. For a Native researcher to distance and objectify Native people in the research process is inappropriate, is offensive to the participants, and limits what can be learned from the research.

Being a woman also influences this relationship between myself as researcher and any Native participants, but it is more difficult for me to articulate on my personal experiences as a woman and how they specifically influence my research. It is difficult because my experiences as a Native person seem to overshadow everything else. Perhaps being raised by a strong and self-assured woman has provided me with a perspective that this is the only type of woman I wish to be, and it is how I expect to be treated and respected by others. But I think that is a culturally learned value, not solely a gender-based value. My mother's prominent role in our family, along with my value for equality and respect, ultimately stems from Navajo culture's value for women. Denetdale (2001) discussed images of Navajo women in creation narratives as evidence of Navajo women's place as central and authoritative figures in Navajo society, who contribute to the continuing vitality of Navajo life and culture:

> Navajo women's status is reflected in the cosmological realm, especially as Navajos continue to revere Changing Woman, the most benevolent of the Holy People. Further, Navajo traditional stories are replete with images of model female and male behavior, which is often referred to as complementary, the notion that gender roles are different, but equal and necessary. (p. 8)

I learned that I should expect to be treated equally and respectfully, and that influences the position I take in conducting research. At the same time, I acknowledge that there are differences regarding women's roles among Native Nations, and the role of "Native woman researcher" may not be so clearly defined in these communities. As a result, I respect the community's protocol for dealing with researchers, and I hope I am helping to define what it means to be a Native woman academic and researcher for Native communities. In any case, my contribution to that definition is not through any direct effort. My main interest is in conducting research that benefits Native people in general and less with focusing on myself. Any barriers I come across because I am a woman, or because I am a Native, or for any other reason, are only obstacles for achieving something greater than myself. I hope that my presence in doing the research and involving Native people will set an example for them to follow as other emerging female Native researchers enter this field. Thus, it is imperative that I do the best I can.

Conclusion

Throughout my life's experiences on the margins in the academy and at home, I have certainly felt out of place and have experienced times of comfort and discomfort. But my grounding in my identity and sense of belonging to my Navajo and my larger Native American community have centered and balanced me. I am empowered by having a strong sense of self and wish that for my children, my relatives, my friends, and my students. I have my mother, and my aunt and uncle who raised me after her passing, to thank for directly teaching me about who I am and for providing me the types of experiences that helped me to learn more about myself. As my mother wished, I have remained strong and will carry and pass on her words throughout whatever future endeavors, struggles, and celebrations life brings.

References

Allen, P. G. (1988). Who is your mother? Red roots of white feminism. In R. Simonson & S. Walker (Eds.), *Multi-cultural literacy: Opening the American mind* (pp. 15–27). St. Paul, MN: Graywolf Press.

Brayboy, B. M., & Deyhle, D. (2000). Insider-outsider: Researchers in American Indian communities. *Theory into Practice, 39*, 163–169.

Churchill, W. (2001). The crucible of American Indian identity: Native tradition versus colonial imposition in post-conquest North America. In S. Lobo & S. Talbot (Eds.), *Native American voices: A reader.* Upper Saddle River, NJ: Prentice-Hall.

Clark, B. R. (Ed.). (1987). *The academic profession: Natural, disciplinary, and institutional settings.* Berkeley, CA: University of California Press.

Corson, D. (1999). Community based education for indigenous cultures. In S. May (Ed.), *Indigenous community-based education* (pp. 8–19). Clevedon, UK: Multilingual Matters.

Deloria, V., Jr. (1991). Commentary: Research, redskins, and reality. *American Indian Quarterly, 15,* 457–468.

Denetdale, J. (2001). Representing changing woman: A review essay on Navajo women. *American Indian Culture and Research Journal, 25*(3), 1–26.

Deyhle, D. (1998). From breakdancing to heavy metal: Navajo youth resistance and identity. *Youth and Society, 30,* 3–31.

Enos, A. D. (2001). A landscape with multiple views: Research in Pueblo communities. In B. Merchant & A. Willis (Eds.), *Multiple and intersecting identities in qualitative research* (pp. 83–101). Mahwah, NJ: Erlbaum Associates.

Henze, R. C., & Vanett, L. (1993). To walk in two worlds or more: Challenging a common metaphor of Native education. *Anthropology & Education Quarterly, 24,* 116–134.

Holm, A., & Holm, W. (1995). Navajo language education: Retrospect and prospect. *Bilingual Research Journal, 19,* 141–167.

Lawrence, B. (2003). Gender, race, and the regulation of Native identity in Canada and the United States: An overview. *Hypatia, 18,* 3–31.

Lee, L. (2004). *Utilizing Sa'ah Naaghai Bik'eh Hozhoon as part of the research process.* Paper presented at Doing Indigenous Research: Theory and Practice Seminar, School of American Research, Santa Fe, NM.

Lomawaima, K. T., & McCarty, T. (2002). *Reliability, validity, and authenticity in American Indian and Alaska Native Research.* (ERIC Clearinghouse on Rural Education and Small Schools Document No. ED470951).

May, S. (Ed.). (1999). *Indigenous community-based education.* Clevedon, UK: Multilingual Matters.

McCarty, T., & Watahomigie, L. (1998). Indigenous community based language education in the USA. *Language, Culture, and Curriculum, 11,* 309–324.

Meck, L. V., Goedegebuure, L., Kivinen, O., & Rinne, R. (Eds.). (1996). *The mockers and mocked: Comparative perspectives on differentiation, convergence, and diversity in higher education.* Guilford: Pergamon and IAU Press.

Mihesuah, D. (Ed.). (1998). *Natives and academics: Researching and writing about American Indians.* Lincoln: University of Nebraska Press.

Romero, M. E. (1994). Identifying giftedness among Keresan Pueblo Indians: The Keres study. *Journal of American Indian Education, 34*(1), 35–58.

Smith, L. T. (1999). *Decolonizing methodologies: Research and indigenous peoples.* London, UK: Zed Books.

Smith, L. T. (2000). Kaupapa Maori research. In M. Batiste (Ed.), *Reclaiming indigenous voice and vision* (pp. 225–247). Vancouver, BC: UBC Press.

Stringer, E. (2004). *Action research in education.* Upper Saddle River, NJ: Pearson Education.

Tierney, W. G., & Rhoads, R. A. (1993). *Enhancing promotion, tenure, and beyond* (ASHE-ERIC Higher Education Report No. 6). Washington, DC: The George Washington University and ASHE.

Valimaa, J. (1998). Culture and identity in higher education. *Higher Education, 36,* 119–138.

Endnotes

1. I use the terms *Indian, American Indian, Native American,* and *Native* interchangeably, for they are each widely used in the Southwest. Pueblo communities tend to use the term *Indian*. Academic circles use *Native American* or *American Indian*.

2. The BIA is a federal agency charged with operating schools for Native students. The schools are typically located on Indian reservations, and it was not until the 1970s or later that Indian people held leadership positions in operating these schools. My mother was one of the first Native women to hold a significantly high position.

3. Pueblos are Native American tribes that share characteristics such as agricultural, linguistic, and cultural practices. There are 19 Pueblos in New Mexico. *Pueblo* has many meanings, such as a village, a community, a culture, a tribe, and a reservation.

4. *Diné* is the Navajo word for "the People" and is often used in place of *Navajo*. Navajo people frequently use both terms in speaking and writing.

5. "Feast Days" are held in every Pueblo in New Mexico and are days that the community celebrates its harvest. The people from the community dance all day, and many families feed visitors, other family, and friends at their homes. Many Feast Days also coincide with a particular Catholic saint's day, because many Pueblos incorporate Catholicism into their traditional activities.

6

TRANSITIONS

Finding My Voice

Tinaya Webb

The Author

Tinaya Webb is a mother, an educator, and a graduate student at the University of Illinois–Chicago. Working in the Chicago public schools, Tinaya has dedicated her life to the improvement of public education for African American children. Her professional undertakings include working with Trinity United Church of Christ's research team to create the church's position on the No Child Left Behind Act and researching the outcomes for African American children from the 1989 desegregation case *People Who Care v. Rockford Public Schools District 205*. Her doctoral research examines the effects of schooling on the cultural loss/retention of African American children. Other interests include the effectiveness of professional development, reading and African American children, and the politics of race and class.

Tinaya works as a lead literacy teacher at Webster Elementary School and as a graduate assistant in the University of Illinois Reading Clinic, which focuses on remedial reading tutorial services for members of the community and serves as a practicum for master's students. Tinaya loves spending time with her children, reading, and contributing to the fight for liberation of the minds of African people.

I n U.S. society, Black women are often asked to accept existing forms of knowledge, instead of adding their interpretation and voice. Early in our development, our thoughts are labeled as emotional, instead of intellectual, and this is the beginning of one form of female oppression. My most vivid memory of this phenomenon occurred in the 10th grade. I was attending a science fair in Champaign, Illinois (sponsored by a young scholars' program), where I was to present a project outlining the layers of the skin. I had a pictorial display and a typewritten report neatly packaged inside a plastic cover. I was excited to be attending a science fair away from home, but my expectations for how my project would be critiqued were higher than how it was actually evaluated.

I eagerly waited for the evaluators to see my display, but my confidence was quickly shattered as the judges questioned me about my topic in depth. I was unable to answer questions, stumbling over words and referring to my drawing of the skin as if I had not done the work myself. By the third question, tears were streaming down my face. Pretending I was having an allergy attack allowed me to avoid further questioning as I excused myself to go the bathroom. I thought I had escaped such an embarrassing situation, but when I returned one keen judge was waiting for me. He picked up on my unpreparedness and calmly discussed the things I did not do well and offered suggestions for improvement.

The feeling of failure was so overwhelming that I still cringe when I reflect on that experience. I felt so dumb! I could not share my encounter with my peers. In no academic experience had I been asked the type of open-ended questions that these judges had asked. In no classroom dialogue had I been pushed to support claims I had made. Like many Black women, I internalized a debilitating belief that I was unable to express myself in certain spaces. I made good use of the familiar scapegoat, "I don't know; I just feel that way!" to dodge the exercise of having to explain fully my thoughts. Emotion is a form of intellect. When talking with your girlfriends, everyone understands that your perspective and the full context of a situation do not need to be explained. Feeling that your opinion is correct without substantial evidence is unacceptable in the world of academia. Black women, especially in academia, must demonstrate an ability to string their thoughts together in a cohesive manner, be critical, and master standard English. Ten years after my science fair disaster, I have confronted and am conquering my learned silence.

My contribution to this book is an examination of the transition from sheltered womanhood to, as hooks (1989) discusses, "talking back." Drawing from Africana womanism, Black feminism, and Critical Race Theory (CRT) (Delgado & Stefancic, 2001). I wish to share my thoughts on finding my liberated voice as a doctoral student, a mother, and a spouse. The first component of this essay reveals my personal insecurities and my ideas of what I believed was expected of me as a woman and then later as a wife. I then discuss the tension between my spouse and me as I gained more knowledge and developed a logical perspective on various topics as a graduate student. This also entails the struggle of single motherhood and my battle to continue with my studies. Finally, I toss around the consequences of finding my voice and its worthiness for a budding African American scholar.

This is *my* story. I highly caution readers against fitting their own personal experiences into mine. The ideas I express can arguably be antifeminist. I believe that in the continuity of male and female relationships we inflict pain equally upon each other. I have witnessed healthy relationships, and I think women and men are complements to each other. The African family cannot survive if we do not believe this.

In the Beginning

Growing up in a two-parent home, I was blessed to see the inner workings of a relationship between a man and a woman. My impression of my mother was mixed, to say the least. At times I felt she was gullible and submissive. Then, I would witness a strong, opinionated force that challenged my father's views. She and my father both took care of the home, and my father, of Southern roots, made sure his children knew and understood the tenets of hard work. He held strong views on how a woman should carry herself:

having soft hands, acting and dressing "like a lady," no spitting, and so forth. These things were not necessarily wrong, but they did not fully represent my identity. I had calluses on my hands, wore baggy shorts (easily interchangeable with biker pants) and mismatched socks, and made it a habit to spit. My dad actually paid for me to go to modeling school so I could develop some etiquette. Funny, I do not and never did see his beliefs as being oppressive. I truly believe my dad was acting out of love and concern.

I learned many things from my mother. Her modeling as a nurturer and supporter is one behavior I strive to exemplify throughout my life. I find it more pleasant to do things for others than for myself and understand that some take my kindness for weakness. At an early age I was practically an "othermother" (Collins, 1991), and my frame of reference revolved around being there for others. As Collins (1991) writes,

> Community othermothers' actions demonstrate a clear rejection of separateness and individual interest as the basis of either community organization or individual self-actualization. Instead, the connectedness with others and common interest expressed by community othermothers models a very different value system, one whereby *Afrocentric feminist* [italics added[1]] ethics of caring and personal accountability move communities forward. (pp. 131–132)

Personal insecurities about not being well spoken, combined with the belief that a woman is defined by her ability to support a man, made me quite traditional. The only criticism I have of traditional ideas is that they pigeonhole women into a particular role. This confinement begins to hurt Black women's development, especially when we are not exposed to other ideas about womanhood. This is what happens when the community places a high value on gender roles and does not allow room for exploration. A boy learns it is okay to be aggressive and dominant in spaces, and a girl learns to be silent and passive. Women and men internalize these roles, and women begin to feel oppressed. Strict gender role setting without compromise becomes the problem, not males hating and hurting women. Communication gaps persist, expectations are set, and conflicting ideas are not accepted. The choices I made looking through a traditional lens blinded me to my own insecurities, and I developed a narrow concept of Black womanhood.

Spousing

I recall being surprised at the independence of some Black women in the 1800s as I read *Black Feminist Thought* (Collins, 1991). To think that they did not believe marriage is for everyone is a refreshing idea in that it makes marriage a choice, not a need or an expectation. When I was pregnant with my first child, my mother promptly mentioned that I should be getting married. A telephone conversation with the father's mother bore the same question, "So, when are you two going to get married?" My answer was never! This was disappointing for my parents, but I could not see being married to someone just because a child was involved. This event pushed me a bit outside of my original views of womanhood. I thought I was claiming my independence—until I met my future husband. Here I describe the progression of my relationship and its parallel to my growth in academia.

I accept the thought that "The Africana womanist is also *in concert* with males in the broader struggle for humanity and the liberation of all Africana people" (Hudson-Weems, 1993, p. 61). My husband introduced me to the studies of African and African American people, and as I grew in my understanding of our unique situation, I felt more strongly that my duty as a woman was to be strong and steadfast in my support of the Black man.[2]

There was never a time when I was not there for my husband. Not being as well read as he at the time, I listened faithfully to many of his ideas. I never thought he was wrong and never used logic to weigh in on any contradictions he made. He is very well spoken and quite opinionated (dominating every conversation he was in), a bit arrogant, and proud to be Black. As I read more on the history of African Americans, we were able to engage in more substantive conversations. These conversations led to a more serious relationship, and we married during the final year of my undergraduate degree. We made babies, and he continued his education. After being a classroom teacher, I decided to get my master's in education.

We had a busy life with both of us being in school and raising two (and later three) children. My interest in the education of Black children grew, and as he continued his educational pursuits, we were quite happy being the scholar/spouse duo. During this time of intellectual growth and mothering, I noticed that my opinions still did not mean much to him. Comments such as, "That's stupid," or "That doesn't make any sense" came out of his mouth frequently. I never argued much, but objections to these statements yielded counters such as, "Stop being so sensitive," and "That's not what I meant." His statements only fostered the personal insecurity I already had. Although I am not absolving him from his reactions to my thoughts, it is imperative for Black women to be honest about the ideas and emotions we bring into our relationships with Black men.

During this time, I believe he was in a period of self-defining and wanted to complete his goals. I never wanted to be the one he blamed for not allow-ing him to work through his plan. Four years into our marriage, his personal drive led to his desire to move to Georgia so he could study at a university there. I knew he loved his family but after several incidents felt he wasn't accomplishing his goals. His move meant that I would be spending the last year of earning my master's with three children by myself. I supported him and said it was okay for him to leave.

hooks's (1989) notion of speaking out was something I had begun to do in the university setting but not in my relationship. What Black man wants to hear a liberated voice when he himself cannot talk back in certain arenas? After adopting White patriarchal tendencies, a Black man must feel he is in control, and when he is demeaned in the world, his home makes him feel secure. Waves from a spouse can often cause dissension in the ranks. This speaks to the dynamics of CRT. The laws and philosophies of our society based solely on the construction of race play into our daily relationships with one another. For Africana men and women, it has spilled over into our un-derstandings of each other, making our interrelationships a struggle to main-tain.

My husband left for Georgia, but a more severe event called him back and put a deep wound in our relationship. By this time, I had decided to continue my education and had started my doctoral studies, but hurt and pain caused by both of us to each other made for a highly sensitive space. The university setting really pushed me to use logic and analytical skills in a way that was new and refreshing for me. My newfound ability to be more critical, along with our sensitivities, played into our conversations, and he began to think I was always against him. One observer noted that my hus-band did not like the fact that I refused to agree with him uncritically.

As I began experiencing academic success in the classroom and shared praise professors would give to me, it seemed he was unable to share my joy. His congratulations were always countered with a comment about himself or seemed strained. I did not like that my husband was not wholly supportive, especially when I had always been there for him. One world was falling apart while another was emerging. Would my relationship be better if I remained silent? I did not think so, but before we could begin balancing the two worlds, tragedy struck, in the form of abandonment, leaving me with three children to raise on my own.

Mother and Scholar—Making Choices

The immediate reaction to my new situation was to leave graduate school so I could focus on the mental, emotional, and physical well-being of my children. It was painful to think that I would have to leave the space where I was growing, learning, and debating. I also felt that the completion of my studies was important to my mission of improving public education for African American children. Comments from other students such as, "Here comes the militant one," further solidified my growing commitment to and articulation of the oppressive situation of African American people. The academic world is very demanding; so are my children. Choices had to be made.

After consulting with a close professor, friends, and family members, I made the decision to continue my studies. I have not yet felt the oppressive weight of being a woman in academia as I have of being Black and having strong views about our experience. Being in an institutionalized setting, I do realize the nature of the beast and know that my race and gender will define me to others. To counter that, I find comfort in consorting with other women of color who are in the doctoral program.

I am a true picture of a balancing act. I juggle working at two jobs, completing my doctoral studies, caring for three children, and carrying out other duties into a weekly routine. This persistence to survive and still be an active force in the Black community is the reality that further separates the Black woman's fight from that of her White counterparts (Collins, 1991; hooks, 1984, 1989; Hudson-Weems, 1993). Survival is not anything new, and I do not dare make any comparisons of my life situation with anyone else's. This is only another testament to the dynamics of being considered an "other" and the detrimental pressure it puts on Black people to perform, produce, provide, and still proceed.

Finding My Voice

It is difficult for Black women to filter their personal interpretations into strong societal perspectives on race, class, and gender. Being liberated and finding the ability to speak out against any oppression is a constant battle among (1) internalized perceptions of the role of women, (2) commitment to the community, (3) awareness of oppression caused by societal values, and (4) being honest.

Finding my own voice in both academia and my relationships has had its ups and downs. Playing the part of both mother and father to two boys and a girl calls me to wrestle continually with how I present gender roles while not hindering my children's individual growth and freedom to make choices. Because of my own experiences, I push them to rationalize the statements they make. Saying "I don't know" in response to any question is not acceptable, and I encourage my children to explain their actions. If I hear one child say to the other, "You're acting like a girl!" I ask what acting like a girl means. I correct statements that qualify objects as being for girls or for boys, and I give them room to express their emotions. In addition, I impress on them values and beliefs of their culture and responsibility to the Black community. Being a mother pushes me to develop my voice continually.

The role of wife has impacted my life in an enormous way. It called for me to challenge my traditional ideas of womanhood. Tension between my spouse and me made me reach deep into myself and expose my personal insecurities. When acceptance of the traditional gender roles broke down, so did our communication. The collision of interests as both of us worked on our academic pursuits, in combination with life-changing events, created a sensitive space. I questioned how he viewed me as a Black woman, and how I perceived my duties as a spouse. The role of spouse forced me to find my voice.

As a doctoral student, I am finding that I have to operate under a pre-scribed set of rules that influence the way I communicate my ideas. Now that I have found the means to speak out, it has become difficult to keep the momentum going. I often comment on how much easier my life was when my speech did not have to contain much substance. Determined to keep my doctoral studies relevant to uplifting my community is forcing me to main-tain my voice.

References

Collins, P. H. (1991). *Black feminist thought—knowledge, consciousness, and the politics of empowerment.* New York: Routledge.

Delgado, R., & Stefancic, J. (2001). *Critical race theory.* New York: New York University Press.

hooks, b. (1984). *Feminist theory—From margin to center.* Cambridge, MA: South End Press.

hooks, b. (1989). *Talking back—Thinking feminist, thinking black.* Boston: South End Press.

Hudson-Weems, C. (1993). *Africana womanism: Reclaiming ourselves.* Troy, MI: Bedford.

Endnotes

1. Here, I must make my claim for the term *Africana womanism*. I italicized "Af-rocentric feminist" to highlight my rejection of the term *feminist* to define the strug-

gle for Black women. Although it should not be a distraction for the solidarity of Black women, how we name ourselves, our views, and our fight is critical. In her book *Africana Womanism: Reclaiming Ourselves,* Clenora Hudson-Weems (1993) sites the fact that the feminist movement as defined by middle-class White women does not fit the issues of the Africana woman because it does not adequately address the issues of race and class. These two factors are endemic to the Africana woman's situation.

2. The intent of this section is not to bash males nor is it to place blame. I have come to understand the choices I have made and place my life's struggles in the broader context of the difficulties and stresses that accompany being Black and a woman.

7

IN BETWEEN CHINA AND NORTH AMERICA

Ming Fang He

The Author

Ming Fang He is an associate professor in the Department of Curriculum, Foundations, and Research in the College of Education at Georgia Southern University. Her work focuses on cross-cultural curriculum studies, narrative/narrative inquiry, and curriculum theory. She currently serves as the editor of *Curriculum Inquiry* and associate editor of *Multicultural Perspectives: An Official Journal of the National Association for Multicultural Education,* as well as program chair for the International Studies Special Interest Group of the American Educational Research Association. Dr. He is the 2003 recipient of the Jack Miller Educator of the Year Award and has authored numerous publications including her book *A River Forever Flowing: Cross-Cultural Lives and Identities in the Multicultural Landscape* (2003). She received her Ph.D. from the Ontario Institute for Studies in Education/University of Toronto in 1998.

The assumption in the phrase "oppression to grace" implies development and growth from being freedom impoverished to freedom enriched. As I thought about writing this chapter, this phrase, and its implications, kept coming into conflict with my experience as a Chinese woman faculty member moving back and forth between continually changing Eastern and Western cultures. My experience is not, I have decided, easily or even best captured by the phrase "oppression to grace." As I thought further about this, I realized that a more appropriate way of articulating how I felt about my experience within the academy was one of in-betweenness. My experience is not one of being in between oppression and grace but, rather, something more complex, historically narrativized, and culturally contexualized. My position and experience in the academy are part of this complexity, but by no means all, or even the most important. The issue, I think, essentially comes to a question of cross-cultural movement between landscapes that are themselves moving. Herein I articulate this sense of in-betweenness and discuss the dilemmas, tensions, and advantages associated with my life within the North American academy.

In-Betweenness: Cultural Movements in China

I am a woman of color, born and raised in a dramatically different culture and language, teaching and working in an American university. My sense of in-betweenness, at one level, is easy to understand based on the forces of color, language, and culture that sweep through our intellectual landscape. But what are the origins of this feeling? Why do I feel in between rather than oppressed?

The reasons, I think, were inscribed in my being as a child. Though I did not know it, I was in between at birth, having been born during the Anti-Rightist Movement and the Great Leap Forward in the late 1950s. My parents were teachers and, as such, were relatively privileged, being considered "engineers of human beings' brains." But the forces in the Anti-Rightist Movement and in the Great Leap Forward led to dramatic changes in my family's status within Chinese society. These changes culminated during the Cultural Revolution (1966–1976), when social values were turned upside down. Intellectuals were considered bourgeois and were to be "reeducated." My father, for example, was removed from his position as teacher; chastised in a street parade, in which he wore a high paper hat and placard on his chest with his name upside down and crossed through with a red X; and eventually imprisoned on a reforming farm to "confess his antirevolutionary bourgeois pollution of students' brains." Thus, for me, the in-betweenness I was born into in the Anti-Rightist Movement and the Great Leap Forward became physically visible in the upside-down values of the Cultural Revolution. As a child, my values and beliefs were in question. Once my parents were highly revered, but suddenly I witnessed my father being publicly chastised, which sharply put basic values and beliefs in conflict. As a child I held onto those values while also adopting the values of the Cultural Revolution without questioning. I was, I now understand, in between. As a child, of course, I neither thought of this as in-betweenness nor understood that there were fundamental intellectual threads at work, which, I now see, are tied to my current academic life. I have written about this as a key moment in my cross-cultural life and identity development (He, 2003). From the point of view of this chapter and the purposes of this book, this was, I believe, a key moment in creating the sense I now experience of being in between.

These cultural movements and the sense of in-betweenness were particularly poignant for me because, I believe, these were intellectual reforms and the in-betweenness was essentially an intellectual in-betweenness. Now I find myself working in the university as an intellectual. What began as anguish over family and social values is now with me as an intellectual sense of not belonging here or there, but of being in between.

What began in the Anti-Rightist Movement and the Great Leap Forward had at least one other major revolutionary expression important to the development of my sense of in-betweenness. It was the intellectuals who were primarily targeted in the Anti-Rightist Movement; in the Cultural Revolution; and in another form, later, in what the world has come to know as the Tiananmen Square Student Movement (1989).

I was, I believe, somewhat characteristic of my generation in that following the Cultural Revolution, when the universities reopened, it was, for the most part, the children of the intellectual group who went to university. Their in-betweenness was brought to life during the Cultural Revolution as they secretly were tutored, read banned adult books, and listened to foreign radio broadcasts. This is how my education continued, secretly in between.

I was successful at university and became a teacher of English as a foreign language. Even then, during that comparatively stable time, the sense of in-betweenness born during the earlier cultural movements was strengthened. My students, most of whom were born during the Cultural Revolution and, therefore, had no direct experience of it, were out of sync with their teachers such as myself. The China they knew and the China I knew were different. This is a difference that continues to this day, for people of different generations speak very differently of the China they know. This difference intensified my sense of in-betweenness within my own culture.

My years as a teacher created, I now realize, yet another thread in my sense of in-betweenness, this time the foreigner versus the Chinese, with the position I now find myself in as being neither the foreigner, that is, the American, nor the Chinese. How did this occur? The post–Cultural Revolution was a time of opening up to the West. Specifically, I encountered four American teachers, two Canadian teachers, and one British teacher on my Chinese campus. I studied with them and learned ways of teaching and learning dramatically different from those I had learned from my parents and other Chinese teachers. I tried to bring these ideas to my own teaching and, as always, struggled to find the balance. I was, intellectually, in between.

This thread of being in between the Chinese and the foreigner became intensified during the Tiananmen Square Student Movement in 1989. Even though China's open-door policy (1978–present) was intended as an opening to the Western economic world, Western values and ideas, as I have already noted, flooded into China, particularly Western ideas of democracy. Tiananmen Square, the largest square in the center of Beijing, has been a national symbol of central governance for centuries (China National Tourist Administration, 2003). Tiananmen Gate, "Gate of Heavenly Peace," is the gate to the imperial city—the Forbidden City. It has functioned "as a rostrum for proclamations to the assembled masses," with the Great Hall of the People on the western side; the Museum of the Chinese Revolution and the Museum of Chinese History to its east and west, respectively; the Monument to the People's Heroes at the center of the square; and the Chairman Mao Memorial Hall and the Qianmen Gate on the south side (China National Tourist Administration, 2003). Democracy-oriented students used this symbolic location to make a stand on democracy and request that the government move toward a democratic modern China. The student movement ended with a military crackdown, political persecution, the arrest of student leaders, and the exodus of large numbers of students and intellectuals abroad.

As a university teacher, I was once again in between, pushed and pulled in several directions at the same time. My sympathies with my own students' desire for Western democratic ideas paralleled my sympathies with Chinese situations and their history. I was caught between advising my students to be cautious, to respect traditional values and the current government, and to reach out to the West and exercise democratic rights. The Tiananmen Square Student Movement catapulted my thinking on my China-foreign in-betweenness, and I left China to study in Canada.

In-Betweenness: The North American Academy

My journey to North America dramatically shifted my positioning on what was foreign. Now I was the foreigner, but still, perhaps even more intensely so, in between. I brought my Chineseness, which was far more of a living presence in my new environment than was Western foreignness a presence in my Chinese environment. I was now living in a culture, actually cultures, that I had mostly read about and had experienced only indirectly in China. I earlier noted that the cultural in-betweenness into which I was born was, ultimately, an intellectual in-betweenness. This became strengthened on my arrival in North America. First and foremost, as in the Cultural Revolution, the experience was one commonly referred to as "cultural shock." Values that held me together and guided me were, as in the Cultural Revolution, turned topsy-turvy as I landed on North American soil. But I soon found, or at least it now seems, as I reflect on my experience, that landing on North American soil meant an intellectual shift. What might have been seen as cultural in-betweenness became, and was, intellectual in-betweenness.

One of the special features of in-betweenness as I experienced it in North America, and that made even more distinct my sense of in-betweenness, was diversity. I moved to undertake my doctoral studies in Toronto, recognized by the United Nations as the most multicultural city in the world. Diversity and multiculturalism were key words everywhere: on the radio; in the newspapers; on the streets; and, of course, in the ideologies and reference lists of the courses I was taking. Whereas I may have thought of myself as coming to North America and into something that could be more or less thought of monoculturally, I found myself in the midst of diversity and wondering, even more so than before, where I fit within this diverse, multicultural landscape. The intellectual work complicated, rather than simplified, this sense of in-betweenness. In search of theoretical positions, I found a diversity of positions. If there was a key note that rang through my course work, it was an intellectual world of multiplicity that one needed to sort through and choose ideas, theories, and ways of thinking suitable to oneself and to various topics of concern.

Some aspects of this intellectual in-betweenness were surprising from another point of view in that they were unexpected connections to the intellectual roots of my upbringing. I found myself studying John Dewey and reading about his trips to China (Clopton & Ou, 1973). I recognized, as did Hall and Ames (1999), intellectual links between Confucian thought and Deweyan thought. Indeed, my sense that Dewey shortened, rather than lengthened, the in-between bridge may have, at least partially, been behind my special interest in Deweyan theory as I pursued my doctoral studies.

Though I had encountered, and even tried, Western thinking and teaching methods, and had worked through master's degree programs at two different universities, I found the spirit of inquiry required in doctoral research to be quite different from the sense of authority and certainty that tended to accompany my ways of Chinese teaching and learning. Again I found myself very much in between because I sensed a different way of thinking and reached out to it while being held from it by the in-betweenness I was born into and the in-betweenness I lived. I was in between a self becoming intellectually inquiry oriented and a sustained self who thought of knowledge in formalistic ways. Just as I now understand that I can never escape the in-betweenness to which I was born, I cannot escape the in-betweenness of knowledge as inquiry (Clandinin & Connelly, 2000) and knowledge as certainty. This in-betweenness permeates my academic life in North America.

This in-betweenness, in another form, continues to develop as I live in the North American academy as a faculty member. A woman of yellow color, as who I was, and will always be, I often find myself caught up in between Black and White tensions. This Black and White in-betweenness is compounded with multiple in-betweenness: in-betweenness within my own culture in China, in North America, and in between. This complex in-betweenness blurs the boundaries between "colonizer and colonized, dominant and subordinate, oppressor and oppressed" (Ang, 2001, p. 2). It creates ambiguities, complexities, and contradictions. I find myself constantly entangled in between. As I encouraged my American students to challenge their

White privileges, I realized that as a Han, the dominant cultural group among 56 ethnic groups in China, I was privileged even though I was intellectually suppressed during cultural movements in China. I also realized that I was privileged as one of the very few Chinese women who could afford to step out of my own country to experience this complex in-betweenness even though I kept losing my sense of belonging in North America. I became, in the Mainland Chinese vernacular, an Overseas Chinese woman with "longer knowledge and shorter hair" (more educated and independent, and less "feminine"), and a woman with a "sandwich mind" (partially Chinese and partially Western).

This in-betweenness became more complicated as I moved back and forth in between cultures in China and North America. In May 2001, I was invited back to China as a Chinese American professor to attend an educational convention on women and minority education and give public lectures. As I flew across the North American continent back to the Asian continent, the cross-cultural, intellectual in-betweenness led to political in-betweenness. On April 19, 2001, the U.S. Department of State issued a public announcement "cautioning Americans—especially Americans of Chinese origin—that they should carefully evaluate their risk of being detained by Chinese authorities before deciding whether to travel to China . . ." (U.S. Department of State's Bureau of International Information Programs, 2001). The announcement states "that individuals who have at any time engaged in activities or published writings critical of Chinese government policies . . . are particularly at risk of detention, even if they have previously visited China without incident" (U.S. Department of State's Bureau of International Information Programs, 2001). As a Chinese-born American, I was advised not to travel back to China. That incident led to tensions. My writing on my experience of the Cultural Revolution (He, 1998) might be perceived as carrying out implicit criticism against the Chinese government. I was, again, captured in between. This time, the in-betweenness was political. I was proud of my writing but frightened by its political potential. This fearful feeling was intensified when the Chinese graduate students at the conference warned me in a friendly way to be careful about what I said and what I did in public, because there was a group of security officers housed just above my residence room. My sense of in-betweenness became traumatized.

This political aspect of intellectual in-betweenness became magnified as I translated my talk and my North American colleagues' talks into Chinese. I found myself stumbling through translation at the very beginning of the conference, being recognized by my Chinese colleagues as an American professor who "dressed like a Chinese and talked like a foreigner" while they themselves dressed in Western ties and suits and talked about the Western paradigms of research in eloquent Chinese English. To borrow a phrase from Hoffman (1989), I felt "lost in translation," because the academic language of multiculturalism and qualitative research was not mentioned in my Chinese education. The political in-betweenness with which I approached the conference turned into linguistic in-betweenness during the conference. I found myself gaining confidence in my translation throughout the conference, and, although still in between, I felt myself moving toward my Chinese self. Being "lost in translation" was, for me, as it was for Hoffman, a metaphor for in-betweenness and the sense of not belonging here or there that comes with cultural movements.

Conclusion

For the purpose of this chapter, it is important to note that it was an academic conference that I was attending in my role as an American woman faculty member. The nuanced cultural, political, and linguistic sense of in-betweenness that accompanied my attendance at the conference characterized my role as a woman of color in the North American academy. I did not feel oppressed at this conference, nor in the experiences I have described that gave rise to my academic life. I am, and always will be, I believe, in between. A recognition of this in-betweenness, is the starting point, perhaps the turning point, of my inquiry in the North American academy.

References

Ang, I. (2001). *On not speaking Chinese: Living between Asia and the West.* New York: Routledge.

China National Tourist Administration. (2003, October 27). *Tian'anmen* [On-line]. Retrieved July 29, 2002, from www.beijingtrip.com/attractions/square.htm

Clandinin, D. J., & Connelly, F. M. (2000). *Narrative inquiry: Experience and story in qualitative research.* San Francisco: Jossey-Bass.

Clopton, R. W., & Ou, T. C. (Trans. & Eds.). (1973). *John Dewey: Lectures in China, 1919–1920.* Honolulu: The University Press of Hawaii.

Hall, D. L., & Ames, R. T. (1999). *The democracy of the dead: Dewey, Confucius, and the hope for democracy in China.* Chicago: Open Court Publishing.

He, M. F. (1998). *Professional knowledge landscapes: Three Chinese women teachers' enculturation and acculturation processes in China and Canada.* Unpublished doctoral dissertation, University of Toronto, Canada.

He, M. F. (2003). *A river forever flowing: Cross-cultural lives and identities in the multicultural landscape.* Greenwich, CT: Information Age Publishing.

Hoffman, E. (1989). *Lost in translation: A life in a new language.* New York: Penguin Books.

U.S. Department of State's Bureau of International Information Programs. (2001, April 19). *Public announcement on detention of U.S. citizens in China (State Department warns travelers of increased risk)* (Press Releases and Announcements 2001) [On-line]. Retrieved October 27, 2003, from http://usinfo.state.gov/regional/ea/uschina/chpr.htm

8

BOTH OPPRESSOR AND OPPRESSED

An Asian Indian Woman's Experience
within the Academy

Kiran Katira

The Author

Kiran Katira is an East African Asian Indian woman, born in Africa and raised in England. She received her bachelor's in elementary education/multicultural education in England and taught in a multiracial urban elementary school for three years. After emigrating to the United States to join her husband, she received her master's in educational administration from New Mexico State University. She is currently pursuing a Ph.D. in educational thought and sociocultural studies at the University of New Mexico. For the past six years, Kiran has worked and served in a community-schools project in inner-city Albuquerque, where she learns and works to build community-university collaborations to serve inner-city youth of color. She has also taught courses to graduate and undergraduate students at the University of New Mexico that focus on race relations and education, community-based initiatives, and critical multicultural education. Her academic interests include antiracist teaching/learning for social justice within urban schools, community-based learning projects, and university settings.

A udre Lorde (1984) wrote, "[T]he true focus of revolutionary change is never merely the oppressive situations which we seek to escape, but that piece of the oppressor which is planted deep within each of us, and which knows only the oppressors' tactics, the oppressors' relationships." This is what needs further exploration within the Asian Indian experience, and this is where my story begins. I am a young, East African, Asian Indian, immigrant woman of color and community activist, and every self-identifier I list has immense bearings on my life in academia. Through these multiple identities I come face-to-face with what it means to be both oppressor and oppressed on a regular basis. In this chapter, I explore the theoretical under-pinnings as well as the practical manifestations of this experience.

An East African Indian's Developing Race Consciousness

What does it mean that I identify as an East African Indian? I am an Asian Indian born in Kenya, East Africa. There is a substantial Asian Indian community in Kenya and other countries such Tanzania and Uganda in East Africa. The history of this group's migration to East Africa dates back to colonial times and before. However, it is during colonial times that the British brought a vast number of Indians over to Africa. The colonial context did not end there, though. The British set up a three-tiered racial hierarchy within Kenya that had the Whites in leadership positions of power and the Indian Africans in retail, service, and middle-management positions. The Black Africans had access to those in the lowest economic tier, many of whom were in manual positions in which they had interaction with Indian Africans more than they did with Whites. Obviously this created a great deal of tension between the Indian Africans and the Black Africans. We worked, lived, and often studied side by side with Black Africans yet within distinct power relations (Alibhai-Brown, 1999). The experience of growing up there gave us all a very racialized identity, a race consciousness that would influence the way we view the world and our place in it.

This would be further heightened when tens of thousands of us emigrated to England in the early 1970s as the result of political unrest in East Africa. The mass arrival of immigrants of color was met with a violent backlash from the British right wing, especially the politically and racially motivated National Front. During this period, there was an alignment of people of color in the United Kingdom, where the Black British and Asian immigrants came together under a "Black collective" to form a coalition of cross-racial solidarity against White supremacy (Sivanandan, 1990). Unfortunately, this coalition fell apart at the seams once any small victories were won. Through the 1980s and into the 1990s, there was a sharp turn in the success and acceptance of East African Indians in the United Kingdom. The success was tied to the acceptance but was also owing to several other factors, including the fact that the Kenyan Indians came from a British educational system in Kenya, which more than prepared them to accommodate to the educational system in England. The acceptance is similar to the "model minority" myth in the United States, in which Asians are used to reify the achievement ideology, while completely ignoring the reasons for the success and the many Asian groups that do not have the same patterns of success (Lee, 1996). For example, in the United Kingdom, the Pakistani and Bangladeshi communities are both near the bottom, if not at the bottom, in terms of economic, employment, and educational status compared with all other racialized groups. The reasons for this include the differences in the socioeconomic and educational status of these communities before they arrived in England and the acceptance of them once they were settled (Prashad, 2001; Sivanandan, 1990; Wu, 2002). The differences in how they are perceived is also tied to the levels of inclusion and exclusion in the national identity of "British," and even though there may be differences in levels of acceptance, all people of color are seen to be incompatible with authentic forms of national identity (Gilroy, 1987). This migration and the ensuing experiences in England exposed us to yet another layer in our race consciousness and thus informs our racial ideology.

Fast-forward to the 1990s. My experiences of race relations between people of color is very similar to that seen in England, with internalized racism keeping us from knowing each other. The difference here in the U.S. Southwest is that I find myself in a situation in which I am surrounded by people who have little understanding of who I am and the history of my people. For the past seven years, I have worked, learned, and served in a community-based project that collaborates with the university. Guided by the tenets of critical multicultural education, university students team teach with Latino/Latina and African American urban communities to provide educational experiences for youth after school and in summertime. Here I am mentored by strong African American women and Latinas who have helped me discover the unearned privilege I have as a university student and what it means to be part of an institution that is seen by many as a colonizer. In this experience, I also learn of the territoriality within and between communities, which bares great resemblance to the colonial history of "divide and conquer" that my countries of origin experienced (Kenya and India).

Meanwhile, I have been teaching and learning at the university and writing and presenting within the fields of antiracist education, development of Asian American racial identity, community activism, teacher education, Critical Race Feminism (CRF), and leaders of color. My multiple worlds,[1] which exist within the university, within Latino/Latina and African-American urban communities, and within my own East African Asian Indian cultural/racial group identity, are all coming together. Where they intersect is where my dissertation begins, which is also where the reality of my multiple identities surfaces. Utilizing CRF and globalization of whiteness theory, I shall show how my dissertation is helping me realize my situatedness.

Through the insights of Collins (2000), Alibhai-Brown (1999), hooks (1994), Grewal and Kaplan (1994), and Spivak (1993) I shall put forth a case of why it is not enough to hear my story, to hear the subaltern speak and empathize with her plight. All these authors critique identity politics and deconstruction that has no connections to larger power relations. For example, Collins (2000) helps us visualize ourselves within intersecting oppressions that are embedded in a matrix of domination, giving us a sense of how we have multiple identities that can be oppressive in some instances and oppressed in others. By contrast, Spivak (1993) articulates the need for strategic essentialism, which calls for us to acknowledge complexity yet stay grounded in the reality that there are patterns to inequity and that only by aligning with others and taking a stand against inequities can we hope for change that is just. Through the lens of these critical race feminists, I came to understand my subject position in relation to others and how my multiple worlds must come together for me to be whole.

Exploited and Exploiter: Asian Indians as the Middle Group

As an Asian Indian working in Latina/Latino and African American communities, I am constantly reminded of my racial positionality within the larger racial hierarchy of the United States. I am neither as privileged as my White colleagues within the community and academia nor as oppressed as the Latina/Latino and African American population with which I work. Globalization of whiteness theory helps me understand how the United States is within a global racial hierarchy (Du Bois, 1996; Lipsitz, 1998; Mills, 1997), in which new immigrants are placed based on their color, class, education, socioeconomic background, and skills (Allen, 2001; Prashad, 2000; Wu, 2002). Within this context, even though Asians are people of color, they are more readily accepted by White culture than other racialized groups. This group is used to symbolize and reify the achievement ideology. The unspoken and invisible underclass of Asian Indians is kept under covers. Those who come seeking economic opportunities or are sponsored by family members are living a different reality, as can be seen in the motel industry and taxicab companies around the United States (Prashad, 2001). In looking at the multiple subject positions of Asians through the work of Collins (2000), I see that Asians are both exploited and exploiters. Collins's analysis makes me aware of a hierarchy of oppression, in what she labels the "matrix of domination," in which all people can be either the oppressed or the oppressor relative to another group. Within my role in academia, and now as a researcher within community settings, I must keep this in mind and not slip into a false sense of reality.

East African Indian Woman Researcher within Communities of Color

How apt is it that, on the one hand, I am theoretically grappling with Asian Indians as the middle group that perpetuates the status quo and, on the other hand, I find that my lived experience exemplifies this very phenomenon? For example, within the hierarchy of power in our organization, a White male holds the highest position, and even though I am not from these communities I have held one of the senior positions for many years, unlike my Black and Latina/Latino colleagues. There is also the stigma and burden that others and I carry of being a representative of a university. There is a rumbling within the communities that I work with regarding the exploitative nature of universities. One of my mentors within the community, a Black female community activist, openly accuses the university of "pimping the poverty of the community to acquire funds, which the community never sees." Another mentor, a Chicana activist, would constantly question our commitment to being in long-term relationships with community members and neighborhoods. How long do we intend to stay and work with community members? Are we in it for the long haul? Or, as often happens with university people, once our needs are met we leave. So, as I embark on research within these communities, I am painfully aware of the reputation of universities.

Through the teachings of these strong women of color, I have unlearned many misconceptions I had about communities of color being patriarchal and in the process learned that I too have the potential to lead. The teachings of these women have also led me to question not only what I study but also why I study what I study. For the past six years in the community-schools project, most of my roles have been directly connected to the Service Corps, university students whom we recruit to serve in these communities. These university students, unlike other educators whom these local neighborhood youth are likely to encounter, are predominantly students of color, many of whom are from the same inner-city communities, and a good number are males. As trainer, evaluator, support staff, liaison to the community, colleague, recruiter, learner, and teacher for the Service Corps, I have witnessed the corps members grow, learn, and unlearn the racial and educational myths about themselves, the communities they serve, and the youth with whom they have built relationships. There is almost too much for me to capture here. Therefore, my research will focus on the racial realism in the stories of the Service Corps with regard to the members' perception of the achievement ideology, the need for antiracist education, their own development of racial identity, their understanding of education for urban communities of color, and how this experience has influenced what they want to do with their lives.

Meanwhile, I find myself in a duality, one that is very common to researchers of color within Critical Race Theory (CRT) (Lopez & Parker, 2003). On the one hand, I am a researcher of color speaking to communities of color as an insider; the communities I work with see me as an ally and advocate who wishes to communicate their world to others. On the other hand, I seek to inform the academic community in the college of education, within which I am an outsider, the ways in which race functions within these communities through educational practice. These two audiences for my work are both important to me. What is foremost in my thinking as I navigate these worlds is, How useful is my research to the people being researched and the communities within which they serve? I want to do everything I can to make sure that at a minimum, my research does not take advantage of the researched and the communities they serve. And in more optimistic moments, I take my lead from Paulo Freire's (1992) notion of liberatory and emancipatory research, which has a political and social agenda for undoing racism within the field of education.

East African Indian Woman Researcher within Academia

The duality experienced transcends itself to my own subject position within these contexts. I am both an "insider" as a person of color in communities of color and university student within a university program, yet, at the same time an "outsider" as a representative of university in community and as a person of color in a mainly White establishment. Even the university students of color see me as an outsider; because I am Asian they do not see me as a part of the politics of race within the United States. I have discovered from my Black and Latina/Latino friends that Asians are basically ignored by more marginalized people of color; sometimes dismissed as hopelessly as-similated to White culture, they have internalized the myth of Asian-in-action for justice. I too have had to unlearn this internalized racist myth through the vast body of literature from Asian critical race theorists. They have shown me the long history, tradition, and present-day reality of Asian social justice activism, much of which has been omitted from the mainstream education we receive.

Within the college of education, I have an added convolution to my dissonance in that I am surrounded by White advisors and mentors. What is most disheartening here is that within my world of community work I am surrounded by strong females of color who mentor me, whereas in my university life I find myself surrounded by mostly White males and some White females for guidance. There are very few female tenured faculty of color to begin with, and of those there are even fewer who address the issues that I am passionate about. Many in the college of education here in the Southwest are more interested in issues of language and culture. The language focus is predominantly on Spanish or Native American languages, so it is of little significance that I am bilingual in a language other than these. Whereas the focus on culture in the college of education is more from an anthropological perspective, I tend to have a more sociological perspective of connecting life in the barrios to national and global patterns of race and race relations. Ironi-cally, it is through the very readings these White professors provide me that

I learn not to be surprised by my predicament. And to bring it full circle, these readings are predominantly by people of color.

In addition to these struggles, I am constantly projecting the notion that the Southwest is not in a vacuum, which is complicated to no end by the fact that I am not from the Southwest. I also struggle with my biases about Western feminism as presented within academia. When I read or am presented with CRT I embrace it with open arms. However, when it comes to feminist theory, I, like many women of color, have steered away from feminist courses within the university. The reasons for this are well articulated by Grewal and Kaplan (1994):

> Asian women from various cultures and locations, for instance, are seen within such scholarship by Eurocentric feminist analyses as an oppressed, monolithic category . . . creating an anthropological totality in which all Third World women are considered passive, nonresistant, living in destructive, uniformly and similarly repressive, patriarchal families. (pp. 238–239)

I too am a woman, yet I feel I lack the patience it would take to help my fellow women unlearn the myths about Asian women before we can even begin the process of learning anything new together. Authors such as Inderpal Grewal, Patricia Hill-Collins, and bell hooks have helped me unpack and understand some of this. For example, hooks (1994) helps me realize that not speaking up about the Asian Indian feminist perspective is in itself an act of oppression; I am perpetuating the status quo and allowing the myths to stand unchallenged.

I also grapple with the reality of using the colonizer's language and educational system to make sense of my world. The collective history of my people, East African Asian Indians, is one immersed in the brutality of British colonization in India and Kenya. This family history is a lived reality in the minds of so many Asians (Alibhai-Brown, 1999). And according to many postcolonialists, we are not free from colonization yet. I have many family members who exemplify this; they value the English language and educational system and ideology above their own. The colonized mind plays many a trick on the colonized. I have witnessed similar things within the neighborhoods I work with, where many parents and community members have great faith in the educational system being just and fair, and push their youth to fit into the system and succeed at all costs.

Having grown up in one of the most economically deprived and racially tense neighborhoods in England, a town called Luton, I am well aware of how miseducation can result in internalized oppression. In Luton, the racial politics are predominantly among Whites, Blacks (West Indian and African), and Asians (Bangladeshi, Pakistani, Punjabi, and Indian). What is unfortunate here is that two parallel manifestations of internalized oppression are occurring. The first is that race relations between people of color are very unhealthy and many people of color blame each other for the struggles they face. The second manifestation is that most people of color strive to be efficient in the English language and system, even at the cost of assimilation and acculturation, for they believe this to be the path to social mobility.

Many of the Indians in this community came to the country from a higher socioeconomic background and are more readily accepted by the Whites in England than the other Asians. For Pakistanis this lack of acceptance is partly owing to the religious bigotry against all Muslims in England, and for Blacks it is mainly owing to anti-Black racism. This difference results in some geographical, employment, and educational segregation from the other people of color for the Indians. This is further compounded by the racist portrayal of West Indians and Pakistanis as "the problem" in the media. For example, the recent race riots in the country were portrayed by the media as initiated by Pakistanis, which was further convoluted by a minority of the Pakistani population who did commit acts of hate against other groups, all of which, plus many other factors, results in all the respective groups internalizing the myths of their superiority or inferiority.

I have now had the privilege of unlearning some of these myths, making me an outsider within, as Collins (2000) would suggest. She articulates that this is a tension we will constantly grapple with, and we learn to live with the inherent contradictions of this status. This relates to Du Bois's (1996) notion of double consciousness: the idea that people of color live within and internalize the consciousness of two worlds—that of the dominant and that of the subordinate culture. Only, in the case of most women of color, this would be more than two worlds; it would be multiple worlds and multiple subjectivities (Soja & Hooper, 1993).

East African Indian Woman as Herself

So, where in all of this am I? And if there are conflicting group identities, which one is to be privileged and when? I have learned that the farther away you are from the power norm (Protestant, White, male ethic in our society), the greater the dissonance you will experience and feel. I have learned to navigate each territory I am in based on my understanding of my subject position—who I am in that space. For example, in community settings, I am accepted because I am seen as a young woman of color who goes out of her way to earn the trust and respect of community members and advocates for community concerns. However, I am also seen as an Asian outsider, not from the Southwest. And above all, I am seen as a university representative and, as such, must always keep in mind the history of the power relationships between community and university, which means constantly maintaining a level of trust that I will not exploit these communities. To navigate these contradictions, I must do one of many things, such as the following:

- Be true to myself and my quest for justice and know in my heart why I do what I do.
- Constantly learn about the larger sociopolitical contexts of identity and apply it to my life.
- Be aware of my surroundings and who I am in that space.
- Always assume that the exploiter role is more prevalent in any given situation.
- Earn trust and respect through listening and focusing on how I can best serve in that space and time.
- Do not get offended when my "differences" are highlighted and used to keep me at a distance, and learn to know the history of why this is the case.
- Try to be authentic by accommodating to all settings but not assimilating, even when I am in community settings. This is based on the notion that I can love and respect others without mimicking them.

Maintaining a strong sense of who I am and my multiple subjectivities will help center me and ground me as I navigate the various territories.

There is an innate contradiction of oppositional identity, in which I, as a marginal woman of color, am allowed to emerge, live, work, and write within a hegemonic, racist, and sexist culture (Grewal & Kaplan, 1994). As an East African Indian, as a transnational woman trying to make sense of my place in the micro and macro positionality I find myself in, multiple identities and postmodern understandings of self have always been problematic to me. Even though I understand and embrace my multiple subject positions, I am fearful of any rhetoric that will blur my identity to the point of making me invisible. However, I am learning through feminist writers such as Grewal and Kaplan (1994) that "a nonessentialist position does not imply a nonbelonging to a group, nor does it imply loss of agency or of coalitions and solidarities." I am learning to become "strategically essentialist," as Spivak (1993) would say. It does my heart no end of good to find meaning in the words of these Asian women, who have helped me realize how to be an agent of change for undoing racism in a sociopolitical way without losing the complexity of who I am. In fact, there is strength in these overlapping positions that may enable me to build coalitions and solidarity among my multiple subject positions.

References

Alibhai-Brown, Y. (1999). To be or not to be Black. *Race and Class 41*(1/2), 163–170.

Allen, R. L. (2001). The globalization of white supremacy: Toward a critical discourse on the racialization of the world. *Educational Theory, 51*(4), 467–485.

Bell, D. (1992). *Faces at the bottom of the well*. New York: Basic Books.

Collins, P. H. (2000). *Black feminist thought: Knowledge, consciousness, and the politics of empowerment*. New York: Routledge.

Du Bois, W. E. B. (1996). Concepts of race. In E. Sundquist (Ed.), *The Oxford W.E.B. DuBois reader* (pp. 37–96). New York: Oxford University Press.

Freire, P. (1992). *Pedagogy of hope: Reliving pedagogy of the oppressed*. New York: Continuum.

Gilroy, P. (1987). *"There ain't no black in the Union Jack": The cultural politics of race and nation*. Chicago: The University of Chicago Press.

Giroux, H. (1992). *Border crossings: Cultural workers and the politics of difference*. New York: Routledge.

Grewal, I., & Kaplan, C. (Eds.). (1994). *Scattered hegemonies: Postmodernity and transnational feminist practices*. Minneapolis: University of Minnesota Press.

hooks, b. (1994). *Teaching to transgress: Education as a practice of freedom*. New York: Routledge.

Lee, S. (1996). *Unraveling the model minority stereotype*. New York: Columbia University.

Lipsitz, G. (1998). *The possessive investment in whiteness: How white people profit from identity politics*. Philadelphia: Temple University Press.

Lopez, G., & Parker, L. (Eds.). (2003). *Interrogating racism in qualitative research methodology*. New York: Peter Lang.

Lorde, A. (1984). *Sister outsider*. New York: The Crossing Press.

Mills, C. (1997). *The racial contract*. Ithaca: Cornell University Press.

Prashad, V. (2000). *The karma of brown folk*. Minneapolis: University of Minnesota Press.

Prashad, V. (2001). *Everybody was kung fu fighting: Afr-Asian connections and the myth of cultural purity*. Boston: Beacon.

Sivanandan, A. (1990). *Communities of resistance: Writings on black struggles for socialism.* New York: Verso.

Soja, E., & Hooper, B. (1993). The spaces that difference makes. In M. Keith & S. Pile (Eds.), *Place and the politics of identity.* New York: Routledge.

Spivak, G. C. (1993). *Outside in the teaching machine.* New York: Routledge.

Wu, F. (2002). *Yellow: Race in America beyond Black and White.* New York: Basic Books.

Endnotes

1. The idea of *multiple worlds* is tied to the notion of multiple subject positions.

9

MENTORING AND ITS ROLE IN SCHOLARLY DEVELOPMENT

Beatrice Bridglall

The Author

Beatrice L. Bridglall is currently editor and assistant director of the Institute for Urban and Minority Education (IUME) at Teachers College, Columbia University. She is coauthor of *The Affirmative Development of Academic Ability* (in process) with Professor Edmund W. Gordon, and coeditor of *Supplementary Education* (in press). Ms. Bridglall is also coeditor of the College Board's and IUME's *Pedagogical Inquiry and Praxis Newsletter*, which is designed to meet the needs of practitioners, policy makers, scholars of practice, and research scientists as they produce and utilize knowledge and techniques to improve the quality of academic achievement in diverse learners. The newsletter emphasizes the bidirectionality of knowledge production through practice and research, and issues associated with increasing the number of high-academic-achieving students who come from African American, Latina/Latino, and Native American families.

With Professor Gordon, Dr. Bridglall codirects the documentation and connoisseurial evaluation of several institutional programs of education that are considered highly effective in the education of potentially able and gifted students from ethnic minority backgrounds. This study is part of a larger program of research that is directed at investigating the personal, environmental, and institutional correlates of high academic achievement in minority students.

Dr. Bridglall holds a master's degree in health policy and management from the Wagner Graduate of Public Service at New York University and has recently received her doctorate from the Department of Health and Behavior Study at Teachers College, Columbia University, in student academic development, program evaluation, and public health.

T he idea of mentoring seems to be interpreted differently by both mentors and mentees. In this chapter, I take the perspective of a mentee. The stage is set with a brief literature review concerning the significance of mentoring for students of color. This is followed by a discussion of my exposure and developmental experience with a uniquely singular mentor, Professor Edmund W. Gordon. I conclude with a suggestion for how mentoring needs to be reconceptualized as not only necessary experience for students of color but also as part of educational institutions' core infrastructure of services to students.

Literature Review

One of the nation's most critical educational dilemmas is the long-standing gap in academic achievement between African American, Hispanic, and Native American students and their European American and Asian American counterparts. Apparently, students of color underachieve as a result of "prejudicial beliefs on the part of faculty and other students, exclusionary social practices on the campus, and other factors that make up a 'chilly' campus climate" (Gandara & Maxwell-Jolly, 1999, p. 52). Other variables include motivational and performance vulnerability in the face of negative stereotypes; low faculty and peer expectations for academic success; academic, social, and cultural isolation; and perceived and actual discrimination (Allen, 1992; Maton, Hrabowski, & Schmitt, 2000; Seymour & Hewitt, 1997; Steele & Aronson, 1995). Additionally, Steele and Aronson's (1995) idea of stereotype threat, referenced above, suggests that when students find themselves in situations (e.g., classes or exams) where they perceive an external expectation based on their minority status, their anxiety that they may confirm the stereotype can lead to diminished performance. Other explanations include:

- Fear of disapproval or rejection by peers, including fears of acting White (Fordham & Ogbu, 1986)
- Hostile or unsupportive environments associated with residual racism (Aronson, Lustina, Good, Keough, Steele, & Brown, 1999)
- Absence of adequate socialization to the attitudinal and behavioral demands of the academy (Ogbu, 2003)
- Limited contact with and exposure to models of academic excellence and exemplars of scholarly practice (Gordon, 2001)

Additionally, it appears that the development of short-term and/or longer-term goals, and understanding the relationship between current efforts and future outcomes, can be more difficult for students of color because role models, mentors, and an adequate support system are often lacking for many in this population. Students of color also seem to face greater difficulties than White students in adjusting to the dominant campus culture, resulting in further academic and social isolation. Once in college, underrepresented students often have difficulty forming relationships with faculty and staff (Johnson, 1996; Nettles, 1990).

Research, however, suggests that these relationships are crucial to persistence and graduation (Fries-Britt, 2000). Davidson and Foster-Johnson's (2002) review of the literature on mentoring graduate researchers of color concluded that mentors are a critical part of these young scholars' success. Successful mentors are often aware of the many cultural and racial variables with which their mentees struggle. Mentors' personal and academic support are also significant correlates of grades, retention, and graduation for African Americans (Tracey & Sedlacek, 1989); women (Ancis & Sedlacek, 1997); and students in special support programs, including Asian Americans, African Americans, and European Americans (Ting, 1997). Clearly, a lack of mentors and faculty who positively reinforce the relationship between effort and positive outcomes is the reality for most students of color. Although it is distressing, it is not surprising that relatively minor obstacles often result in low academic achievement and/or attrition for these students (Mallinckrodt, 1988), who are usually never heard from again (Allen, 1992).

Alternatively, those students who are academically successful have been exposed to a wide range of formal and supplementary education efforts

(Bhattacharya, in press; College Board, 1999); actively engage in school events and extracurricular activities (Everson & Millsap, in press); identify with high achievement values; have good study skills and other learner behaviors (Maton et al., 2000); demonstrate personal skills such as independence, interpersonal facility, and flexibility; and maintain positive ties with peers and adults, such as parents and mentors who continually advocate high expectations for achievement (Bloom, 1968; Gordon & Song, 1994). Clearly, high levels of achievement, scholarly or otherwise, appear to be associated with the attitudes and behaviors that develop under the guidance of a significant supportive other. In the academy, one's mentor is often such a person. That is certainly the case for me.

My Mentor: Edmund W. Gordon

As a recent recipient of a doctoral degree, I would characterize the course of my developmental experience as remarkably singular. The developmental cause of this achievement rests almost entirely on the kind of mentor I am fortunate enough to have worked closely with in the past four years. Some prominent educators consider this mentor a national treasure, and it is not difficult to recognize the accuracy of this judgment when it refers to Edmund Wyatt Gordon. Indeed, currently in his ninth decade of life, Professor Gordon continues to play a pivotal role as a scholar, mentor, educator, and senior researcher in education and psychology—an inspiration to younger scholars—and to me, a woman of color and mother of two young boys, as an emerging scholar concerned with the underserved and underrepresented.

Professionally, I work with Edmund Gordon as editor and assistant director of the Institute for Urban and Minority Education (IUME) at Teachers College, Columbia University. I am also responsible for conducting a program of research that is directed at investigating the correlates of high academic achievement for students of color. This research program emphasizes the identification, documentation, and connoisseurial evaluation of those correlates referable to the characteristics of individuals who are high academic achievers; the characteristics of programs of educational treatment; and the ecological or institutional contexts that are associated with such achievement. In the referenced emphases, I design instruments and conduct validation studies, conduct interviews and focus groups, and administer surveys. I am also closely involved in the conceptualization, development, and implementation of supplementary education services for students, their families, and their schools in the community of Central Harlem, New York. Additionally, I am responsible for writing and editing IUME's publications, including books, newsletters, and monographs, as well as representing and interpreting Professor Gordon's position to a variety of audiences.

Admittedly, some have questioned my commitment to such issues as equity and high-quality education and health care for the underserved and underrepresented despite knowing that as a Southeast Asian American, I identify myself as a woman of color. Perhaps I am a bit naïve to think that my commitment to the referenced issues should matter more than my ethnicity. Fortunately, this has not been an issue for my mentor, an African American male, who reminds his protégé that many people of color around the world, not just African Americans, face racism and discrimination, ingrained poverty, little or low-quality education, and exclusion from the political process. It was thus established early in our association that our resonance to each other's ideas, values, and ubiquitous concern for underrepresented people of color boded well for our research and writing together.

Gordon's role as mentor has exposed me to some of the best minds in the country, including his own. Informal conversations with him and other scholars of education suggest that the nation is at a juncture where the field of education is not only trying to get a handle on what works for certain populations, but also on a conceptual grounding relative to how differing strategies and approaches can function individually and interactively. Gordon's concern for understanding the theory and practice of pedagogy from differential perspectives informs some of his major ideas concerning how the diverse characteristics of urban youth of color necessitate differentiated treatments and configures a part of his rationale for how pedagogy should be conceived, developed, implemented, and evaluated. Clearly, unlike some high-achieving majority students for whom schooling constitutes only one form of support, for most ethnic minority and low-income students, schooling is usually the only support for academic learning to which they are exposed.

This ubiquitous concern also includes the issue of assessment, which Gordon (2000) suggests needs to be more systematically integrated with qualitative and quantitative ways of knowing and understanding with respect to the differential learning patterns and modes of intellective performance that may be crucial to rigorous intellectual and academic development. Indeed, knowing and understanding the properties of one set of behaviors as enabling of even more comprehensive behaviors is at the core of his advocacy for the differential analysis of learner characteristics and the differentiated design of learning experiences. Gordon advocates that schooling for students in urban communities needs to begin to converge around the criteria of good educational planning, wholesome and purposeful developmental conditions, greater diversity of curricula and goals, and greater attention to the needs of individual learners. He argues that the purposes, goals, and practical strategies informing teaching, learning, and assessment need not only to value the backgrounds and situations of students of color but also to enable them to achieve higher levels of intellective competence by facilitating the mastery and transfer of indigenous as well as hegemonic knowledge, skills, and dispositions. In addition to the ideas referenced above, I have come to understand and appreciate the educational implications of the following conceptual issues:

- The instrumentality of knowing and understanding to doing; that is, purposeful human agency
- The requirement of contextualist and perspectivist thought for critical analysis
- Skepticism regarding all that is given and/or assumed
- The utility of interactional and relational adjudication of social phenomena
- The bidirectionality of the flow of knowledge between inquiry and praxis
- Sense making as the core of human agency, defined as intentionality, forethought, self-reactiveness, and self-reflection (Bandura, 2001)

Although these ideas and conceptual issues have informed Professor Gordon's and my work together, the more functional dimensions of my experience as a mentee have included a variety of challenging intellectual and professional experiences. Among these are

- Professor Gordon's insistence that our work and approach to practical problems be informed by sound theory
- An emphasis on reading widely and critical discussion of what is read
- Extensive exposure to human exemplars of scholarship
- The opportunity to perform in real-life professional situations

With respect to reading widely, thinking, and critically discussing what I have read, I have begun to appreciate more fully Gordon's notions of the conjoint importance of knowing and understanding through his guidance of my exposure to the work of scholars such as Kenneth Gergen, C. Wright

Mills, Carl Bereiter, Pierre Bourdieu, Alexander Luria, Lev Vygotsky, Richard Schweider, Michael Jackson, Edmund Sullivan, and Jerome Brunner. Through the reading and continuing discussion of the work of these scholars, I have learned to appreciate the roles of critical analysis, contextual analysis, perspectivism, and skepticism in the development of understanding. I struggled through my initial reading of Gergen's *Social Understanding and the Inscription of Self.* In a discussion with Gordon, I realized that Gergen (1990) is arguing that we need to "shift from an individualist to a relational orientation to understanding selves" (p. 570) partly because our current ethnographic procedures for observing and recording human action do not provide satisfactory understanding of others' actions, and partly because of the dilemmas associated with validating interpretations. In this essay, Gergen analyzes existing Western assumptions concerning individualism, a dualistic conception of persons, and the categorization of people's rational and irrational processes of mind (underpinning understanding). He finds that these are flawed approaches because they influence characterizations about other cultures and peoples that are not accurate representations. He attempts to justify his ideas by characterizing the Wittgensteinian, hermeneutic, and deconstructionist alternatives to modes of traditional empiricism as not sufficiently valid.

In my discussions with Gordon, it occurred to me that these methods may not be wholly flawed because they not only function as one way of knowing and understanding but also provide a basis for either challenge or support of these assumptions. Gergen (1990) both proposes and attempts to anchor an alternative theory of social understanding in assumptions about relational nuclei; individuals as intersections in a variety of relational units; the adjudication of relational phenomenon; and the generation of "understanding" as a social category.

Perhaps my mentor exposed me to scholars who advocate nontraditional systems of thought in part not only because he resonated to their thinking but also to encourage critical reflexivity and out-of-the-box thinking on my part. As we continued to read and reflect on Gergen's ideas, for example, I discovered that he (Gergen) challenged Wittgensteinian language games, hermeneutic methodology, and deconstructionist thought to conclude that Wittgenstein does not provide adequate alternatives to conventional language use. Similarly, the hermeneutics do not allow us to "probe the depths of others' intentional systems," and their projected meanings cannot be subjected to disconfirmation; and, from the deconstructionist perspective, "we can never escape from the prison of tropes that isolate us one from the other" (p. 582).

Given his view of the inadequacy of the Wittgensteinian, hermeneutic, and deconstructionist schools of thought, Gergen (1990) attempted to provide an alternative theory of social understanding called *relational adjudication*, which is grounded in three interdependent assumptions (relational nuclei, individuals as intersections in a variety of relational units, and adjudication and the generation of "understanding" as a social category). From Gergen's perspective, relational nuclei means that the mutual interdependency of members in a society necessitates that "all personal outcomes are essentially contingent on interchange." As such, individual well-being cannot be removed from the web of relationships in which a person is engaged; thus, the nature of these relationships is a function of the subtle and overt processes of adjusting and readjusting actions (Geertz, 1973). One could argue that actions signifying adjustment and readjustment are based on the interpretation of someone's behavior (Geertz, 1973). Gergen, however, did not reference Geertz (1973), who asserted that individual expressions or symbols are valid within the context of communication with others, thus creating "webs of significance." By definition, then, these many and uncertain meanings are fertile ground for generating interpretation (Sullivan, 1984).

My mentor's juxtaposition of Gergen, Geertz, and Sullivan against a background of our having read Michael Jackson's *Paths toward a Clearing* left my mind reeling, even as it was stretching. Gergen's idea of *the individual as intersection of relational nuclei* suggests that individually, we comprise a range of relational patterns. Thus, when any two of us meet, we each bring the webs (of relationships) in which we are enmeshed to the association. Consequently, these webs of relationships influence how effectively (or ineffectively) we coordinate our actions and reactions. This leads to Gergen's idea of the adjudication and the generation of understanding as a social category. This concept suggests that given the variety and multitude of webs that we are each a part of, we need a public standard for deciding whether one action, compared to another, rightfully or wrongfully follows from the preceding.

Further conversations with Gordon revealed that Gergen's concept of adjudication has undertones of morality; that is, those who are positioned to determine whether a sequential action is wrong or right are guided by their values or underlying morals. Although Gergen argues that these difficulties in coordination situate the adjudication (which arises primarily within the context of multiple relationships) of public judgments that specific (individual) actions are out of "synchrony or do not fit within the emerging pattern" (p. 586), it seems to me that the adjudication itself, with its underlying morality, contributes to the criteria for understanding coordinated actions. Consequently, we can posit that by negating or ignoring some parts of the relational sequence, any single individual may be considered exemplary or, alternatively, guilty. Gergen stresses that it is this deliberate use of standards that allows individuals to attribute ignorance or misunderstanding to others.

My emerging role as a researcher concerned with accurately representing phenomena under study is informed by critical exposure to Gergen's perspective that the ethnographer can achieve success (as judged from the criteria of those studied) only when he or she coordinates his or her activities with those studied. This notion is especially significant given his idea that the enlightened ethnographer, upon returning home, comes up against the "task of specifying an ontology that differs from that which is normative within the home culture." Gergen also suggests that the ethnographer needs to be aware that while this ontology cannot be entirely unusual, he or she can and should "play at the margins of the unacceptable—unsettling and reconstituting the language of representation so as to undermine the traditions and carve out a new domain of intelligibility" (p. 590). In this situation, "erosion and emancipation are close companions" (p. 590). Gordon and I find it interesting at this point in Gergen's argument that he did not reference Sullivan's claim that emancipation is one of the ends of a critically interpretative psychology.

Exposure to thoughtful conversations between Gordon and his senior colleagues suggests that emancipation and social justice in individual, interpersonal, and societal levels are among the implicit goals they strive for. These goals seem to be especially important given the (1) current levels of knowledge dissemination that are insufficient to achieving educational goals; (2) self-affirming attitudes and behaviors that need to be shaped and reinforced (Glanz, Lewis, & Rimer, 1996); (3) self-regulation and a sense of self-efficacy (Bandura, 1986) that must be developed; and (4) insufficient awareness of the amount and quality of time that must be invested in attaining high levels of academic achievement (Resnick, 1999). Clearly, these problems go beyond the simple dissemination of information to finding ways (including those that are culturally sensitive) of influencing people's capacity and disposition to utilize information and services to change their behavior (Freire, 1973; Gordon, 1999; Wallace, 2000).

Given this context, it seems to me that a discussion by Gergen of the responsibilities of social scientists, which according to Gordon (2000) included (1) the production of knowledge that has relevance for meaningful human enterprises, and (2) the pursuit of understanding of that knowledge and its consequences for the human condition, may have enhanced his argument. Additionally, Gergen's challenge of the traditional Western ways of knowing would have been more defensible if he had acknowledged that the social scientist is caught in a paradox between "the investigation of the mechanisms and meanings of the behavioral adaptations of diverse populations of peoples, living under differing conditions and circumstances" (Gordon, 2000). It appears to me, however, that Gergen may agree with Gordon's notion that social scientists must select components of the phenomenon for observation and analysis because they cannot examine most phenomena in their entirety. Similarly, because he may agree that this truncation results in research that is not conducive to producing complete knowledge and understanding (Gordon, 2000), some of Gordon's ideas can serve as a beginning for operationalizing the notion of relational adjudication. It also appears that Gergen did not explicitly frame or recognize, on a macro level, what he is reacting to in his challenge of traditional empirical methods. He did implicitly concur with Gordon, however, that in our research on different people and cultures, "potentially important aspects of the diversity and its implications are ignored in order to produce accepted knowledge concerning these people" (Gordon, 2000). Thus, it seems that part of what is driving Gergen's reaction to traditional empiricism is its tendency to produce often "incomplete or questionable knowledge that seems counterintuitive to the person being studied by others and sometimes contributes confusion rather than clarity to our understanding of the behavior in question" (Gordon, 2000).

Can some of Gordon's ideas of what it means to pursue understanding enable Gergen to operationalize his notion of relational adjudication? I believe they could serve as a beginning, especially since we can agree that traditional western conceptions do not account for the knowing and understanding of particular and idiosyncratic phenomena (Gordon, 2000). Relational adjudication can also be related to some elements of McGuire's (1983, 1989) ideas of contextualism and perspectivism. One of the premises of contextualism concerns the character of human activity. Gordon and McGuire advocate the fluid and dynamic rather than static nature of human activity. As such, reality can "no longer be considered stable or necessarily ordered" (Gordon, 2000). It appears then that because context contributes to shifting interpretations, our intentions shape and mold a certain situation, while simultaneously our intentions are shaped and molded by the dynamics of that situation. Context, in other words, is not an unchanging phenomenon (Gordon, 2000; McGuire, 1983). Because Gergen did not make specific reference to context, I wondered if he hoped that his idea of relational adjudication would influence the unearthing of universals that may displace traditional Western conceptions of knowing.

The contextualists claim that given differing contexts, circumstances, temporal factors, and even constraints (Keil, 1983), more than one perspective or theory can simultaneously apply to the same human behavior (McGuire, 1989). Given Gergen's dismissal of hermeneutics, he may not give much credence to this claim. It appears, however, that he may be substituting one set of inadequate methods for another without realizing it. Additionally, given shifting theories of intelligence, and the recognition that people learn in different ways, Gergen's idea of relational adjudication, although useful in some unexplored instances, may be lacking or inadequate in others. Had he considered the contextualist perspective, his argument about relational adjudication might be stronger.

It bears reiterating that I am reading Gergen through Gordonian lenses. Thus, in my discussions with Gordon and my observations of other scholars, I am impressed by the way in which scholarly debate and arguments are scaffolded with ideas drawn from various sources to make conceptual connections or to introduce different perspectives on the phenomenon under question. For example, Keil's (1983) concept of constraint parallels Gordon, Rollock, and Miller's (1990) idea that when the researcher develops a way of interpreting a phenomenon, he or she also develops a way of not seeing. It seems to me that relational adjudication is only one way of knowing and understanding, and it is limited because it does not acknowledge other perspectives, their value or their utility. Both Gordon and McGuire suggest that researchers have to experiment in different ways because one of their purposes is to understand the phenomenon, not merely to prove the hypothesis. Additionally, it is important that researchers understand and perceive a situation the same way as indigenous folk; otherwise, despite the accuracy with which the researcher describes the observed situation, unless she understands it in the same way as the indigenous folk, she would miss a pivotal aspect of the situation, "since that indigenous perspective is going to influence the behavior observed" (Gordon, 2000).

Unlike Gergen, Gordon struggles with questions that focus, among other things, on achieving consistency across differing interpretations and establishing criteria by which to judge the usefulness of cross-situational interpretations. From Gordon's perspective, interpretational psychology requires that context, perspective, and intention should be considered privileged constructs. While critical theorists would posit that under social conditions that privilege openness in communication, hermeneutical validity is likely to be achieved (Gertz, 1973; Habermas, 1970), both Gordon and Gergen reject this notion, with Gergen suggesting that

> [T]here are principled difficulties underlying the hermeneutic attempt to establish validity in interpretation. The problem commences when one treats the text (or other social action) as opaque, and presumes a second level (an internal language) that must be located in order to render the overt transparent. Yet all we have at our disposal in the process of understanding is a domain of public discourse (or action). We imagine that there is a domain of private discourse to which this must be attached. Yet we possess access neither to the private discourse itself nor to the rules by which it is translated into the public domain. It follows that any attempt to translate (or understand) must be based on an analytic as opposed to a synthetic procedure. That is, readings or translations can only be rendered true by definition—by virtue of circularity rather than verification. (pp. 579–580)

In the circles I have traveled in during the past four years, the conversations I have been privy to, and the reading I have done, it seems to me that Gergen, Gordon, and their colleagues seem to be rethinking how we validate knowing when traditional methods no longer seem adequate. Although these scholars appear to have different ideas that are developed in various directions, there seems to be more convergence than divergence. Given the postmodern era we are thought to be in, this search for different ways of knowing is a reflection of the notions among modern scholars that, except for some earthly physical constants, conceptions about reality are often consensus judgments that are subject to change given different contexts, perspectives, intentions, and situations. Gergen not only thinks broadly and deeply, but he also expresses himself quite well. It is easy to see why Gordon refers to him as one of psychology's most seminal minds, and why he chose Gergen's work as one of the vehicles for my continued intellectual development.

Conclusion

Clearly, some of Gordon's ideas and conceptual frameworks are informed by his political beliefs. In his writings and in our conversations, he acknowledges the tension between the value that society seems to place on the perceived outcomes of the educational process and its parallel social recalcitrance when it comes to investing in the resources necessary to improve access and participation for some ethnic minority groups, especially when benefits might devolve to those who tend to cluster in the lower end of the socioeconomic scales. The clarity of Edmund W. Gordon's ideas and their lucid elaborations will continue not only to inform the field but may also spur radical ways of approaching the issues of teaching, learning, and assessment for students of color. He believes it is toward such developments in our students that we must continue to direct our efforts and our endorsement of education in general. Our continuing work together shifts the debate away from majority and minority differences in levels of intellectual functioning to understanding the mechanisms and meanings between the developmental patterns, cultural and learning styles, and temperamental traits of learners and the educational experiences to which they are exposed.

Thus, in working with Professor Gordon, I have come to appreciate that

- Thinking about explanations and the limitations of solutions may be more important than the solutions themselves.
- While theories provide useful ways of looking at phenomena and solving problems in specific contexts, it is in the nature of theories that they are subject to disconfirmation.
- Questions concerning *why, what if,* and *why not* should follow naturally from questions of *what is, how much,* and possible relationships between phenomena.
- A way of seeing is a way of not seeing.
- Knowing and understanding are eternal human endeavors.
- Reasoning, reflexivity, and agency just may be the most critical of human behaviors.
- There are few problems that I cannot solve given appropriate and sufficient effort.

Given this continuing singular mentoring experience, it is not possible to generalize to other mentors. As a mentee who continues to benefit in many ways from a mentor such as Professor Gordon, my experience is an illustration of what outstanding mentoring can look like for young scholars of color. Additionally, given the growing recognition that mentoring is necessary for developing intellectual and social competencies for students of color, educational institutions need to reconceptualize the structural supports they provide for their students to achieve academic excellence. The

Meyerhoff Scholars Program at the University of Maryland, Baltimore County (UMBC), is an example of an exemplary student academic development program that has situated mentoring at the core of its infrastructure. Professor Gordon and I have examined this program extensively and are impressed with how students and exemplary upperclassmen mentor each other; the commitment of the faculty to the academic excellence of students of color; the parental surrogacy roles played by the program staff; and the spirit, drive, and commitment of their president, Dr. Freeman Hrabowski. UMBC's mentoring emphasis appears to work because the university believes that once a student is admitted, it is the university's responsibility to enable that student to achieve academically by providing the requisite supports, motivation, monitoring, advisement, and social capital.

On a personal level, Edmund Gordon takes this commitment to mentoring very seriously. Indeed, one of his mantras could very well be that *with great privilege comes great responsibility*. Because Professor Edmund W. Gordon is my mentor, colleague, and friend, it is an understatement to say that being one of his mentees has influenced my personal and professional lives. On the personal level, not only has my understanding of and respect for myself as a thinking person been enhanced, but many of my values have been clarified and grounded in systematized knowledge. As a professional person, Professor Gordon continually challenges me to produce work that is not only excellent but also morally, ethnically, and empirically defensible. Along the way, I have come to appreciate the bi-directionality of theory and practice, with each having the capacity to inform the other, and a new appreciation for the critical importance of context and perspective for the achievement of understanding. These personal and professional dimensions of my life come together in growing recognition that scholarship is not only another manifestation of human agency but also informed and responsible human activity directed at the liberation of the mind and the achievement of social justice.

References

Allen, W. R. (1992). The color of success: African-American college student outcomes at predominantly white and historically black public colleges and universities. *Harvard Educational Review, 62*, 45–65.

Ancis, J. R., & Sedlacek, W. E. (1997). Predicting the academic achievement of female students using the SAT and noncognitive variables. *College and University, 72*(3), 1–8.

Aronson, J., Lustina, M. J., Good, C., Keough, K., Steele, C. M., & Brown, J. (1999). When White men can't do math: Necessary and sufficient factors in stereotype threat. *Journal of Experimental Social Psychology, 35*(1), 29–46.

Bandura, A. (1986). *Social foundations of thought and action: A social cognitive theory.* Englewood Cliffs, NJ: Prentice-Hall.

Bandura, A. (2001). Social cognitive theory: An agentic perspective. *Annual Review of Psychology, 52,* 1–26.

Bhattacharyya, M. (in press). Community and faith-based support for supplementary education. In E. W. Gordon, B. L. Bridglall, & A. S. Meroe (Eds.), *Supplementary Education.* The College Board and Rowman and Littlefield.

Bloom, B. S. (1968). *Human characteristics and school learning.* New York: McGraw-Hill.

College Board. (1999). *Reaching the top: A report of the National Task Force on Minority High Achievement.* New York: The College Entrance Examination Board.

Davidson, M. N., & Foster-Johnson, L. (2001). Mentoring in the preparation of graduate researchers of color. *Review of Educational Research, 71*(4), 549–574.

Everson, H., & Millsap, R. (in press). The impact of extracurricular activities on standardized test scores. In E. W. Gordon, B. L. Bridglall, & A. S. Meroe (Eds.), *Supplementary education.* The College Board and Rowman and Littlefield.

Fordham, S., & Ogbu, J. U. (1986). Black students' school success: Coping with the "burden of acting White." *Urban Review, 18*(3), 176–206.

Freire, P. (1973). *Education for the critical consciousness.* New York: Seabury Press.

Fries-Britt, S. (2000). Identity development of high-ability Black collegians. *New Directions for Teaching and Learning, 82,* 55–65.

Gándara, P. (with Maxwell-Jolly, J.). (1999). *Priming the pump: A review of programs that aim to increase the achievement of underrepresented minority undergraduates* (Report to the Task Force on Minority High Achievement of the College Board). New York: College Board.

Geertz, C. (1973) *Interpretation of cultures.* New York: Basic Books.

Gergen, K. J. (1990). Social understanding and the inscription of self. In J. W. Stigler, R. A. Shweder, & G. Herdt (Eds.), *Cultural psychology* (pp. 407–606). New York: Cambridge University Press.

Glanz, K., Lewis, F. M., & Rimer, B. K. (Eds.). (1996). *Health behavior and health education: Theory, research, and practice* (2nd ed.). San Francisco: Jossey-Bass.

Gordon, E. W. (1999). *Education and justice: A view from the back of the bus.* New York: Teachers College Press.

Gordon, E. W. (2000). Production of knowledge and pursuit of understanding. In E. W. Gordon & C. C. Yeakey (Eds.), *Producing knowledge and pursuing understanding.* Stamford, CT: JAI Press.

Gordon, E. W. (2001). *The affirmative development of academic ability* (Pedagogical Inquiry and Praxis, No. 2). New York: Institute for Urban and Minority Education, Teachers College, Columbia University.

Gordon, E. W., Miller, F., & Rollock, D. (1990). Coping with communicentric bias in knowledge production in the social sciences. *Educational Researcher, 19*(3), 14–19.

Gordon, E. W., & Song, L. D. (1994). Variation in the experience of resilience. In E. W. Gordon & M. Wang (Eds.), *Educational resilience: Challenges and prospects.* Mahwah, NJ: Lawrence Erlbaum.

Habermas, J. (1970). *Toward a rational society: Student protest, science, and politics.* Boston: Beacon Press.

Johnson, I. H. (1996). Access and retention: Support programs for graduate and professional students. *New Directions for Student Services, 74,* 53–67.

Keil, F. (1990). Constraints on constraints: Surveying the epigenetic landscape. *Cognitive Science, 14,* 135–168.

Mallinckrodt, B. (1988). Student retention, social support, and dropout intention: Comparison of Black and White students. *Journal of College Student Development, 29,* 60–64.

Maton, K., Hrabowski, F., & Schmitt, C. (2000). African American college students excelling in the sciences: College and postcollege outcomes in the Meyerhoff Scholars Program. *Journal of Research in Science Teaching, 37*(7), 629–654.

McGuire, W. J. (1983). A contextualist theory of knowledge: Its implications for innovations and reform in psychological research. In L. Berkowitz (Ed.), *Advances in experimental social psychology.* New York: Academic Press.

McGuire, W. J. (1989). A perspectivist approach to the strategical planning of programmatic scientific research. In *The psychology of science: Contributions to metascience* (pp. 214–245). New York: Cambridge University Press.

Nettles, M. T. (1990). Success in doctoral programs: Experiences of minority and White students. *American Journal of Education, 98*(4), 494–522.

Ogbu, J. U. (2003). *Black American students in an affluent suburb: A study of academic disengagement.* Mahwah, NJ: Erlbaum.

Orfield, G., Kahlenberg, R. D., Gordon, E. W., Genesee, F., Slocumb, P. D., & Payne, R. K. (2000). The new diversity. *Principal, 79*(5), 6–32.

Resnick, L. B. (1999). From aptitude to effort: A new foundation for our schools. *American Educator, 23*(1), 14–17.

Seymour, E., & Hewitt, N. M. (1997). *Talking about leaving: Why undergraduates leave the sciences.* Boulder, CO: Westview Press.

Steele, C. M., & Aronson, J. (1995). Stereotype threat and the intellectual performance of African Americans. *Journal of Personality and Social Psychology, 69,* 797–811.

Sullivan, E. (1984). *Critical psychology: An interpretation of the personal world.* New York: Plenum Press.

Ting, S. R. (1997). Estimating academic success in the 1st year of college for specially admitted White students: A model combining cognitive and psychosocial predictors. *Journal of College Student Development, 38*(4), 401–409.

Tracey, T. J., & Sedlacek, W. E. (1989). Factor structure of the non-cognitive questionnaire: Revised across samples of Black and White college students. *Educational & Psychological Measurement, 49*(3), 637–648.

Wallace, B. C. (2000). A call for change in multicultural training at graduate schools of education: Educating to end oppression and for social justice. *Teachers College Record, 102*(6), 1086–1111.

Appendix A
Example of Previous Field-Based Learning Assessment

Collaboration: Demonstrate the ability to work in teams in inter-professional settings across traditional lines of programs, agencies, disciplines, and diverse communities to establish common missions and purposes; and to collaborate with others in decision making, learning, completing tasks and applying knowledge of group processes and group interaction.

_____   _____
  Student's Signature & Date   *Mentor's Signature & Date*

CHHS Common Grading Rubric

This form contains the common grading rubric used by all CHHS course instructors and contains the standards and criteria instructors in all learning experiences use to assess student performance.

Department of Health, Human Services & Public Policy
Collaborative Health and Human Services
Standards and Criteria for Ranking/Grading Competency Levels

STANDARDS FOR QUALITY OF WORK

	Ranking	Score	Grade	Academic Criteria	Field Criteria
Outstanding/ Excellent	4	90 - 100	A- to A+	**The work (oral and written) is excellent.**	**The work (oral and written) is excellent.**
				It shows creative and critical thinking, original responses to the material; strong analytical skills; strong descriptive and bibliographic skills; and the ability to synthesize material.	*Takes responsibility for own professional development (including Field Learning Agreement) *Eager to learn—seeks and utilizes training *Enthusiasm for the work
				The work draws critical connections between research materials; their historical, cultural, political, social and economic contexts and uses an excellent level of detail to demonstrate knowledge and skills.	*Written work is publishable within the agency, e.g., reports, brochures, court reports, etc. *Ability to synthesize information and apply to the job
				The work draws on multiple sources and shows excellent bibliographic, annotation and synthesizing skills.	*Understands political and professional culture *Incorporates feedback
				Written and oral work shows logical and clear thought and expression, unity and coherence of analysis and creativity.	*Works beyond expectations, which includes the following: —Stays beyond the scheduled hours as needed —Goes the "extra mile" to help out when needed —Ability to work independently —Demonstrates leadership
				Excellent spelling, punctuation and grammar are evident. Student is always prepared and strongly contributes to the group learning process.	*Understanding of micro and macro systems *Ability to collaborate with broad range of clients and coworkers
				Presentations are professional, original and engaging.	*High level of self-awareness as a developing professional

	Ranking	Score	Grade	Academic Criteria	Field Criteria
Commendable/ Very good	3	80 - 89	B- to B+	**The work is better than average.** There is some original thought and response to the material. The work demonstrates good interpretive, descriptive and synthesizing skills. The work shows the ability to make critical connections between the historical, cultural, political, social and economic contexts. It provides an appropriate level of detail to demonstrate knowledge and skills development. The work draws on multiple research sources and shows good bibliographic, annotation and synthesizing skills. Written and oral work shows logical and clear thought and expression, unity and coherence of analysis and creativity. There are a few spelling, punctuation and grammar errors, but they do not seriously interfere with meaning or reading. Presentations are generally professional and somewhat original. Student is usually prepared and contributes to the group learning process.	**The work is better than average.** *On time—punctual and reliable *Dresses appropriately *Produces high quality work, both written and oral *No spelling, punctuation or grammar problems *Ability to work with minimal supervision to complete assignments *Dependable, consistently follows through on assignments *Takes responsibility for on-the-job training *Ability to respond to constructive feedback *Ability and willingness to ask for assistance and information as needed
Adequate *(Note: C- is not a passing grade.)*	2	70 - 79	C- to C+	**The work is average.** It remains at a surface level and is more descriptive than analytical. It does not make use of original thought or response to the material. There is evidence of difficulty in synthesizing material and reflecting critically its context. The work draws on limited (one or two) research sources and is lacking in bibliographic completeness and accuracy. Written and oral presentations lack sufficient, clarity or accuracy.	**The work is average.** *Fulfills contractual requirements for learning agreements and job duties at a minimum level *Ability to complete entry-level tasks and assignments

Sufficient errors in spelling, punctuation and grammar interfere with meaning and reading.

Presentation of the work is incomplete, minimal or unclear.

The student is sometimes unprepared and often unable to contribute to the group learning process.

| Unsatisfactory | 1 | 60 - 69 | D- to D+ | The work is significantly below average. | The work is significantly below average. |

The work is significantly below average.

The work lacks organization, thoughtfulness and shows difficulty in understanding the readings and expressing ideas.

There is evidence of an inability to interpret the material beyond a minimal description.

There is an inability to critically interpret materials and analyze connections between materials.

Multiple errors in bibliographic sources, spelling, punctuation and grammar seriously interfere with meaning and reading.

The work is not presented with originality or care.

The student is frequently unprepared and unable to engage in the group learning process.

The work is significantly below average.

*Not able to synthesize information and apply to job

*Difficulty maintaining consistent schedule, not dependable

*Unethical practice

*Does not complete required paperwork within scheduled due dates

*Does not respond to training

*Does not take responsibility for learning experience

The work is unacceptable or not submitted within established deadlines.

| None | 0 | 59 - 60 | F |

The work is unacceptable or not submitted within established deadlines.

Appendix C
The Collaborative Health and Human Services Assessment Protocol

1. Assessment of CHHS Major Learning Outcomes (MLOs)
   • Entering Student Self-Assessment: First Semester Junior
   • Exiting Student Self-Assessment: Last Semester Senior
   • Portfolio Review: Graduation Assessment by faculty and mentor
   • Postgraduate Self-Assessment: One year post graduation

2. Assessment of CHHS MLOs in Field Placements
   • Field Learning Agreement and Student Assessment Matrix
   • Student Assessment of Agency and Mentor
   • Mentor Assessment of CHHS Field Practice Program

3. Pathway Options and Instructions for Assessment
   • MLO Academic and Field Evidence
   • MLO Pathway Guidelines
   • Criteria for Assessment/Ranking: Academic and Field
   • Standard syllabus format
   • Portfolio Assessment instruction for reviewers

4. Student Contact and Data Collection
   • Entering student information
   • Exiting student locator

5. Program Summary Data
   • Student competency summary matrix
   • Postgraduate status summary: graduate school acceptance and employment trends

Note: From *Assessing student learning: Lessons from an outcomes-based health and human services program,* by B. Simmons and K. Judson, 2004, Anaheim, CA. Presented at the 50th Annual Program Meeting of the Council on Social Work Education. Adapted with permission.

Appendix D
Cover Letter to External Readers of the Portfolio

CALIFORNIA STATE UNIVERSITY MONTEREY BAY
INSTITUTE FOR COMMUNITY COLLABORATIVE STUDIES
100 Campus Center Seaside, California 93955-8001
Phone (831)582-3565 Fax (831)582-3899 http://iccs.csumb.edu

Dear Portfolio Reviewer:

Thank you for agreeing to review the portfolio of one of our graduating seniors. This is an important piece in the assessment cycle that our students experience during their time here.

In reality, however, your participation serves two functions. The first and most obvious is your feedback on the student's collection of evidence in support of a minimally acceptable level of knowledge, skill, and attitude in the twelve areas that we have defined as learning outcomes. The second function is to provide feedback to the CHHS faculty regarding the program itself. I'll say more about that in a moment.

Assessing the Student's Work

While reading the portfolio, we strongly encourage you to be in front of a computer that is opened to the "MLO Pie" on the CHHS website. There you will find the definition that CHHS uses for each learning outcome, the "Knowledge-Skill-Attitude" (KSA) statements for each MLO, and what we call the "supporting competencies" for each MLO. Ultimately what we are looking for from each student is evidence that is "Adequate" or better for each MLO as defined by the KSA statements. The supporting competencies are meant to be suggestive (not exhaustive) of the kinds of evidence the student might put into the portfolio.

You will receive a hardcopy of an assessment form and a sheet that defines the standards that CHHS uses. The assessment form uses a Likert-like scale. We ask that you read enough of each portfolio section to get a good sense of the student's level of work and circle the number that represents your assessment of the work for that MLO. We have also provided space for you to offer feedback to the student.

You will undoubtedly find that the student is using a piece of evidence in support of more than one MLO. The explanation of how the evidence supports the respective MLO should be found on the table of contents for each MLO. We have asked the students NOT to reproduce multiple copies of the evidence. Rather, you will find instructions where to find the evidence if it is being used in more than one section.

Programmatic Feedback

The second function served by the outside reader is to provide feedback to the CHHS faculty regarding the program itself. In many ways, we rely on the outside portfolio reviewers to provide a quality control check on the program. We want to collect in a systematic way your thoughts, observations, reflections, and wisdoms gathered from your experience as a portfolio reader. The purpose of this exercise is to take your feedback and use it to improve our curriculum, assignments, pedagogy, field program, etc.

So, as you read through each portfolio, we would appreciate your recording your questions, thoughts, and observations on this form. For example, if you conclude that a student's evidence is minimally sufficient to pass the MLO, but that you think more evidence in a certain area or of a certain type would have strengthened the student's case, jot that down. Perhaps the evidence of knowledge or attitude is more implicit than explicit; you are comfortable that the student knows what needs to be known, but wish that something more concrete had been presented. Note that. If there seems to be a disconnect between the student's written work and the observations of the field work mentor(s), note that. If you have a question about how something was presented or wonder how something is being taught, put that down too. If you found a particular assignment to be useful or intriguing (or not so useful), let us know that. If you think the content being presented to the students is dated or otherwise not useful, feel free to say so.

You need NOT record the name of the student on this form. We are more interested in your reactions that might be representative of systematic issues or things that need to be addressed. If you are reading more than one portfolio, you need keep only one set of notes and turn that in when you are finished. You also should not feel the need to record things if you have no questions or observations that you would like to share.

The form is broken down simply by MLOs for you to record whatever observations you might have for that particular section. Additionally, there is space on the back for general questions or comments. If this particular structure does not fit how you would like to pose your question(s) or state your observation(s), feel free to do it however you would like and we will figure it out. Use additional sheets as needed.

We hope during the next year to use your responses to this rather open-ended exercise to create a more structured, closed-ended (but not entirely so) form that will make this a little easier in years to come.

We are the only academic unit on campus that uses external community reviewers for the graduation portfolios and have been acknowledged by our peers for taking this approach. We do so to honor our commitment to our community partners, but in turn we recognize that your taking the time and making the effort to be part of this process reflects your own commitment to CHHS and CSUMB. We thank you.

Be sure to pick up your complimentary hat or t-shirt when you turn in your portfolio. Thanks again for this important contribution to the teaching and learning that we do at CHHS.

Brian Simmons and Jerry Endres
Capstone Advisors

FIGURE 1
CHHS's cross cultural competence MLO

Definition: Demonstrate the ability to be comfortable with differences between self and others, to engage in a process characterized by mutual respect and sensitivity, to assess the needs and capabilities of culturally diverse populations, and communicate effectively across cultural groups to deliver appropriate health and human services.

Core Competencies:

Knowledge: The cross-culturally competent worker in the health and human services knows the basic issues associated with cultural competence, knows her or his own culture and the impact it has on professional practice, and has knowledge of the specific beliefs and practices of the different cultural groups (broadly defined) with whom she or he will be working.

Skills: The cross-culturally competent worker in the health and human services knows how to access available information and resources to improve services to the groups he or she is working with, and adopts professional practices to meet culturally unique needs.

Attitudes: The cross-culturally competent worker in the health and human services acknowledges the importance of culture and maintains vigilance toward the dynamics of cultural differences.

Supporting Competencies:

The entry-level cross-culturally competent worker in the health and human services has the ability to:

- recognize the limits of one's own knowledge, competencies, and expertise and how those limits affect interactions with people from other cultural backgrounds
- demonstrate a positive attitude and approach to learning about the characteristics of different cultural communities and the resources available to serve them
- demonstrate an understanding of one's racially and culturally bound values and attitudes and seeks to cultivate a nonracist worldview
- challenge assumptions, stereotypes, and paradigms of others
- demonstrate a basic knowledge of how oppression, racism, discrimination, and stereotyping affect all people, including a history of the oppression of some groups by the dominant culture and the role of internalized oppression
- claim one's own cultural identity; to have a working knowledge of that culture, including an awareness of how it affects one's his or her own beliefs, values, and behaviors; and be able to present that culture to others
- contrast his or her own beliefs and attitudes with those from other cultures and challenge one's own biases and practices

- demonstrate an understanding of communication style differences
- establish an approach that actively seeks out educational and social experiences that foster her or his own knowledge, understanding, and cross-cultural skills
- adapt practice to different cultural situations
- acknowledge that one individual need not have all the answers and to be open to himself or herself and others taking risks, reaching out across cultures, and learning from her or his mistakes
- acknowledge the role of indigenous helping practices and respect intrinsic help-giving networks in the community
- seek professional experiences (e.g., training, education, consultation) to improve effectiveness in working with others who differ culturally
- think critically on matters of cultural diversity

FIGURE 2
Mentor Field Assessment

MLO 1—Collaboration: Demonstrate the ability to work in teams in interprofessional settings across traditional lines of programs, agencies, disciplines, and diverse communities to establish common missions and purposes; and to collaborate with others in decision making, learning, completing tasks and applying knowledge of group processes and group interaction.

Circle the number that best reflects the students' level of competence at the beginning and end of the field experience

Collaboration Competencies	Planned Assignments and Projects	Progress on Projects and Evaluation of Student		Assessment of Entering & Exiting Level of Competency				
				None/N/A	Limited	Adequate	Commendable	Outstanding
Knowledge: Demonstrate what collaboration means, why it is important and how community conditions can be improved by employing the collaborative process.			Entering	0	1	2	3	4
			Exiting	0	1	2	3	4
Skills: The ability to build consensus and sustain participation with an interprofessional group solving problems and resolving conflict using different decision-making processes relevant for collaborative groups.			Entering	0	1	2	3	4
			Exiting	0	1	2	3	4
Attitudes: Demonstrate the ability to share resources, expertise and responsibility to achieve a common goal in a collaborative setting.			Entering	0	1	2	3	4
			Exiting	0	1	2	3	4

Required Comments on Student Performance for this MLO:

This evaluation has been reviewed and discussed with the student

_____   _____   _____   _____   _____   _____
Agency Mentor   Date   Student   Date   CHHS Faculty Advisor   Date

MLO 1—Collaboration: Demonstrate the ability to work in teams in interprofessional settings across traditional lines of programs, agencies, disciplines, and diverse communities to establish common missions and purposes; and to collaborate with others in decision making, learning, completing tasks and applying knowledge of group processes and group interaction.

Circle the number that best reflects the students' level of competence at the beginning and end of the field experience

Collaboration Competencies	Planned Assignments and Activities	Completed Assignments and Evidence for Portfolio		Assessment of Entering & Exiting Level of Competency				
				None/N/A	Limited	Adequate	Commendable	Outstanding
Knowledge: Demonstrate what collaboration means, why it is important and how community conditions can be improved by employing the collaborative process.			Entering	0	1	2	3	4
			Exiting	0	1	2	3	4
Skills: The ability to build consensus and sustain participation with an interprofessional group solving problems and resolving conflict using different decision-making processes relevant for collaborative groups.			Entering	0	1	2	3	4
			Exiting	0	1	2	3	4
Attitudes: Demonstrate the ability to share resources, expertise and responsibility to achieve a common goal in a collaborative setting.			Entering	0	1	2	3	4
			Exiting	0	1	2	3	4

Required Comments on Student Performance for this MLO:

This evaluation has been reviewed and discussed with the student

Agency Mentor _____ Date _____

Student _____ Date _____

CHHS Faculty Advisor _____ Date _____

PART TWO

PRIDE AND PREJUDICE: FINDING YOUR PLACE AFTER THE DEGREE

10

BEING ALL THINGS TO ALL PEOPLE

Expectations of and Demands on
Women of Color in the Legal Academy

Danielle Conway-Jones

The Author

Professor Conway-Jones joined the faculty at the University of Hawai'i William S. Richardson Law School in 2000 and currently serves as an associate professor of law and director of the Hawai'i Procurement Institute. She teaches intellectual property, government contract law, international intellectual property, and Internet law and policy. She also served as the interim director of the Law and Methods Program for 2002–2003. Formerly, Professor Conway-Jones was on the faculties of The University of Memphis, Cecil C. Humphreys School of Law, teaching torts, toxic tort litigation, and government contract law; and Georgetown University Law Center, teaching legal research and writing and legal writing for foreign lawyers.

Professor Conway-Jones graduated from New York University, Stern School of Business in 1989, with degrees in finance and international business and a United States Army commission. She attended the Howard University School of Law, where she served on both the *Howard Law Journal* and the National Moot Court Board. After graduating from law school in 1992 and attaining her bar memberships, she fulfilled her military commitment by graduating from the Judge Advocate General's School in Charlottesville, Virginia, and receiving an appointment to the Chief Counsel's Honors Program, United States Army Corps of Engineers, Washington, D.C. Professor Conway-Jones primarily practiced in the procurement law section, representing the U.S. government in complex bid protest litigation. While on active duty, she earned a dual Master of Laws degree in environmental law and government procurement law from George Washington University Law School in 1996. Currently, she is a major in the United States Army Reserve assigned as a professor at The Judge Advocate General's School in Charlottesville.

Professor Conway-Jones's LLM thesis and other writings appear in the *Howard Law Journal, University of Richmond Law Review, Santa Clara Law Review, Asian-Pacific Law and Policy Journal, Washington University Global Studies Law Review,* and *Michigan Journal of Race and Law.* She has spoken and presented at various conferences in the United States, China, Micronesia, and Mongolia on topics including globalization, distance education, intellectual property, e-commerce, and indigenous peoples' rights in traditional knowledge.

There is a historical military principle called center of gravity, which depicts one force's ability to identify a weakness of an opposing force and the contemporaneous exploitation of that weakness to achieve a strategic or tactical advantage in battle (Paret, 1986). The employment of center-of-gravity tactics by one force usually causes friction to the opposing force (Addington, 1994). Oftentimes, friction is defined as the fog of war—the fortuitous presence or deliberate erection of obstacles that create hurdles or impediments for an opposing force (Addington, 1994). As I reflect on my membership in the legal academy, I cannot help but think of these historical military principles and their nonmilitary application to my experiences coming through and up the ranks in the legal academy. As in battles and wars, there are times of great accomplishment and unalterable belief about the necessity of engaging an opponent; just as equally, there are times of severe disappointment and disillusionment about the need for such conflicts. The application of the principles of center of gravity and friction to my experiences as an African American woman law professor in a majority institution and my vacillation between feelings of success and defeat are keenly apropos when placed in the context of an ongoing battle for respect; acceptance; external validations of worth and contribution; and, most important, inclusion and integration without assimilation.

One might say that I have achieved significant success in the legal academy: I am tenured; I am at one of the more diverse, if not the most diverse, law schools in the United States; I have achieved notoriety in the State of Hawaii's legal community and in the overall community; and I am sought out for my expertise and for participation in various university and community initiatives and activities. Yet, I ponder: "Is it really a success to be the one who fills all of the slots at my institution, and has a battle really been won when the price of that 'success' yields significant collateral damage?" Terms such as *filling all of the slots, success,* and *collateral damage* will necessarily require definition and discussion with respect to their meanings in the context of teaching and achieving in the legal academy as an African American woman. But before I get to this, I would like to present a subtheme, which is plainly this: Women of color on law faculties are just as entitled to academic freedom and support for individual intellectual exploration as those colleagues representing the majority; anything less negatively impacts on the woman of color's scholarly productivity, agenda, value, and resources. Thus, social and equal justice for women of color in the legal academy demand that majority institutions reevaluate their commitment, if any, to a diverse faculty to protect the academic freedom and the sustainability of women of color on a faculty.

Woman of Color as a Role Model

A common and often relied upon argument to support diversity initiatives in the legal academy is that students of color need and desire law professors who look like them and who can serve as role models for them during their tenure in law school (Young, 1995). On the surface, I have always been persuaded by this argument, and, in fact, the role model theory was the primary reason that I chose to attend Howard University School of Law, a historically Black college. I wished to be surrounded by people who looked like me, and, more important, I wished to, at last, see a face in the front of a higher-education classroom that was my mirror image. Thus, the significance of the role model theory is not lost on me, but it does have negative side effects when applied at a majority as opposed to a historically Black institution. Specifically, when students of color attend a historically Black college or law school, the number of faculty of color is plentiful. In such a situation, there is no need for students of color to flock to or focus on just one faculty member when several are available who teach myriad subjects. This is not the case for the one woman of color on a law faculty. Application of the role model theory to a woman of color on a majority faculty immediately presents inequitable conditions, having multiple negative impacts.

Most apparent, the woman-of-color law professor is deluged with requests for attention by all students, not just students of color and women. It is true that part of the role of any faculty member is to serve as a resource and a model to students. Unfortunately, women of color, particularly African

American women, are viewed as compassionate caregivers, counselors, and symbols (Young, 1995). Although in the abstract these qualities are notable, there is left very little room to function outside of these stereotypes. And, even less attention is paid to the woman-of-color law professor's true role as intellectual, academic, and scholar. In fact, if you operate "out of character" by being a challenging, stern, and "tough" professor in the classroom, somehow you will be viewed as betraying your "position" as a woman of color. Thus, as one author noted, "Being a role model imposes professional limitations and can be psychologically burdensome. Because role models are under intense scrutiny, our human weaknesses must be hidden in order to display the desired image" (Young, 1995, p. 281).

There is even more support for the proposition that the role model theory imposes far greater burdens on the woman-of-color law professor than on her majority counterparts, both male and female. For example, Professor Anita Allen-Castellitto argues, "that the expectation that black women will be role models for black female students 'signals to faculty members who are not black females that they may abandon efforts to serve as positive role models for black women . . . it lets most faculty off the hook when it comes to educating black women'" (Allen, 1990–1991, p. 40). Professor Allen-Castellitto also observes that "being a positive black female role model often seems to require acting as much like an educated upper-middle-class White person as possible, consistent with an ability to participate meaningfully in elite African-American community life. Looking and speaking like Whites has always helped would-be role models" (p. 40). Conversely, "if you're not black enough, you are seen as unqualified to be a role model" (p. 40). These observations are critical in that they demonstrate the gauntlet that a woman-of-color law professor must run on a daily basis to project the façade of the "good role model," who is rarely seen out of costume or character. Thus, the requirement to be a good role model for students of color and a "good" race or ethnic representative is just one example of the requirement to "fill all of the slots." The woman of color must retain upper-middle-class characteristics in order to legitimate her presence in the legal academy. In addition, the woman of color must present an image of overqualification in order to justify her position as the leader in the classroom in order to gain that respect that is presumptively offered to her White male counterparts. If you, the woman of color, successfully hurdle these obstacles, have you succeeded? For those of us who have "succeeded," meaning retained the foothold in the door of legal academia, have we really been included and integrated as vested equal partners in the law-teaching community?

The next two sections discuss whether the woman-of-color faculty member can truly be said to have succeeded, where success is measured by the complete integration of the woman of color as law professor with full rights of academic freedom.

Woman of Color as a Resource to Faculty and Administrators, and as a Bridge to the Community

In no other context is the "fill all the slots" paradigm more evident than in the area of university and community service, notably the least regarded variable in the calculus for a faculty member's worth and value to a majority institution. Despite this truism, the demands placed upon the woman-of-color faculty member—as the "go-to" person for department, university, and community programs and initiatives—is immense. Here is how it unfolds: In addition to being the subject of conventional department and university assignments, you as a woman of color are identified as a resource to law review students writing about race, gender, and ethnic issues who just need to bounce ideas off of you to get your perspective; moot court students who are dealing with issues related to race, gender, and equality and are in need of your insights as a judge and a woman of color; administrators who are conducting brown bag activities or constituting committees around issues of race, gender, and culture and who insist your presence is required to add balance or provide guidance to the group; university officials who identify you as a woman-of-color potential mentor who should make herself available for those faculty of color coming through the ranks to ensure the latter's preparation for tenure and promotion. Furthermore, the university requires your participation on systemwide committees to add "diversity" to university decisions and actions, community organizations require your contributions so that their groups are representative of the larger community, and so on. Any one or all of these activities is important in its own way; however, taken together, these activities work a threefold disadvantage on the lone woman-of-color faculty member.

First, one lone voice representing an entire racial community assumes that that racial group is homogeneous in thought, expression, and experience. This we know is furthest from the truth, yet the mentality to all committees "identify and appoint that one woman of color" bespeaks this truth. Second, the overuse and exploitation of the one woman-of-color faculty member casts her in the position of servant to all in the community, with little time or resources remaining for her individual scholarly production—

the sole measure, in reality, of a faculty member's worth in the legal academy. Third, if the woman-of-color faculty member does engage in race and gender discourse, she runs the risk of being labeled "biased" by majority faculty who, ironically, placed her in this position by adherence to the "we have one" paradigm.

The undervaluation of administrative duties and university service is demonstrated by the investment of financial resources and the bestowing of laudable recognition, without exception, to law faculty who publish. Although they realize that scholarly publication is the measuring stick for productivity, administrators as well as university and community leaders who insist on overtaxing and overburdening women-of-color faculty with non-publication tasks imply that scholarship and publication by women of color is not valued or respected. The untenable position in which a woman-of-color faculty member is placed is either one of not being considered a team player or, worse, one of having to produce twice as much or more in the service arena while not compromising the quantity or quality of scholarly publications. There is no greater truth that the majority will consider a decline in the latter, for any reason, to be unacceptable; hence, the majority's erroneous observation will be that the woman-of-color faculty member is inferior and incapable of producing at the level of her White male and female counterparts.

Professors Deborah J. Merritt and Barbara F. Reskin (1992) found after extensive empirical study that

> tokenism . . . compounds ordinary teaching problems for those members of subordinated groups who manage to be hired; their obligations beyond teaching and research, for example, community responsibilities, counseling students, and committees, are widely reported in the surveys to be more onerous for them than for white male colleagues and to have a crippling effect on faculty performance and promotion. Mentoring by senior faculty is less likely to be available or offered, [and] support mechanisms to compensate for these disadvantages are often not available. (p. 20)

In this context, you can begin to see the negative results, or collateral damage, of the "we have one" theory. The woman-of-color faculty member is placed in the unenviable position of having to shoulder a disproportionate burden of activities in order to achieve "success," with the collateral damage being the inability to take full advantage of the academic freedom enjoyed by majority faculty.

Woman of Color as an Ethnic Representative

Connected to the "we have one" theory is the notion that hiring one woman-of-color faculty member will provide a point of reference for race, gender, and ethnic issues. The argument "we have one and need only one woman of color on the faculty" is a form of tokenism, whether intended or not. Appointing one woman of color allows the majority to continue to presume that ethnic minorities are one-dimensional in thought and expression and that one voice as ethnic representative is all that is necessary to explain fully the passions and concerns of the group. Professor Peter Halewood (1995) observes, "It is likely that the introduction of a small number of marginalized voices will be tolerated only because they are unlikely to unseat the dominant group or fundamentally challenge its perspective. The dominant group remains unwilling to admit different groups in numbers sufficient to facilitate real change" (pp. 18–19).

However, the more detrimental effect of the "we have one" paradigm is the assault on the academic freedom of a woman-of-color scholar. To illustrate this point, I refer to my own scholarly and teaching agenda and then compare that with the de facto expectations of students, administrators, and faculty colleagues. My area of scholarly expertise includes extremely technical subjects. I teach and consult in the areas of government procurement law, domestic and international intellectual property law, and Internet law. I am particularly sought out by the practicing bar and the military for my expertise in handling issues related to the intersection of government contracts and intellectual property, particularly federal government use rights in technical data and computer software and software documentation produced by federal government contractors prior to and during the performance of government contracts. In fact, I have been engaged in one way or another in this field since my graduation from law school and my subsequent service as a judge advocate in the United States Army. When I began teaching, particularly at law schools where I was the only woman of color, I observed that students, faculty, and administrators primarily sought my advice and guidance on issues of race and gender and only secondarily on my areas of expertise. This is not to say that I do not carry strong opinions about issues involving race and gender, but my overarching concern is that as a woman-of-color faculty member I am viewed as an expert in areas of race and gender when, in fact, such experts have devoted their lives and scholarly agendas to this complex area of study, whereas I have not. Thus, the problem I see with the conflation of my very existence and legal issues surrounding race and gender is the devaluation of an entire area of scholarship.

I have encountered well-meaning and sensitive faculty colleagues, students, and administrators who expressly or implicitly urge me to become involved in tackling race and gender issues on a macro level, which, if I do, will only cause my primary scholarly agenda to be compromised. Thus, I would be no longer free to explore the rich and complex issues presented by government contract law and intellectual property law. In fact, if I retreat from this scholarly agenda in favor of dealing in the race and gender arena, I, as one of the few experts in this field, would be ignoring the social, political, and economic implications that must be explored, analyzed, and discussed for the benefit of contractors innovating for the federal government and society at large. I propose that majority law faculty members are not presented with the dilemma regarding the expectation of scholarly agenda and output on issues of race and gender, on the one hand, and the chosen area of expertise, on the other. As a woman-of-color law professor, I am placed in the position of having to choose between a perceived obligation to address issues of race and gender as a tangential requirement imposed by the ethnic representative theory of faculty hiring and the obligation to research and write in my areas of expertise—where, at the end of the day, production in these areas will be the only measure the majority will use to assess my scholarly performance—or to engage in both areas as a scholarly agenda and, thus, carry a disproportionate burden of production and output that necessarily belies academic freedom. This dilemma alone suggests that majority institutions truly committed to diversity must support the development of a critical mass of women-of-color law faculty as a good-faith showing of support in the hiring, mentorship, and retention of the woman of color. Without this good-faith showing, there will be no real opportunities for the woman of color to succeed and flourish in the legal academy, because the specter of collateral damage will always loom.

Conclusion: Woman of Color as a Resource

The dilemma confronting a woman of color in the legal academy is a real one. Whether a woman of color could, should, or would want to make herself available as a pedagogical resource on issues of race and gender is not an institutionally fair or reasoned approach to promoting diversity or academic freedom. In addition, placing this responsibility on a woman of color by sheer adherence to the "we have one" paradigm is tantamount to exploitation; as well, it dilutes the heterogeneous richness and diversity of legal scholarship produced by the varying voices of women of color in the diaspora. To avoid the collateral damage that will necessarily result from the "we have one" theory in the construction of a diverse law faculty, a majority institution must make significant commitments to critical mass when constituting a truly diverse faculty. Women of color can demand parity in academic freedom, but such demands are only theoretical battles that are lost to the reality that having just one on the faculty breeds disproportionate burdens that impede full acceptance and integration into the academy.

References

Addington, L. H. (1994). *The patterns of war since the eighteenth century* (2nd ed.). Bloomington: Indiana University Press.

Allen, A. (1990–1991). On being a role model. *Berkeley Women's L.J., 1*(6), 40.

Halewood, P. (1995). White men can't jump: Critical epistemologies, embodiment, and the praxis of legal scholarship. *Yale Journal of Law & Feminism, 1*(7), 18–19.

Merritt, D. J., & Reskin, B. F. (1992, August 31). Hidden bias of law school faculties. *Legal Times,* p. 20.

Paret, P. (1986). Clausewitz. In P. Paret (Ed.), *Makers of modern strategy: From Machiavelli to the nuclear age.* Princeton, NJ: Princeton University Press.

Young, D. E. (1995). Two steps removed: The paradox of diversity discourse for women of color in law teaching. *African-American Law & Policy Report, 270*(2), 274.

II

THE "INTERCULTURAL SPACE" WHERE WORLDS COLLIDE

Amanda Kim

The Author

Amanda Kim, Ph.D., is currently a postdoctoral scholar at the Center for the Study of Higher and Postsecondary Education, University of Michigan. She was born in South Korea and later immigrated to the United States with her family and grew up in the Midwest. She completed her doctoral degree in counseling psychology and practiced for two years as a staff psychologist. Her research interests in diversity and multiculturalism are the result of her personal and professional experiences that set the stage for social-justice-based research that would have an impact on the developmental experiences of young adults within university settings.

I began my graduate studies in counseling psychology in the year 1992; it marked the beginning of my consciousness as a woman of color and what it means to be a Korean American. As the eldest daughter of a Korean immigrant family of working class, my home life was nothing like the world that I knew existed outside the walls of our apartment. I remember coming to this awareness after having Michele over to my home after school one day. Michele and I were both in 7th grade. Michele was blonde, blue eyed, and beautiful, but other kids teased her for being fat; she was my best friend and I was her ardent admirer. I felt proud of having her friendship. However, in my home, she noted how "strange" my home was, commented on the strange "smells" of my house, then proceeded to ask me how often I washed my clothes and my sheets, what kinds of food my family ate, what I got for my birthday, and what kind of a car my parents had. Whatever her intentions, each question had the impact of shaming me further and further. Fighting back the hot tears, I became angry with myself for having invited her into my home. I did not know what to do with the shame I felt in seeing my "ethnic" world through her eyes. Our friendship soon ended. I think the abrupt introduction of the differences between Michele's home and mine were too much for either one of us to handle. I never told my parents what happened that day. I swallowed the bitterness I felt at Michele, at my parents, and at myself.

Twenty years later, I still remember the feelings I experienced in that moment when I had wished so badly that I could undo everything so I could be friends with Michele again and so she could be oblivious to the other world in which I lived. And, still, I struggle with how to bridge the life of my family, my home, and the heritage and ways of who I am with who I wish to be, who I am expected to be, and who I think others see me to be in the world that exists outside the walls of my parents' home.

Harro's *Cycle of Socialization* (2000) provides a nice framework for understanding and dissecting the impact of the dual socialization experiences that I had with my parents and society at large that provided the foundational framework for my bicultural lens.

Since 7th grade, I have learned much about the differences between American culture and ethnic minority culture as well as the desire to assimilate and be, like everybody else, in constant tension with the desire to honor, respect, and live in the cultural identity of who I am. Some learnings came from inside and outside the academy regarding social systems, institutional systems, and the historical legacy of America's struggle with cultural identity and racism. Other learnings came from painful recognition of the racist, classist, sexist experiences that I was able to recognize and label. And still other learnings came from the obstacles I faced in "trying on" or sharing the enthusiasm of my new learnings with family and friends. The sources of support and the motivations I have for integrating these learnings into my identity and the choices I am able to make in my life are ripe for a critical consciousness experienced in the "intercultural space" of the worlds I occupy.

I use the term *intercultural space* to refer to the space of conscious awareness of not feeling fully comfortable in the space of my home life kept alive by my parents nor in the space of the academy or as an ethnic minority member of a predominantly White American society. Berry (2001) defines *intercultural space* to be the intersection of two or more contact groups where cultural boundaries and social relationships are negotiated. In this place of "intercultural space," I am sharply aware of the vantage point I have in being able to step outside the cultural spaces that I occupy and my ability to be conscious of the choices I make and the spaces that I choose to occupy. In this intercultural space, however, I am also painfully aware of the precarious nature of my membership. The fear that my membership may be challenged or taken away from me is coupled with the alienation of being relegated to the position of "other" in both worlds. The emotion of living in this space is one of "feeling alive," painful and exhilarating all at once, in the conscious recognition of where I choose to be and what it means to make that choice, but it is also a vulnerable and alienating place that is bereft of comfort, security, and acceptance. It is a space that I believe is ripe for learning about myself, others, and the world(s) in which I live. The challenge of this space, I believe, is that it is devoid of the web of social supports that makes for a community, which is so critical to the sense of belonging and feeling connected to others.

Upon completion of graduate school, the notion of "work" and the value systems that were implicated became very clear. Having enjoyed graduate school and the passion for learning that I had developed, my hope was to be immersed in higher-education environments. I envisioned myself being a university faculty or staff member. My attraction to this line of work came from a value system of wanting to do "meaningful" work that would be gratifying to my enjoyment of learning and being around others who wished to be engaged in similar ways. My value framework was very much supported by the faculty mentors and peers of my program, most likely because it was the value system that they bought into.

The reaction from family and friends within the Korean American community was quite different. It is not uncommon for individuals of immigrant backgrounds to privilege status, power, and money over "meaningfulness" in one's work. I made numerous attempts to explain and justify my position, without much success. Because I am of a stubborn nature and because I am female, my desire to engage in "gratifying work" over lucrative work was reluctantly accepted. Looking back, I now recognize the positionality of others who could not support me in my choices. In talking with my family over the years, I became keenly aware of how different their understanding and experiences of power were from mine. In their critical learning of how to be successful, empowerment came in the form of status, prestige, and money. It was through those avenues that they experienced power within their environments. I came to recognize through my learning experiences that I am empowered in my ability to learn and critically evaluate the structures of power. This lesson was critical to my capacity to empathize with different positionalities of those whom I love and with whom I will continue to have a close relationship. Sometimes I long to go back in time and feel the comforts of what it was like not to have the divide in our perspectives.

Excited about my own reflective learning experience, I often wanted to share my thoughts and engage with others in my community on issues of multiculturalism, racism, structural systems, and social justice. I quickly became labeled as a "liberal hippie" in my idealistic notions of wanting and working for change and transformation. On occasion, I was even labeled an "honorary whitey" for imitating the talk of "liberal white America" that is privileged enough to protest against racism and discrimination. Sadly, I became aware that many of my friends and family recognized the inequities in society, and the racism experiences in their own lives, but felt powerless to change what already was. People said to me, "At some point, you have to accept how things are and just make the best of it." Those words haunt me to this day. It is the notion of "making the best of it" that catches me every time.

In my consciousness, I have come to see what my interpretation of making the best of it means for me, a collaborator in perpetuating the status quo. Consequently, making the best of it is the dangerous place of disconnect from the power that I have in shaping the world. So as much as I love, honor, and take pride in the relationships that I have with the members of my community, I have to fight feelings of disappointment, sadness, and sometimes anger at what I perceive to be their disempowerment.

On the flip side, I have come to see that my reactions to collisions with the majority culture offer a different experience. Along with the critical consciousness came a critical lens that expanded my horizon for recognizing the inequities, injustices, and acts of "isms" perpetuated by those around me. Having acquired this critical lens, I no longer have the luxury of ignorance. Subsequently, I am more critical and aware of the various issues infused in my interactions with others. At times it is very much a burden and at times I have to remind myself not to take things so seriously and to remember to challenge my interpretations. What I find to be the most difficult in my interaction with others in the majority culture is when my voice is dismissed or silenced. Let me provide an example.

One year, I attended a department gathering at a faculty member's home. I was enjoying the casual interactions and seeing the different faces. An older White male enthusiastically greeted me. We began a casual conversation about the need to provide "social outlets" for academics who tend to be introverted and workaholics. I could not have agreed more. The connection I felt to this man disappeared the instant he complimented me on my English. I had a visceral reaction to his comment, which I tried to hold, as I reminded myself that I did not know his intentions. I thanked him and added that English was my primary language. My intention had been to be polite and gently remind him that he may have mistakenly made some assumptions about me. He added fuel to the fire burning in the pit of my stomach as he continued to talk about how laudable it is that Japanese International students work so hard at immersing themselves in the American culture. He spoke of how much he had enjoyed his interactions with students like me. I had to walk away then—fuming. Years later, I read Elena Tajima Creef's (1990) "Notes from a Fragmented Daughter" and smiled at the familiarity of the personal scenes recounted.

I wonder, even as I recollect this past incident, what it would have been like to say the words that were burning in my brain even as I smiled weakly and walked away: "Stop complimenting me on being such a good Japanese International student. Instead of putting all these assumptions on me in the name of being 'nice,' why don't you just ask me who I am?" I have mixed feelings about having silenced my voice and questions about what then happened to the mix of emotions I felt in that situation and countless other times when I have silenced myself or have been silenced by others. I acknowledge my complicity in silencing myself, but I also know the costs involved in refusing to be silent. That is the place of my struggle. What will I risk? How much will I risk to have a voice in the dominant culture?

I think if I had spoken in a friendly, open, and caring way that man might have been able to hear what I had to say. But I was not in a place where I could have been caring and friendly in that moment. I was in a place of insecurity, anger, and resentment, described by Phinney, Horenczyk, Liebkind, and Vedder (2001) as a potential by-product of engaging in learning about one's ethnicity. In hindsight, I can see how I might feel more comfortable and able to do that. Other times, I can also see the broader picture of the impact in reacting to those situations with tact and openness as part of my choice in doing my share in trying to change the spaces in which I move. At times, though, I wish that I could casually laugh off the mistaken assumptions and walk away untouched by those moments.

Regardless of the specific nature of these collisions that I speak of, I think the impact is always a visceral one of wanting to give up, feeling frustrated, alone, and helpless. However, past these affective reactions are the moments for critical learning and self-reflection that allow me to locate myself in the "intercultural space" where I have the privilege of struggling with issues in a meaningful way and living with the juxtapositions, contradictions, and realities of being at the center as well as being at the margins. Consequently, despite the frustrations, anger, and powerlessness I feel when faced with collisions of my world(s), they also provide the opportunity to redefine and rework my understanding in critical ways that have become critical aspects of who I am and who I choose to be. Nevertheless, when I feel tired or scared, I always find myself nostalgic for those moments in the past when I felt safe, comfortable, and secure in the not knowing. Sometimes I just want to go home again.

References

Berry, J. W. (2001). A psychology of immigration. *Journal of Social Issues, 57*(3), 615–631.

Creef, E. T. (1990). Notes from a fragmented daughter. In G. Analdua (Ed.), *Making face, making soul: Creative and critical perspectives by women of color* (pp. 82–24). San Francisco: Aunt Lute Books.

Harro, B. (2000). The cycle of socialization. In M. Adams, W. Blumenfield, R. Casteneda, H. Hackman, M. Peters, & X. Zuniga (Eds.), *Readings for diversity and social justice* (pp. 15–21). New York: Routledge.

Phinney, J. S., Horenczyk, G., Liebkind, K., & Vedder, P. (2001). Ethnic identity, immigration, and well-being: An interactional perspective. *Journal of Social Issues, 57*(3), 493–510.

12

SIDES OF THE TENURE AND PROMOTION PROCESS

Can I Be a Parental Figure, Scholar, and Spouse?

Cassandra Sligh DeWalt

The Author

Dr. Cassandra Sligh DeWalt has a Ph.D. and an M.Ed. in rehabilitation counseling and has held several positions in academia, other educational agencies, and counseling agencies, including assistant professor, assistant director of the Practicum and Internship Experience at North Carolina Central University, distance education course developer/instructor, and program coordinator of the rehabilitation counseling program. Dr. Sligh DeWalt was also employed at ACT in the minority student development office, as a case management supervisor, and as a mental health counselor/social worker at a psychiatric hospital. She is certified in North Carolina as a Qualified Mental Health Professional and a Qualified Developmental Disabilities Professional. Dr. Sligh DeWalt's research concentrates on the value of mentoring in graduate programs, such as teacher education programs, counselor education programs, and elementary/secondary programs. Her dissertation, "Black and White Graduate and Professional Students' Perceptions of Mentoring in Higher Education," has generated other publications such as a 2001 publication in the *Annals Journal*.

The responsibilities and expectations of a college or university professor are numerous and often as diverse as the missions and submissions of the institution to which a faculty member serves. Specific responsibilities and expectations of higher-education faculty generally fall under the categories of research, teaching, and service. University and college faculty are expected to research, write, and publish articles, books, or chapters thereof, monographs, and other instructional resources and make presentations of research findings to collegial peers for information and/or assessment. Faculty members are often expected to provide quality instruction in their field of expertise and assess student learning against scholarly or professional standards. A faculty member may be expected to recruit, admit, and advise students as well as serve as their mentor, counselor, and role model, while also providing services to the community.

College and university faculty are expected to attend numerous meetings that sometimes take time away from research or scholarly pursuits that count toward promotion or tenure, such as a research agenda or grant-writing opportunities. Additionally, attendance in regalia of convocations, baccalaureate, and commencement events is an expectation of faculty, because it is a contractual responsibility.

Some faculty members, in addition to these duties, are responsible for other administrative tasks such as hiring faculty, developing and implementing curriculum, and monitoring departmental budgets and grants. University and college faculty members may also be expected to pursue tenure and/or promotion. Achieving tenure and promotion at historically Black colleges or universities (HBCUs), however, is often easier said than done.

In this chapter, I provide narratives that exemplify categories of challenges to obtaining tenure and/or promotion at an HBCU. The narratives focus on both the political and academic challenges. At the same time, they focus on the multiple roles of being a parental figure or guardian, scholar, and spouse. I then offer suggestions for coping with these challenges. The following narrative focuses on some positive interventions after being thrust into so many roles.

First Year on Tenure Track

The first year as a tenure-track faculty member, I really was overwhelmed by a lot of service. I felt like there were always meetings to attend. I enjoyed the service component and teaching, but I was bewildered at how I would effectively do the research according to my own standards and according to the university's policy. I call my first year as a tenure-track professor the year of revelations and the year of learning how to circumvent a system filled with criteria and rules for the tenure and promotion process. I also found this was the year I learned I could become an effective researcher by saying a political "no." Saying no to certain projects would not mean losing tenure or promotion, but learning how to say no was important. By the end of the first year, I began to process saying no but not fully understanding the need to say no. As a first-year faculty member, if you do not say no to certain things, you may experience "the dump." Believe me, being dumped with too many duties may drain you to the point where you may not have the energy to pursue the tenure or promotion process effectively.

During year one, I also signed up to teach every day during the summer. I felt overwhelmed, and I learned that some faculty members choose not to teach during the summer. I later found that teaching summer courses is an easy way to burn yourself out as a new faculty member. You should never try to teach too many courses over the summer, even when the money looks inviting. I found that summertime may be used to restore your writing or research. It may also be a time to do proposals and apply for grants for the next year. Unfortunately, I did not utilize my first summer as I could have, but this experience helped me to understand the process of pursuing tenure and/or promotion and how to deal with the challenges along the way. At the end of my first year and the first session of teaching summer school, I vowed never to teach an entire summer again, because it weighed me down with too many teaching duties and afforded less time toward the research component of the overall process.

I did not see that a person may burn out if a coping plan is not developed. I developed my coping plan by reading information on surviving and thriving through academia. Reading about other faculty members' difficulties allowed me to see how I needed to take care of myself better. For instance, I did not see the possibility of burnout, which can happen when trying to meet the tenure and/or promotion requirements, until the culmination of my first year as a faculty member. After I realized what I needed to do to meet the tenure requirements, I was able to add more meaning to my "coping plan." I had some questions: How can I meet the tenure requirements when service is so demanding? How will I be able to meet tenure when I am not sure of the requirements because the requirements seem to change?

Second Year on Tenure Track

During the first year, I learned many lessons. I learned not to burn myself out and to cultivate ways to master the tenure and promotion process during the second year. For instance, during the second summer session (while teaching the second summer session) preceding my second year as a tenure-track faculty member, I worked diligently to find my own way to "master" the tenure and promotion requirements. I spent many days writing proposals for articles I could pursue in the future. I also began to pull out old papers and manuscripts that could be presented at conferences and/or submitted as journal articles at a later date. In addition, I began to think of an area in my home where I could concentrate on my research. Finally, I began to ask myself, "Is it the research that will sustain tenure more than the service?" and "How will I continue to balance the service and the research requirements?"

As I pursued my second year as a tenure-track professor, I saw service and teaching as huge requirements at my university. I again went back to the coping plan I had developed, and I said to myself, "Okay, I can and will do my best to cope with the service, research, and teaching." I further developed the coping plan by reviewing the ways to survive academia in the literature. I wrote these down and I followed them. I learned that I had to take care of myself by understanding the politics of academia. I had to learn how to survive my environment. The teaching and service requirements are a large part of the faculty requirements, and I found that these two combined with the research requirements are and were quite challenging.

I gained a better understanding of the process toward achieving tenure and promotion during my second year; I can now value the interactions that I have with faculty who have been at the university longer, for example, four or more years, and I see the value in continuing these working relationships. For instance, faculty who may be at the same level or a higher level of promotion can be effective mentors who can continue to sponsor, advocate, and assist me through the tenure process and in my overall professional career. Faculty can also assist me by sharing with me the hardships they faced while pursuing academia and by helping me to understand certain things that I cannot change about academia. I would find it very difficult to survive as a junior faculty member if I did not have a faculty member with whom I could at least discuss certain aspects of the tenure process. Having other faculty to discuss this process with has also assisted me in understanding that there may be a waiting period for the tenure and/or promotion process even if the requirements have already been met. This allowed me to understand further that things beyond my control can happen.

New Roles during the Tenure-Track Process

A new development during the spring of my second year on tenure track was the addition of a family member, a child who came to live with me. This forced me to deal with three major roles: parental figure, scholar, and spouse. Throughout my first and the beginning of my second year on tenure track, I truly felt that I was finally able to deal with the dual role of spouse and scholar. However, the role of parental figure was challenging. For instance, now I had to assist my spouse with picking up the child from school and also help this child with homework and other everyday challenges. Things such as caring for my child when the child became sick added so much more than I realized to my schedule and interfered with my ability to remain focused on my writings. After about two months of this new situation in my life, I finally became acclimated to a schedule, but it did not happen overnight. I often found myself off track. I found that I had to work diligently at balancing family time, work time, research time, and service time. When faculty committee meetings were held on certain days, I could no longer depend on my past flexible schedule, which was always open for major changes. Now, if things changed for the faculty schedule at the university, I had to make sure my spouse or another individual was available to pick up my child or provide basic care such as day care. Whew! The multiple roles allowed me to understand that I was a human being. I could look at myself and be okay with my progress.

Third Year on Tenure Track

At the beginning of my third year of the tenure-track process, I can clearly see that some of the efforts that I have put forth toward research and publishing have been beneficial, as a result of lessons learned from years one and two. However, dedicating enough time to the research process is still a tug-of-war. I have learned that I must dedicate a chunk of my schedule toward writing research articles, researching information on the Internet, researching research engines for articles, and continuing to network with other colleagues outside of the university. Developing professional relationships with faculty and staff outside of the university where I am located has been a huge part of extending my networks during the beginning of my third year. This part of the learning process has been a worthwhile experience. I never valued the power of knowing someone in my area or related areas until I started presenting at national conferences. Developing relationships outside of the university has provided me with contacts with other individuals who can keep me abreast of worthwhile research proposals, grant ideas, and so forth. I have also learned to collaborate with other universities and colleges to continue to develop partnerships that can later foster possible research effort.

I have begun to value not always wanting to collaborate with others. I do not mean this in a negative sense. I enjoy collaborating with others as long as it is beneficial and not adding more challenges to the process. I have learned that you can possibly be more passionate about an area of research, teaching, or service than another individual, and it is best sometimes to focus on that area on your own. It may prove more challenging to your tenure and/or promotion process if you try to force others to collaborate with you on projects. It is best to distinguish between those persons who can assist you and those persons who can later be more of a detriment to your overall process or goals.

In essence, by the beginning of my third year, I had to weed out some of the things that were counterproductive to my overall process toward tenure or promotion. I had to decide which external and internal committees were actually beneficial for my productivity. I then also had to decipher when I felt I was being "dumped on." When I experienced the "dump," I could now say no. I could say no without feeling like I had to do everything. I could be productive but not be "stretched" in the process. Believe me, when you start saying no, it is a real eye-opener in the tenure and promotion process. We should not feel that we have to sign up for everything. We need to learn to be productive without forever yielding without concern for our overall physical and emotional health. Without your health, you cannot continue to pursue tenure or promotion. In fact, you may be left behind, without tenure, without promotion, without employment, without ever being able to be a fruitful worker. Do not lose yourself to meet tenure or promotion. Do your best without sacrificing all of your roles to your family, your spouse, or your children. Think of it this way: if you do not get tenure or promotion, whom do you want standing by your side? I want my family and all the roles that make up me as a person. This was a major epiphany for me by the beginning of my third year.

I even continue to examine my research goals closely since I now see the value of examining my portfolio externally. It is of great value to have another colleague read your portfolio and give you pointers on where to go with your research. I now know of other sources that I can pursue as I strive to strengthen my research. I also continue to examine my research agenda each year closely to see what I have accomplished and what I need to spend more time on. Never forget your research agenda even when "service" seems to be a huge undertaking. It is a part of the tenure or promotion process, so it is worth spending time on. Additionally, I have learned to be more productive during my time at the university by scheduling time to work on research weekly. Never go weeks without working on your research. This is the worst mistake you can make on tenure track.

Course of Action

I would like to offer two courses of action that have been of significant benefit regarding the tenure and promotion process at my HBCU, one therapeutic and the other strategic. These courses of action have also assisted me in dealing with several roles I have taken on as I began the tenure and promotion process: parental figure, scholar, and spouse. In developing the narratives, a therapeutic process occurred. As the result of this therapeutic process (venting about the tenure process with another faculty member and writing this chapter), collectively, I developed a proactive approach for faculty to cope with the tenure process, which I discuss next.

Identify Another Person as a Support Person

Identifying another person as a means of support can assist in pursuing the tenure process. As Berger (1992) and Sligh DeWalt (1999, 2002, 2004) stated, a support person can assist in understanding the environment and can listen to your thoughts and venting. Identifying your situation may assist in your psychosocial and professional development (Sligh DeWalt, 1999, 2002, 2004) regarding the tenure process. Without this means of support, there may be moments when the tenure process may seem overwhelming and un-approachable.

Collectively Define the Problem/Reach Rational Resolutions

Throughout the challenging process of tenure and promotion, do not let the process overwhelm you to the point where you cannot continue the process. In other words, it is highly important to protect yourself as the investment. As person-centered theory articulates, it is important to understand "listening, accepting, respecting, understanding, and responding" (Corey, 2000, p. 179). It is, at the same time, important to know and understand "yourself" during the process of tenure and promotion. In identifying a problem you may have while pursuing either tenure or promotion, it is possible to remain rational and productive. Try not to lose yourself by inundating yourself with too many external areas not related to tenure or promotion.

Another suggestion is to become aware that there are only 24 hours in a day. All things cannot be done in a day. Avoid taking on too much. You may regret it later. Know when to say yes when someone at your university or college requests that you take on additional duties, so that you will not be perceived to be a nonplayer, especially by chairs and deans. More important, know how to say no diplomatically but convincingly or you may be a candidate for "the dump." The time needed for the serious pursuit of a tenure agenda can be easily consumed by the inability to say no.

In pursuing the tenure and promotion process, I became aware that I am my own gatekeeper and how I end up in the process is my own responsibility. Overall, know yourself always. For instance, I developed a deeper religious conviction through my process. I now know that there are some things that I must have in my life in order to be a complete person. I know that prayer and positive meditation are two things that I must always have present. I know also that I have to know who I am at all times and not change my values even though situations in which I may have to make choices may present themselves. I am more convinced that I can remain myself and live a peaceful life even though I have to have a sense of time management and must see through my own lens before I can see through any other lens. In essence, if I know who I am and I know I have put my best effort forward, all else is moot. Whew! It took me a long time to get to this point.

Conclusion

The tenure-and-promotion process can be both a rewarding and a laborious task to pursue. During the process, there are some situations that may occur. Overall, it is important to understand your academic climate prior to developing a coping plan. There can be a disparity in the coping and tenure process; therefore, it is equally important to take care of yourself during the process. Marketing yourself for the "what ifs" is also a great way to deal with the tenure process; try to make yourself as marketable as anyone at any university by matching your research, teaching, and service by other examples. One great way to do this is by aligning yourself with external faculty members who can also review your portfolio according to their standards.

It is also important to remember that with tenure there is always the chance of putting your greatest efforts forward only to find that you do not meet the standards proposed at your college or university. In essence, it is important to understand that the overall result of receiving tenure or not receiving tenure may not always reflect whether or not you are a worthy faculty member. But, without tenure, there would be no guidelines on which to base your discipline. Therefore, keep marketing yourself with the first priority to satisfy yourself and be proud of your accomplishments. And never forget those who stood beside you during the process—your spouse, your children, or your family.

References

Berger, B. (1992). Mentoring graduate students. *American Journal of Pharmaceutical Education, 56.*

Corey, G. (2000). *Theory and practice of counseling and psychotherapy.* Brooks Cole.

Sligh DeWalt, C. (1999). *Black and White graduate students' perceptions of mentoring.* Unpublished doctoral dissertation. Iowa City: University of Iowa.

Sligh DeWalt, C. (2002). *My soul is not broken; I am stronger than ever.* Bloomington, IN: FirstBooks.

Sligh DeWalt, C. (2004). *Counseling through the healing process: And a child shall lead them.* Bloomington, IN: FirstBooks.

13

PERSPECTIVES ON NEGOTIATING IDENTITY AND PROFESSION AT A HISTORICALLY BLACK COLLEGE OR UNIVERSITY

Cassandra Sligh DeWalt and Cheryl Thompkins Horton

The Authors

Cheryl Thompkins Horton graduated from North Carolina Agricultural and Technical State University with a B.S. in biology, and from UNC–Greensboro with an M.A. in biology. She received her Ph.D. in science education from North Carolina State University in Raleigh. Cheryl has K-12 public school experience and has taught high school science. She currently teaches science education methods courses, general education courses, and middle school courses at North Carolina Central University in Durham. Along with her teaching responsibilities, she is the middle grades program coordinator. Dr. Horton has presented at various state and national science education conferences.

Information about Cassandra Sligh DeWalt is on page 138.

We, as African American women, are analyzing our identity and role as assistant professors at a historically Black university. How can African American women as professors find their place in higher education? This question may be difficult to digest or even hard to think about in an academic culture. However, this sentiment may be prevalent at your university or institution. These words may often be wrought with competition and challenges that may come as you continue to achieve in academia (in your roles as, for example, professor, parent, coworker, wife). Also, analyzing the aforementioned question may spark an assessment of the following: (1) who you were before you were a part of academia, (2) who you are or were while matriculating through academia, and (3) who you have become after years of being a part of this academic system.

One purpose of this written rubric is to provide personal narratives and discussions about identity and professionalism. Another purpose of these narratives and discussions is to assist other faculty and persons in academia in understanding and developing proactive interventions to eradicate the negative underpinnings of this intellectual void.

As two African American female professors at a historically Black university, we expound on situations and discussions related to identity and our perspectives on negotiating identity and professionalism. We may experience similar or different experiences, but the main thesis provides "voices" to an area in the academic arena that may sometimes be hidden.

Narrative One (by Cassandra Sligh DeWalt)

As a junior faculty member, it can be disconcerting to not always receive "mentoring" relationships, especially if you possess a positive outlook on professionalism, and the culture of academia. Believe me, I have seen that academia has a hidden culture, one that Aponte and Wohl (2001) and Sue and Sue (2002) state has a distinct set of beliefs and traditions. This hidden culture is one in which you cannot always get intelligible responses to your questions. Often one must ponder whether received information is credible or if one has even asked the proper questions, owing to the vague notions of the responses given. In trying to meet the demands that other roles (researching, service, teaching, administrative, and so forth) bring, it can be challenging and often filled with "I-am-not-sure-if-this-is-what-I-need-to-do" moments. In this narrative, I discuss some issues during my process as a junior faculty member that actually strengthened and motivated me.

Year One

Whew! I remember stating that one word over and over again as I attended committee meetings, taught classes, assisted with national accreditation processes, and still tried to meet the necessary deadlines for submitting required documents. Then, after saying "whew!" in one environment, I also had to say it when I went home. There were times when I wanted to ask an external faculty member some protocol questions, but, for some reason, I resisted this notion. Instead, I began to adjust to staying in my office, working on tasks, and being independent. In academia, I think eventually I concluded that some faculty view collaboration on certain activities as a possible weakness or unwarranted endeavor. However, because I have a propensity for collaboration with others, I wanted to open myself up to participating in joint activities, but, at the same time, I did not want to open myself up to being rejected by others in academia. So, I decided to take on what I thought academia was about. I again went to my office, closed the door, turned the computer on, graded my students' papers, said hello to other faculty members passing by in the hallway, attended meetings, and remained in my academic location. How so unlike my personality! Once I was the talkative individual, but now I was a person who considered getting up in the morning and proceeding in a conservative manner at work the best proactive move.

Year Two

As I continued to examine my identity through the lens of the philosophy "I got mine; you get yours," I then reflected on my second year. I thought there had to be a way that I could choose not to take on this belief and still continue to be a professional and a productive faculty member. I sought support outside the university, because I wanted to identify with others who had had similar experiences. Therefore, I developed collaborative relationships that could foster a new philosophy: "I got mine but I can also assist you with yours." I am in no way saying that I could not find anyone at my present university who fostered this same philosophy. I am only stating that receiving external professional support has greatly heightened my skills, abilities, knowledge, and competencies. Consequently, being active in national and regional conferences has allowed me to develop my network and scholarly activities.

In trying to secure an attitude of "I got mine; I can help you get yours" at my present university, I decided to network collectively with a small group of colleagues who shared some of my goals and similar contextual situations. I was a professor with other duties such as acting as a researcher, grant writer, and committee member. I found that other junior faculty had some of the same challenges. We later began to form a support structure. Through this support system, we began to open doors to one another in reaching the professional goal, that is, to help each other "achieve" the goals in academia. These goals established what all faculty members had to follow for the academic year, such as teaching about four classes, retaining and recruiting students, completing reports, continuing to assist the unit with surveys related to assessments, and developing a research agenda. To continue a positive approach to accomplishing some of these goals, I began to cultivate social and professional relationships, including those encompassing exercise, prayer, and professional and personal mentoring. Therefore, I had to concentrate on three pivotal categories: (1) religion, (2) quiet time, and (3) professional and personal mentors. These pivotal categories were necessary to maintain my positive outlook.

Religion/Quiet Time

Religion assisted me through a lot as I progressed through my academic career. I made specific attempts to pray for things to happen positively. In doing this, I continued to check myself to make sure I did not internalize the statement, "I got mine; you get yours." I would often reflect during quiet time in my office or at home on my daily work activities. I viewed this as a constructive way to make sure I was proceeding in a positive manner in all things. For instance, I would reflect on how I could continue being the same humble person, even though I was successful at achieving goals in my role as a faculty member. I had some successful publications and presentations, but I still wanted to make sure I did not become arrogant or egocentric, which can sometimes happen if one is not careful. My desire was simply to exude confidence.

Personal/Professional Mentors

Having contact with internal and external mentors has been an excellent way for me to deal with certain areas of my professional development. I have also discovered that through this contact I can be productive and still be a collaborator. I have to be patient in waiting on those persons who I know are there to assist me with certain academic areas such as publishing. I also recognize that not everyone in academia has developed the philosophy "I got mine; you get yours." Mentors have guided my steps or informed me of times when I needed to look into certain situations in more depth. Without these personal and professional mentors, I would not always see more covert things in academia. Therefore, I know that having these mentors has been beneficial. They have guided me through some hidden and political aspects of academia. Through our conversations, I now understand what it means to be patient and know what actions I should take at certain times.

Proactive Stance

Tackling the statement, "I got mine; you get yours," has been an eye-opening experience. I chose *not* to change my personality and my culture in order to gain greater acceptance in academia. With my own culture, I am still a competent, professional member of the academic culture. I chose to put community above simple competition in my pursuit of academic goals. In this way, I could remain true to the teachings of my mentor, my father. My father's familiar statement to me was, "Be comfortable with the person you see in the mirror when you are away from the job." My father always believed that the values that a person was "raised" with as a child should not change to make it in life. He believed that a person should know what he or she can and cannot do and not try to do all things. I can say that my father's instilling this in me at an early age has given me a context with which to judge and assimilate my experiences in academia.

Narrative Two (by Cheryl Thompkins Horton)

I was totally shocked by the discrepancy between my expectations and the actual inner workings of academia. The transition from graduate student to faculty member was overwhelming. In graduate school, I focused on research methodology, presentation of research, performance of service in the public schools, preparation for conference presentations, and participation on various committees. These experiences are presumed to assist you with carrying out your duties as a professor. However, as a graduate student, I have interacted with professors from various institutions, but there was no opportunity to have knowledge about the inner workings of academia.

During my undergraduate years, I admired my professors and thought teaching would be an excellent profession. For years I had the urge to teach at a university, especially an HBCU. I wanted to be able to impart knowledge to students in a way they could comprehend. A little voice had been whispering for years to me that I should teach at a university; not only that, my voice spoke loudly and said to teach at a historically Black university. However, while an undergraduate student I did not understand the demands of the job.

I wanted to teach at an HBCU because of my parents' attendance, my childhood memories of participating in the HBCU experience, and my undergraduate experiences. Because of my experiences socially and academically, I thought the transition would be seamless (Resnicow & Ross-Gaddy, 1997). I also assumed that being an African American woman might ease my access to the academic community. With all these positive thoughts, how could I not be successful as a Black female professor at a historically Black university?

During my first year as a faculty member, I realized that there are a number of hidden administrative tasks. I was not aware of all of the committee and administrative duties we as faculty members perform. There is an expectation that you should understand how to do the assignments (reports, provision of advice, end-of-year reports, and so on) without guidance in the tasks at all. However, even though you might not understand a task, you can get reprimanded for not understanding and not completing it a day ahead of the due date. It is important not to burden yourself with menial tasks unrelated to tenure and promotion, which is one of the most frustrating things about being in a new profession and in academia. There was not much opportunity to learn about the aspects of being a professor that would facilitate or ease my way into the position. I felt inadequate as a professor. However, as a professor, you must realize that assignments are part of your job and that you must search high and low to find the answers to complete them.

On the other hand, there is the issue of isolation. I have felt isolated in two ways, by being inexperienced and by being academically challenged. Not knowing which direction you should design your goals, such as in research, teaching, and service, can sometimes make you feel very isolated. I have asked for advice from several professors from other universities, and all have been willing to share information and resources. It is important to have a mentor and someone you can rely on to help you solve dilemmas. However, the person assisting must be aware of the academic culture of which you are a part for the solution to coincide with the situation.

Academically, I am the only science educator at the university, and that leaves me feeling secluded and isolated. With this situation there is no one to team up with for research projects. There have been many opportunities when a science educator was required but I was overlooked. The inclination is to give the project to someone who is strictly a science specialist without an education background or someone who does not have a terminal degree. This practice leads to underutilization of resources and the consequent difficulty in obtaining developmental assignments for growth.

This makes it difficult for one to find one's identity. Nevertheless, as long as I continue to read journal articles, present at conferences, and maintain professional networks I will be able to continue to grow. This is how I will maintain my identity.

Conclusion

Adjusting to the academic culture is a difficult transition from graduate student to junior faculty member. In dialoguing about issues that are of concern for junior faculty members, it is important to be cognizant of the philosophy "I got mine; you get yours." These issues of identity are important to the person, the environment, and the culture. However, confronting and solving issues for identity are important for your psychological well-being.

Junior faculty members are faced with many challenges that can later affect their overall perceptions of the university in having to deal with the demands of the job, which can include teaching, service, administration, scholarly activities, and committee work. This, in turn, can affect whether they continue in higher education or choose to depart. However, this situation exists at many universities, and the novice professor needs to understand that part of academia. Along with the identity issue is the issue of role conflict. There is a conflict between teaching and scholarly pursuits (Settles, Sellers, & Damas, 2002). Howard-Vital (1989) states that African American women not receiving support in the professional arena are not able to carry out research.

Implications

When we were writing this chapter, we did not realize that finding one's identity and role in higher education is a widespread problem. There is a lack of empirical research relating to these issues. Many problems are encountered in this academic culture, but there are solutions and coping strategies. Yet, the positive experiences counterbalance the negative experiences (Settles, Sellers, & Damas, 2002). Teaching experiences and student interactions are positive and motivating aspects of being a university professor.

After analyzing our positions and roles, we devised some recommendations for success in our culture. The following coping strategies will enhance your success:

- Form a research group.
- Make alliances with trustworthy colleagues.
- Learn to prioritize service, research, and teaching goals.
- Collaborate with others in your discipline.
- Seek the requirements for tenure and promotion.
- Focus goals toward tenure and promotion.
- Learn the bureaucracy of your academic environment.
- Free yourself from menial tasks unrelated to tenure and promotion.
- Commit only to required committees.

It is important when matriculating in an academic culture that you continue to rely on the positive aspects of what makes up your identity. As Howard-Vital (1989) said, "Unless we as African-American women take an aggressive, unrelenting, lead in identifying who we are, we will continue to react to distortions and perceptions created by others" (p. 190).

References

Aponte, J., & Wohl, J. (2001). *Psychological intervention and cultural diversity.* Boston: Allyn & Bacon.

Howard-Vital, M. R. (1989). African-American women in higher education: Struggling to gain identity. *Journal of Black Studies, 20*(2), 180–191.

Resnicow, K., & Ross-Gaddy, D. (1997). Development of a racial identity scale for low-income. *Journal of Black Studies, 28*(2), 239–254.

Settles, I. H., Sellers, R. M., & Damas, A., Jr. (2002). One role or two? The function of psychological separation in role conflict. *Journal of Applied Psychology, 87*(3), 574–582.

Sue, D. W., & Sue, D. (2002). *Counseling the culturally diverse: Theory and practice.* New York: John Wiley.

14

CHOOSING MY BEST THING

Black Motherhood and Academia

KaaVonia Hinton-Johnson

The Author

KaaVonia Hinton-Johnson is an assistant professor at Old Dominion University in Norfolk, Virginia, and a freelance writer. She earned a B.S. in English education in 1995 and an M.A. in African American and English literature in 1996, both from North Carolina Agricultural and Technical State University in Greensboro; and a Ph.D. in English education in 2003 from The Ohio State University. Her specialization is English education with an interest in multicultural literature, particularly African American literature for adults, young adults, and children. Her writings have been accepted by *Social Education, Multicultural Review, VOYA, Kliatt, Encyclopedia of African American Literature, Journal of Children's Literature,* and *English Journal.* She is currently writing a book for Scarecrow Press.

The best thing she was, was her children.
—Toni Morrison, *Beloved* (1987, p. 251)

S cholars argue that White feminist theoretical undertakings concerning mothering are not appropriate for studying Black mothers because they rarely take race and culture into consideration (Collins, 1991; Joseph, 1991). Collins (1994) argues that the experiences of Black mothers are paramount to any inclusive discussion about mother/child relationships. Scholars who have turned their attention to the Black mother often do so via literary works and/or criticism (see, for example, Crews, 1996; Morrison, 1987; Wade-Gayles, 1984; Washington, 1990; Williams, 1986) or in reality (Collins, 1991, 1994; Roberts, 1997a). However, a computerized search for studies on the Black mother produces literature that concentrates on single Black "welfare" mothers (for example, Augustin, 1997; Roberts, 1997b). Little research is available on (1) Black mothers who choose to be single, (2) single Black mothers who are professionals, or (3) single Black mothers who are pursuing doctorate degrees.

Storytelling, a rich element of the oral tradition in African American culture, is a significant part of critical race theory (Ladson-Billings, 1998; Parker, Deyhle, Villenas, & Nebeker, 1998). Story is a powerful way to bear witness, to put forth a "counternarrative," and to speak for oneself (Parker et al., 1998). For example, through the character Adam Nehemiah in Sherley Ann Williams's *Dessa Rose* (1986), Williams critiques the academy. The academy is a large part of the national narrative, for it has been paraded as the conduit of superior ways of knowing. However, Williams (1986) suggests that Dessa's life experiences, and her ability to put them into narrative form by way of oral storytelling, have greater value than Nehemiah's—the self-appointed ethnographer who attempts to document Dessa's story—university-obtained knowledge.[1] Needless to say, Nehemiah is perplexed and frustrated when Dessa answers his pointed questions with circular narratives, narratives he cannot fully comprehend. It is these narratives, the narratives of Black women, that have sustained me and made it possible for me to understand the importance of telling and preserving tales. I have chosen to use narrative discourse, a discourse Bell-Scott (1994) refers to as life notes, to talk about my experiences within the academy. This chapter is my contribution to the growing body of literature that focuses on the experiences of Black women as mothers, students, and professionals in a society that often renders them invisible.

Putting Black Women at the Center

Black women writers have a tradition of writing texts that put Black women at the center. These writers create images of Black women that defy the many dehumanizing stereotypes that have been perpetuated about them (Collins, 2000). In these literary works, women confront issues some Black women face in reality: sexism, racism, motherhood, sisterhood, and so forth. Barbara Christian (1994) once wrote, "What I write and how I write is done in order to save my own life" (p. 357). For some of us who do not write, the power lies in what we read. Similar to Christian (1994), I have used literature, Black literature in particular, as a point of reference, as a tool to justify "that I am not hallucinating, that whatever I feel/know is" (p. 357).

One of my favorite novels, *Beloved* (Morrison, 1987), includes several informative portraits of motherhood that intrigue me. Set during slavery, the novel reveals the pain and anguish felt by slave mothers who were not allowed to mother their children. According to Baby Suggs, a mother separated from her children was the "nastiness of life" (p. 23). Baby Suggs's memories of children taken from her and sold to distant plantations are heart wrenching: "She didn't know to this day what their permanent teeth looked like; or how they held their heads when they walked. Did Patty lose her lisp? What color did Famous' skin finally take? Was that a cleft in Johnny's chin or just a dimple that would disappear soon's his jawbone change? . . . Does Ardelia still love the burned bottom of bread?" (p. 139). By the time Baby Suggs's eighth child, Halle, was born, she felt it was no longer "worth the trouble to try to learn features [she] would never see change into adulthood"

(p. 139). Legalities often interfered with the slave mother's (natural) desire to mother her children. Like the mothers themselves, the children were property, chattel, sold to the highest bidder.

For Sethe, the protagonist of *Beloved*, motherhood brought a different set of challenges and disappointments. Pregnant when she escapes Sweet Home, she gives birth just before she reaches Baby Suggs's house, where her other three children are safely awaiting her arrival. However, when that safety is threatened and Sethe fears that she and her children will be returned to Sweet Home, "she just flew. Collected every bit of life she had made, all the parts of her that were precious and fine and beautiful, and carried, pushed, dragged them through the veil, out, away, over there where no one could hurt them" (Morrison, 1987, p. 163). As Sethe recalls her attempt to kill her children and herself she argues:

> [A]nybody white could take your whole self for anything that came to mind. Not just work, kill, or maim you, but dirty you. Dirty you so bad you couldn't like yourself anymore. Dirty you so bad you forgot who you were and couldn't think it up. And though she and others lived through and got over it, she could never let it happen to her own. The best thing she was, was her children. Whites might dirty *her* all right, but not her best thing. . . . No undreamable dreams about whether the . . . bubbling-hot girls in the colored-school fire set by patriots included her daughter; whether a gang of whites invaded her daughter's private parts, soiled her daughter's thighs and threw her daughter out of the wagon. (Morrison, 1987, p. 251)

Paul D, recognizing Sethe's mothering as a demonstration of "thick love," explains the danger of it: "For a used-to-be-slave woman to love anything that much was dangerous, especially if it was her children she had settled on to love. The best thing, he knew, was to love just a little bit" (Morrison, 1987, p. 164). However, Sethe disagrees: "Love is or it ain't. Thin love ain't love at all." Further, Sethe explains the extent of a mother's love, a love that extends beyond adulthood: "Grown don't mean nothing to a mother. A child is a child. They get bigger, older, but grown? What's that supposed to mean? In my heart it don't mean a thing" (p. 164).

In several other novels, Morrison (1970, 1977) provides complex mother/child relationships that I have reflected upon throughout the years. For example, why did Milkman's (*Song of Solomon*, 1977) mother nurse him for so long, and do most mothers metaphorically nurse their sons (and perhaps their daughters) beyond the reasonable time? And why didn't Paulette (*The Bluest Eye,* 1970) feel a greater sense of urgency around mothering?

In *Sula,* another novel by Morrison (1973), Eva teaches that motherhood is often synonymous for sacrifice. For years rumors circulate suggesting that the loss of one of Eva's legs was directly related to her need to provide for her children. Ironically, because Eva does not display physical affection, her daughter, Hannah, wonders if she loves her children. Eva's reply reveals that some mothers define love in terms of their ability to provide for their children:

> You settin' here with your healthy-ass self and ax me did I love you? Them big old eyes in your head would a been two holes full of maggots if I hadn't. . . . With you al coughin' and me watchin' so TB wouldn't take you off and if you was sleepin' quiet I thought, O Lord, they dead and put my hand over your mouth to feel if the breath was comin' what you talkin' 'bout did I love you girl I stayed alive for you can't you get that through your thick head or what is that between your ears, heifer? (Morrison, 1973, pp. 68–69)

As the novel progresses, Eva's love for Hannah seems apparent when she sacrifices her own safety in an attempt to rescue Hannah from a fire that kills her.

Part I

I read these novels before I chose to be a mother, yet I wonder if I really understood the magnitude of the role. In many ways these stories helped me to imagine motherhood, and then, later, they helped me to reflect upon it.

Part II

In eighth grade, I decided I wanted to pursue a Ph.D. But things did not go as I planned. While a junior in undergraduate school, I fell in love and got married. Despite this, I graduated with my class and enrolled in graduate school a few weeks later. After graduate school, I began teaching at a historically Black university, and it was there, three years into marriage, that my husband and I began to plan to conceive our first child. After several months, we were unsuccessful in our attempt. I got nervous; after all, timing was everything. I teach! The baby had to arrive during summer vacation, or I would have to postpone conception for another year. This would not do; my life was already mapped out: have baby by 25, begin Ph.D. program the following year, graduate by 30, find job, evaluate life, squeeze more kids in if there is time, and don't forget about tenure. We conceived just in time. According to the plan, he would be born in August.

Part III

Za'id did not stick to the plan. He was born in September, two weeks off schedule. Though there were no severe complications during my pregnancy, I was often nauseous and lethargic. The only time I truly came alive was when I was in the classroom. It did not matter that my stomach was unsettled 30 minutes before class or that only two hours before I was so sleepy I closed my office door, put my head on my desk, and prayed that my students would not remember when my office hours were. When I entered the classroom and began to engage students in a discussion about African American literature, I would become invigorated while Za'id remained still and listened.

The night I went into labor, I dreamt that my water broke while I was teaching the *Narrative of the Life of Frederick Douglass, An American Slave* (1845, 1986). When I awoke, it was obvious to me that I was in labor, but because of a false alarm the week before, I hesitated before calling the doctor. While waiting, I turned on the television. Ironically, there was a documentary about the life of Frederick Douglass on A&E. While I entertained the thought of taping the program, the labor pains grew sharper. It was not a false alarm.

Prior to feeling those intense labor pains, a degree of pain unlike any I had ever experienced in my life, I told everyone that I would have Za'id naturally. No epidural for me. When the pain intensified, that all changed with only a little persuasion from the doctor. I welcomed the anesthesiologist with open arms. However, I wish I hadn't, because the epidural left me unable to control my own body. I felt nothing. The doctor and nurses had to tell me when to push until, finally, to borrow Sethe's words, "my best thing" was born! Like an anthropologist, I kept field notes about him daily and documented all I had observed each Sunday (the day he was born). In the notebook I wrote:

10/19/97

Five weeks! As I sit at the computer holding you, I marvel at how much you have grown. I took you to get your second immunization shot this weekend; you weigh 10 pounds and 4 ounces. . . . You discovered TV this week. . . . Your dad reenlisted this week. Now we are moving to Ohio for three years.

10/26/97

A lot has happened this week. You visited Norfolk State University, but that doesn't mean you have to attend that school. You might want to go to another HBCU, A&T, like Mommy. You took your first long car ride to Arkansas, which is 17 hours from Virginia. You were a very good baby. You started laughing really loud at your dad this week. . . .

Za'id needed my complete attention that first year, so I decided I would delay returning to teaching.

Part IV

Scholars have written about the mythology that undergirds the image of Black motherhood (Bernard, 2000; Borab, 1998; Collins, 2000; Wade-Gayles, 1984). As Wade-Gayles (1984) explains, "One of the most pervasive images in American thought and in Black American culture is the image of superstrong Black mothers. . . . They are devoted, self-sacrificing, understanding, and wise. Their love is enduring, unconditional, and without error" (p. 8). Similarly, Borab (1998) reminds us that "the depiction of mothers who failed to live up to their responsibilities" was missing from earlier literature, and mothers generally "were not allowed to escape oppression by abandoning their children or even by going insane" (p. 86). After choosing to become a mother, I reread *Beloved* and *Sula* and found that the texts were wrought with new meaning for me. For example, when Eva suggests to Sula that she should consider becoming a mother and Sula retorts, "I don't want to make somebody else. I want to make myself," I applauded (Morrison, 1973, p. 92). Sula realized what I had not: at 25 years old I had no clue who I was or what I really wanted to do with my life. I had made someone else, but what about me? Had I made myself?

Part V

I had no idea that I would be a single mother. After all, I *was* married. But, once again things did not go as planned. After five years of marriage, I separated from my husband and reevaluated my life. I knew what the research said about people like me. I knew "scholars" wrote compelling reports that claimed all "female [read Black female] headed households . . . are dysfunctional and deviant [as] is perpetuated by such patronizing, racist, and sexist writings as the *Moynihan Report* (1965)" (Kuwabong, 2000, p. 68). I was familiar with literature that suggested the blame for social ills rests on female-headed families. And I was also aware that society claimed that "sons of single mothers will have difficulties developing masculine tendencies and normal emotional development with the absence of a significant male" (Gearing & Campbell, 2000, p. 47). Nevertheless, I put these myths aside, made some calls, filled out some papers, and prepared for my/our future.

We chose to move to Ohio because it was home to one of the few universities in the country that offered a Ph.D. in English education. However, I had postponed pursuing a terminal degree in exchange for caring for my newborn full-time.[2] Once I became a single mother, I felt that pursuing the Ph.D. was important for my son and me.

In African American culture, caring for children has most often been viewed as "a collective responsibility" (Collins, 1991, p. 45). This notion of "othermothering" redefines motherhood in a way that includes biological mothers as well as other women and men within the community who take on the responsibility of rearing children (see chapter 6 by Tinaya Webb). My grandmother was one of the best "othermothers" in my community. She unofficially adopted people (Whites and Blacks, young and old) from all around the county, so I knew that "the concept of motherhood [is not] reduced to a biological function" (Joseph & Lewis, 1981, p. 83). I knew that I would need to have several quality "othermothers" in place as well as the support of Za'id's father once I enrolled in school part-time.

Part VI

My academic advisor, also a new mother, fully understood that I had particular needs and concerns that differed from those of traditional students. From the beginning, it was obvious to her that my son impacted every decision I made, and I believe he also impacted the way in which she advised me and served as an advocate on my behalf. It was not unusual for us to decide whether a particular "opportunity" was right for me based on whether or not it interfered with my responsibilities as a mother. For instance, we chose graduate assistantships that allowed me to work when my son was in pre-school.[3] Although one of my assistantships required that I work one Saturday a month, Za'id was allowed to come to work with me when necessary.[4] As a result, when members of the project, a group of K–12 teachers of color, began to have children of their own, they felt comfortable bringing them to meetings. Though this may seem unprofessional or unorganized, it was actually important, because the stability of the project was maintained: members were more likely to attend monthly meetings if they did not have to concern themselves with securing child care.

My experiences led me to conclude that the academy can be a child-friendly atmosphere. At the end of my first semester in doctoral school, my advisor encouraged me to present at a symposium sponsored by the college of education. I had written a paper, "Yet, Artists We Will Be," based on the anthology, *Black-Eyed Susans and Midnight Birds: Stories by and about Black Women* (1990), compiled by Mary Helen Washington. In part of the paper, I discussed the literary works that contained thwarted Black women artists, women who virtually had to steal small segments of time to create art, because their duties as mothers and wives were so demanding. As I stood at the podium discussing my paper, Za'id, who was two years old at the time, tugged at my skirt and insisted that I stop reading the paper and put his shoe back on his foot. Try as I might, I could not gently persuade him to sit down, nor could I simply ignore him and continue presenting. Za'id's act represented both the epitome of my talk and my attempt to balance motherhood and academia.

As it turned out, Za'id would accompany me to a number of presentations, each one more memorable than the next. For instance, two years later, I presented on the Africanist presence (Morrison, 1992) in Judy Blume's novels. After I concluded the talk, I asked, "Any questions?" The first one came from Za'id. He wanted to know if he could eat his crackers. I was always somewhat ashamed that I had to bring my son along to conferences. However, Delpit (2002) officially confirmed what I had begun to notice: it was not just me, the single Black mother, who brought her child to academic functions; a number of parents, mothers and fathers, take their children to conferences when they need/wish to do so.[5]

I am fortunate that Za'id has been such an active participant in this process. But we have had to make sacrifices. Whereas students without children might have written their comprehensive exams at the university library, I wrote mine in McDonald's Play Place. However, I am sure they did not have the attentive study partner I had. Za'id listened as I prepared my job talk. After a few slides, he left the room and went into his own room to play with his toys. When I yelled after him that I was not finished with my presentation, he yelled back, "I can still hear you in here!" as he continued playing with his trucks. He helped me prepare for interviews too. After he finished asking me questions about my work, he said, "My turn, Mommy. You ask me some questions." Of course I did. After all, we are a team. The dissertation defense was the final test for me, and I did not take it lightly. I told Za'id I was worried about not passing the defense. In his nonchalant way he said, "Mom, you've been working on that thing all year. You really ought to know it by now." He was right. I am fortunate that I had Za'id to motivate, encourage, and support me. Before I graduated I wrote,

> [My] son serves as a powerful motivational force for me. He has been with me every step of the way. His mere presence reminds me daily that I must be persistent in my effort to obtain a terminal degree. I cannot tell him we went through the stress and uncertainty of candidacy exams to give up now. He would never understand why during Christmas break I spent more time shut up in my room trying to type a dissertation proposal than I spent playing with him, only to give up and give in. I want my son to see me and know what perseverance looks and feels like. Most of all, I want him to know that our sacrifices, his and mine, have not been in vain. (Hinton-Johnson, 2003, p. 38)

Reflecting on the significant part Za'id played during "my journey to the Ph.D.," I regret more than ever that he did not attend my graduation (Green & Scott, 2003). A few weeks before I graduated, I decided it was best for him to take his annual vacation with my mother because the last-minute details of writing and submitting the dissertation electronically were overwhelming when coupled with planning a move to another state to take a new job.

Part VII

As I write this chapter, Za'id leans over me, peers at the laptop, and immediately recognizes his name. "Why is my name in your story, Mommy?" he asks. "Because you are an important part of my story," I say. He immediately gets an idea. "When you're done, Mommy, staple it, and I will learn to read it all and take it to show-and-tell on Friday." I laugh because I know he is serious; however, I subconsciously note that he is well on his way to appreciating the power of stories.

Today, we are on a new journey. I recently began working as an assistant professor at a university in the Midwest. Once again, we are in a town, a state, a region where we have no family. I teach classes that I absolutely love but dread going to because they are in the evening. Not only does the guilt of being a single mother contribute to the dread, but also the fear of leaving my baby with strangers (Gearing & Campbell, 2000). I search frantically for child care in a town where I know virtually no one. And when I find someone I think will take good care of Za'id for four hours two evenings a week, he tells me the woman is in the wrong profession. I listen to him because, as my mother says, "The boy has been in day care enough to know." Once again, I am frantic! I try to explain to Za'id that I have to work; it is our livelihood. But, my five-year-old only looks at me and says, "Mom, what's more important, your job or your son?"

I think we both know who is *more* important, but we also know that although I realize that choosing motherhood means having great responsibilities, I will not *give up* my personal goals, because they are an important part of who I am. There is no doubt that I will do as Black mothers—academicians—before me have done: I will learn to balance mothering and the academy.

References

Augustin, R. (1997). Learnfare and black motherhood: The social construction of deviance. In A. K. Wing (Ed.), *Critical race feminism: A reader* (pp. 144–150). New York: New York University Press.

Bell-Scott, P. (Ed.). (1994). *Life notes: Personal writings by contemporary black women.* New York: W.W. Norton.

Bernard, W. T. (2000). Bringing our boyz to men: Black men's reflections on their mother's childrearing influences. *Journal of the Association for Research on Mothering, 2*(1), 54–65.

Borab, C. (1998). Freeing the female voice: New models and materials for teaching. In M. Graham, S. Pineault-Burke, & M. W. Davis (Eds.), *Teaching African American literature: Theory and practice* (pp. 75–97). New York: Routledge.

Christian, B. (1994). The race for theory. In A. Mitchell (Ed.), *Within the circle: An anthology of African American literary criticism from the Harlem renaissance to the present* (pp. 348–359). Durham, NC: Duke University Press.

Collins, P. H. (1991). The meaning of motherhood in black culture and black mother-daughter relationships. In P. Bell-Scott, B. Guy-Sheftall, J. J. Royster, J. Sims-Wood, M. Decosta-Willis, & L. Fultz (Eds.), *Double stitch: Black women write about mothers and daughters* (pp. 42–60). Boston: Beacon Press.

Collins, P. H. (1994). Shifting the center: Race, class, and feminist theorizing about motherhood. In E. N. Glenn, G. Chang, & L. R. Focey (Eds.), *Mothering: Ideology, experience, and agency* (pp. 45–65). New York: Routledge.

Collins, P. H. (2000). *Black feminist thought: Knowledge, consciousness, and the politics of empowerment* (2nd ed.) (pp. 45–200). New York: Routledge.

Crews, H. S. (1996). *A narrative of the daughter mother relationship in selected young adult novels*. Unpublished doctoral dissertation, Rutgers, The State University of New Jersey, New Brunswick.

Delpit, L. (2002). No kinda sense. In L. Delpit & J. K. Dowdy (Eds.), *The skin that we speak: Thoughts on language and culture in the classroom* (pp. 31–48). New York: The New Press.

Douglass, F. (1845, 1986). *Narrative of the life of Frederick Douglass, an American slave written by himself.* New York: Penguin Books.

Gearing, R. E., & Campbell, S. (2000). Deconstructing mother guilt: Single mothers can effectively raise an emotionally healthy and well-developed male child. *Journal of the Association for Research on Mothering, 2*(1), 47–53.

Green, A. L., & Scott, L. V. (Eds.). (2003). *Journey to the Ph.D.: How to navigate the process as African Americans.* Sterling, VA: Stylus.

Hinton-Johnson, K. (2003). "Dreams hanging in the air like smoke": A personal reflection of factors influencing enrollment and persistence in higher education. In A. L. Green & L. V. Scott (Eds.), *Journey to the Ph.D.: How to navigate the process as African Americans* (pp. 30–46). Sterling, VA: Stylus.

Joseph, G. I. (1991). Black mothers and daughters: Traditional and new perspectives. In P. Bell-Scott, B. Guy-Sheftall, J. J. Royster, J. Sims-Wood, M. Decosta-Willis, & L. Fultz (Eds.), *Double stitch: Black women write about mothers and daughters* (pp. 94–106). Boston: Beacon Press.

Joseph, G. I., & Lewis, J. (1981). *Common differences: Conflicts in black and white feminist perspectives.* Garden City, NY: Anchor Press/Doubleday.

Kuwabong, D. (2000). Restoring the memories of joining between a mother and son: A reading of Lorna Goodison's maternal poems. *Journal of the Association for Research on Mothering, 2*(1), 66–78.

Ladson-Billings, G. (1998). Just what is critical race theory and what's it doing in a *nice* field like education? *Qualitative Studies in Education, 11*(1), 7–24.

Morrison, T. (1970). *The Bluest Eye.* New York: Washington Square Press.

Morrison, T. (1973). *Sula.* New York: Alfred A. Knopf.

Morrison, T. (1977). *Song of Solomon.* New York: Signet Books.

Morrison, T. (1987). *Beloved.* New York: A Plume Book, New American Library.

Morrison, T. (1992). *Playing in the dark: Whiteness in the literary imagination.* New York: Vintage Books.

Parker, L., Deyhle, D., Villenas, S., & Nebeker, K. G. (1998). Guest editors' introduction: Critical race theory and qualitative studies in education. *Qualitative Studies in Education, 11*(1), 5–6.

Roberts, D. (1997a). *Killing the Black body: Race, reproduction, and the meaning of liberty.* New York: Pantheon.

Roberts, D. (1997b). Punishing drug addicts who have babies: Women of color, equality, and the right of privacy. In A. K. Wing (Ed.), *Critical race feminism: A reader* (pp. 127–135). New York: New York University Press.

Wade-Gayles, G. (1984). The truths of our mothers' lives: Mother-daughter relationships in black women's fiction. *Sage: A Scholarly Journal on Black Women, 1*(2), 8–12.

Washington, M. H. (Ed.). (1990). *Black-eyed Susans and midnight birds: Stories by and about Black women.* New York: Doubleday.

Williams, S. A. (1986). *Dessa Rose.* New York: Quill William Morrow.

Endnotes

1. It is important to note that while Dessa is imprisoned because of her involvement in a slave revolt, she is also pregnant with a son.

2. I returned to teaching when my son was six months old.

3. After a year of taking classes part time, my advisor helped me secure enough funding to take a leave of absence from high school teaching to work on a Ph.D. full time.

4. The director of the program, a Black male, was supportive of me and served as a role model for Za'id.

5. Delpit (2002) recalls a discussion she had with her daughter regarding the use of Black English vernacular versus mainstream American English: " 'I know how to code switch!' 'Code switch,' I [Delpit] repeat in astonishment. 'Where did you hear that term?' The eleven-year-old who has accompanied me to conferences and speaking engagements since she was an infant answered, 'You know, I do listen to you sometimes' " (p. 39).

15

SEEN, NOT HEARD

A Conversation on What It Means to Be Black and Female in the Academy

LaVada Taylor Brandon

The Author

LaVada Taylor Brandon, Ph.D., is an assistant professor of social studies education in the School of Education at Purdue University–Calumet in Hammond, Indiana. A native of Nashville, Tennessee, Dr. Brandon has a B.A. in history from Fisk University, an M.Ed. from Tennessee State University, and a Ph.D. from Louisiana State University. Dr. Brandon's work is centered on the use of oral history and the education of African American children.

When I was asked to contribute a chapter to *From Oppression to Grace: Women of Color and Their Dilemmas in the Academy,* I was very excited by the offer and immediately began tossing questions in my head to situate a conceptual framework for the piece. Often, I found myself torn between writing an autobiographical account of my experiences in the academy or centering students' voices and having them share what it has meant for me as a woman of color to be their professor. Because I am a strong advocate of centering students' voices, I decided that using students' perspectives would be the way to write this chapter. But how could I find out this information without my students feeling like they had to embellish the truth because of our student/teacher relationship? Months passed and the chapter went unwritten. Then a colleague approached me to ask if I would be willing to come to her class and share what it has meant for me to be a Black teacher teaching predominantly White students. Although this was the exact topic of the chapter I was going to write and I agreed to her request, I now found myself asking the same question: What does it mean to be a person of color teaching at a predominantly White institution (PWI)? As the day of my lecture approached, I decided that this would be a perfect opportunity to gather material for my chapter. Instead of me telling students what it means to be a Black female professor, I would give them the opportunity to tell me. The following is a transcription of our conversation. The class comprised 22 students. Seven were students of color. To protect the anonymity of students and the professor who invited me to lecture, their names have been omitted. Instead, student responses are indicated with S, the professor of the course is represented as T2, and I am T.

T: Hello, my name is Dr. LaVada Taylor Brandon. Recently your professor asked me to come and share with you what it means to be a Black teacher teaching in predominantly White settings. Ironically, I was also recently asked to write a book chapter on the same topic due on December 1st. I have not written a word. So, I decided to tape our conversation today to use as my paper—killing two birds with one stone. Is there anyone here that disagrees with us taping today's session?

[*No hands raised*]

T: All right. Now, our first task for today. I want you all to tell me when you see words like Black or female or teacher what are the images that you think of? Who do you think this person is . . . what does it mean to be a Black person or a female? What does that mean? First of all let me put this here [on the blackboard]. Is it natural or am I nurtured to be a female? Is that a natural thing or did somebody make me a female?

S: Natural.

T: That's natural—we're going to put that here. What about being Black?

S: Natural.

T: What about being a teacher?

S: Nurtured.

T: So, I'm made a teacher? Right? Okay, then what makes us a teacher? How are teachers made?

S: Through your education.

T: What is education? What is the purpose of education?

S: To learn new skills and new knowledge.

T: Whose skills, whose knowledge?

S: State of Indiana.

T: Really? Now let me tell you something. I've lived in California, Louisiana, and I'm from Tennessee and have taught in all three states and now I just happen to find myself in Indiana so it's [education] just a little bit bigger than this here place. So, given that what is the purpose of education? What do we do with education?

S: Expand your life so that you learn about the world around you and differences . . .

T: That's good, you've got to expand your mind to learn new concepts about the world and ideas. Okay, any other ideas about education? Let me ask you this. Is education bias?

S: Yes.

T: Okay, then what is the purpose of education?

S: To pass down knowledge from one generation to the next.

T: There you go. Basically, to pass down knowledge from one generation to the next—Right? Do we all agree that that is the purpose of education?

S: Yes.

T: Then whose knowledge is therefore being passed down?

S: Teachers'.

T: Really?

S: The person who came up with that?

T: Who is the person that came up with that? Who is the constructor of knowledge? Because knowledge in and of itself is a political force especially since you have suggested that the purpose of education is to pass down a particular way of knowing from one generation to the next. Whose way of knowing gets passed down from one generation to the next through the political process of education?

S: Teachers before us, our ancestors.

T: Who were the teachers? Who were our ancestors? I want you to name the people.

S: Socrates.

T: Socrates, all right.

S: Aristotle.

T: Who are they? What was their identity? Who were they?

S: Males.

S: A bunch of dead White males.

T: All right. Dead, White males. And I'm going to write that. I didn't say it. You did!

S: [*The students chuckle*]

T: All right, a bunch of dead White males. And, I'm going to write that because I didn't say it, you did. All right, now Socrates, I like Socrates he was a cool brother. That's the reason we have this set up right now. You know it's called the Socratic method he just walked around thinking and asking questions he wasn't really about imparting knowledge he was more about letting knowledge grow and kind of come to you. But around the period of Protestantism education took a totally different spin. Like it used to take 20 years to get a Ph.D. I mean forever. You had to learn and digest and be questioned and all that kind of stuff. But, then Peter Ramus and Johann Comeius created a way to commodify this thing called knowledge and it happened around the period of commercialism; and the rise of a middle class, a group of people that were once serfs wanted to be better than other serfs and peasants but they didn't have the blue blood of the kings. So they wanted to know real quick the ways of being and knowing of the blue bloods and thus curriculum and instruction was born. I know I'm throwing a lot at you but I've only got an hour to do this. All right, so education took a totally different spin. It became something that you attain, you get, you get through textbooks and lesson plans. And, it was not something that you just kind of flow into, taking years to acquire. All right, now whose education did the serfs want to acquire? Who did they want to be most like?

S: The nobility.

T: The nobility! The nobility. Who represented the nobles? And as, as we speak of this, what region are we talking about? We're talking about knights, serfs, and nobles. Where are we? What part of the world are we?

S: Europe.

T: We're in Europe! Okay. So we, we got this dead right now, but you know, the world has a lot of different people. So we've also got a Eurocentric focus, right? Because when they left England and came to the United States your foreparents were those same people, right? And they brought with them not only the religious doctrine—although they claimed that they were running away from that—but they also brought a way of knowing and being, a way to understand the world. As you know. Okay. Now, so they get to the United States. Was everybody allowed to get an education?

S: No.

T: Who could get an education?

S: White men with money.

T: White men with money! So you could have been a White man and didn't own property or have any money and you were still going to be what?

S: Uneducated.

T: Uneducated! So now, we have White men with money. All right. And we're all still in the process of doing what? Constructing . . .

S: Knowledge.

T: Knowledge! All right, this commodity. Now, we have this entity now that has been constructed by a particular people with particular ideas. Right? Right. When did public education become instituted?

S: I don't know.

T: When?

S: We learned this in foundations.

T: Yes! Yes! From your foundation classes.

S: [*Pause*]

T: When?

S: I didn't exactly hear the question.

T: When did public education become, I would say, a part of the American culture? What happened? What was going on? You all can just tell me what happened. What took place?

S: Was it after the war?

T: It was after a war. Which war?

S: The Civil War?

T: Which?

S: [*All speaking at once*]

T: You're exactly right! The Civil War. What happened?

S: [*All speaking at once*]

T: Who are they? They aren't feeling me then. That's okay. We understand.

S: When they signed the Emancipation Proclamation.

T: All right.

S: Freeing all the slaves.

T: All right.

S: And then . . .

T: And then what?

S: Oh, equal opportunity was available to the slaves.

T: Well that was because of what? Before we really got equal opportunity, the slaves wanted something that they had never had before.

S: Their forty acres.

T: In addition to their forty acres and a mule (which they never got to keep) . . . what else did they fight for and get during the period of reconstruction?

S: Public education.

T: Public education. Public education. That is when public education became an intricate part of U.S. culture. That's what they won, right? Now, you have all these people who are now free to go to school! Now, are all of these people coming from an upper-class Eurocentric male background?

S: Nah.

T: Do they have this way of knowing indeed?

S: Nah.

T: So they're coming in here without this; they're immediately classified as what, learned or unlearned?

S: Unlearned.

T: Unlearned and heathens. And the purpose of becoming learned means that you have to go through the what?

S: The indoctrination.

T: The indoctrination process! You have to get an education . . . right? So that's what we know whether you're Black, White, Purple, or Green becomes pretty much what?

S: The same.

T: Homogenized. Right! And you can refute me at any time. Right?

S: Yes.

T: Yes! Yes! Yes! So what we know—Oh, and by the way, the philosophical term for ways of knowing and being is epistemology, all right? Now, there are a couple of pieces of text from which I'm drawing this conversation. The first one is *The Mis-education of the Negro,* by Carter G. Woodson. The second one is a more recent piece by Bill Watkins, called *The White Architects of Black Education.* Okay. All that I'm sharing with you, I'm drawing from these specific texts. If you decide that you want to see what this woman is talking about a little further, you can go take a look at them for yourself. Okay. So now we're at the point of realizing that our total education is the same. According to Woodson, for those of us who are, he'd say, African American, Negro, basically people who have been historically marginalized, this education does something to their personhood. All right. Now, if we used the jargon of being historically marginalized, you would include everybody who is not what?

S: White.

T: Okay. Outside of Whiteness, maleness, middle-classness, and protestantness just plain ole WASP. Those who are marginalized, outside of the center. All right. People of color ways of knowing and being, according to Woodson, is distorted through this indoctrination process. We're all getting the same education. All right. Now, this is important for me anyway to understand because when we add this question of . . . what it means to be a Black female teacher, it becomes kind of convoluted. We see it as only a situation of race, but when we deal with the issue of epistemology and metaphysics, the way I learn is the way most of you have learned. So my teaching may not be out the box. The only thing that is out the box in a racialized context is the color of my skin. The teaching of the subject is not a threat, unless I have a certain political ideology that is found outside of the contexts of my education or as Woodson would say "mis-education." And that is what you would find in both Watkins and Woodson. Question? Comment?

S: I understand that.

T: Good! What do you understand? Because I feel that I'm getting parched and I didn't bring my water. So tell me, what do you understand?

S: When you said, uh, when you said that there's a . . . a center from where it all comes from and the only way that something will be an issue is if you tower outside the center the middle, that the only issue lies in the color of your skin.

T: There you go. And what is that issue that lies within the color of my skin, which brings us to the notion of Black? What do we think of when we think of this term *Black*? What does that mean? And I don't want to hear no color-blind discourse 'cause you already done told me that I was Black, which means you see my color and I want to know what we think about that. Yes. And I've got tough skin. I tell that to my students too. So the other Black folks in here, if you get offended just pretend that they're talking about me! Right. I got to close the door too. It gets heated right about now. We don't have, we don't even have a windowpane in our door. Isn't that something? Okay, Black. We don't! As I say, we talk about all sorts of stuff up in here. What is Black? What does this notion mean?

S: Well, a person being of different political views.

T: Like?

S: Like, uh, on slavery and.

T: So when you think of Black people, you think of slavery?

S: Uh-huh.

T: All right. What else? And I want to come back to this 'cause this is a heavy one. I'm a social studies person and a lot of students have issues with textbook portrayals of slavery.

S: Civil rights.

T: Okay. You think of what else?

S: Ignorant.

T: Ignorant! There you go, girl! Tell it! Tell it like it is! Blacks are ignorant! They don't know anything about what they're talking about. What else?

S: Different cultures.

T: Different cultures. Okay. No, no. That's too broad. What do you mean by different cultures? What makes them different? What are the images that . . . that . . . that stick out that makes them different, because basically I've told you all already, we're all Americanized the same way. So what makes us different? Think about that now.

S: History.

T: Say it! How? No, not really. I forgot about most of my history until I got into graduate school, child, because they told me the same history that they told you.

S: Right. I know.

T: Wow! Okay. So tell me what part of that history is different?

S: Your personal family background may be different.

T: I don't know anything about that.

S: I mean like your traditions.

T: What are they? Name them.

S: I'm trying to think. I don't know. I just don't; I'm ignorant, I'm ignorant when . . .

S: From Africa!

T: From Africa?

S: I don't know.

T: There we go. That will work! Can I tell you all a secret? It is possible for me to share a bit of a secret. All Black folks might not be from Africa. There's a Black group in Australia called Aborigine and they are just as Black as anybody in Africa, so we might be from Australia.

S: There are Blacks from the Dominican, Black Mexicans. I only see just Black people from Africa in that question.

T: Okay, I should, you're right, but even in saying that there are . . . there are people of African descent all over the continent, the history does say that the majority of us were taken from Western Africa and found ourselves displaced in America. All right, but still, because of the negativity that is oftentimes associated with Africa (that is, ignorant), while forgetting a fact that they were the beginning of civilization, all right . . . yet, Africa is still often remembered as the Dark Continent, the Black continent, thus lending itself to negative stereotypes. All right. So that is the reason why I'm kind of troubled with that.

S: [*Students speaking at once*]

T: All right.

S: Uh, I said that there are White people in Africa as well.

T: Uh-huh.

S: So if someone was in Africa consistently and came to America, would they be African American?

T: No. Yes! Yes! They would be. Yes. But, I had a friend in graduate school and she was quote/unquote, as you say, African American, but she was of Dutch ancestry.

S: Oh.

T: She still was considered African American, but that does not mean the same thing as our history.

S: Our history is Black and political [*Inaudible*]

T2: I had a White friend who came from Africa and he marked himself as an African American and his White friends told him that there is a lot of baggage that comes with being African American.

T: 'Cause it means something. Let's get back to what it means.

S: I would say Black and ignorant . . .

T: Uh-huh.

S: And other times, you think of being loud.

T: Ooh! Loud. All right.

S: Please be clear on where you're focusing, where you are trying to lead us in this conversation.

T: I don't have any idea. I told you all already; I'm just basically trying to understand what it means to be a Black female teacher.

S: Are you just looking for the negative stereotypes within the American society?

T: No, I'm looking for whatever . . . whatever images appear when you hear this word; that's what I want.

S: 'Cause we can focus on whatever.

T: Yup.

S: Can I be honest?

T: Yes.

S: When we talking about like culture and stuff . . .

T: Uh-huh.

S: I'm not Black so I'm ignorant to that. I'm not Mexican American. So, I have my culture. It's like I don't know.

T: So you're trying to express that you live within a vacuum outside the understanding of everybody else's culture?

S: I mean White people live in White suburbia, and, you know . . . I mean . . . so I mean we're raised besides our White education is what it is. I mean we have our culture within that, so I admit that I'm ignorant to things that you may not be ignorant to.

T: Yes. So then we would learn from each other. So that is why you're in here for right now. The other of you, what do you see when you think of Black? Those of you that are not living such a role, and obviously turn your TV off, and don't see any Black people at all, and never go to the movies, and that's okay! So you just can't say anything! We got what? Twenty-four kids up in here, twenty-two?

S: Yes, twenty-two.

T: Yes, whatever. Okay. We got enough to populate this board without you. All right.

S: I think of it as complete different languages.

T: Language. What's the language? Y'all know the language. Ebonics, Ebony phonics. All right. I hate these dry-erase boards. They, all right. Okay. What else?

S: Let me ask a question.

T: Yes.

S: Now, I was kind of set in the manner of when you say . . .

T: You're living in a bowl?

S: No, I'm not living in a bowl, but everything that you name is like kind of negative.

T: Not so! Not so!

S: Actually, it is.

T: See! And that in and of itself is a perception. Because to me Africa is the baddest place ever named a continent. Ebonics is the beauty of my language; slavery is what built the economic foundation of this country. So, therefore, the only thing that I see up here is ignorant and that is questionable based on . . .

S: I say . . . I say . . .

T: Now . . .

S: I say almost everything up there is negative.

T: You said everything! Now, you're trying to cover up what you just said. Lord, have mercy! Don't be tripping up. I need some more apple juice.

S: You make me nervous with that.

T: Me too! But I got to get through this before time is up and I die of thirst.

S: [*Students are chuckling*]

T: Well, just know that I'm thinking about that cord. All right. I'll try to go around it this way. Okay, you were about to say?

S: I think Ebonics is a negative thing. Ebonics really is ignorant. I know Black people who are not loud, and they're not ignorant, and they don't speak Ebonics. When I think of Black people, I don't think of Ebonics, ignorant, or loud. And that's . . . I just don't get it, uh, when people see Black people, you said, what do you see when you think of a Black? So you think Ebonics when you see Black people?

S: That is stereotypical. That is like saying . . .

S: Being loud, so I'm not loud.

S: What do you see so . . .

T: Wait a minute!

S: I'm not finished.

T: [*Everyone is speaking at once*] It's me! I'm instigating this!

S: No, what I'm saying, you said, what do you think of . . . Black . . .

T: Right.

S: Or what do you see . . .

T: No, the only reason why I'm troubled with what he suggested is that you all said, as if this was a universal commonality of thinking, that all the things up here were negative. From my perspective . . .

S: The question that you asked. I think Black people . . .

T: What do you think of? That is it!

S: Do you mean from us being Black or for another race?

T: Whoever! You can speak from your perspective!

S: Oh, really?

T: I didn't quantify or qualify anything! Is that the reason why most of you are silent? It doesn't matter. I don't care! This young man asked me if I wanted stereotypical representation. I never asked for stereotypical representation.

S: That's what will come out of most people's mouths, something negative.

T: Okay. Then, if that's what's coming out of most people's mouths—and we're not going to stick on Black because we still got to get to female and teacher, okay—but if that's what's coming out of most people's mouths, chances are that's what's in their what?

S: Mind.

T: In their head. So, see, I will probably get to this epistemology thing. So where do they learn this stuff? Where do we learn this stuff 'cause we're not exonerated from the schools. Where do we learn it?

S: From the media.

T: Media is one place.

S: Family, media, history, culture, and society; it's from the far, far, far . . .

T: Okay. Let's just do it slow. Family, media, who else?

S: I said culture.

T: Culture. Y'all using culture too . . . too . . . too loosely. Yeah, let's be specific. And where else? And I really . . . I want you all to name institutions. History is an institution in and of itself. The typical institutions, where else do we learn it?

S: Okay. I don't have an answer to that, but I have a question.

T: Well, let's get to this first. Can you write the question down? Because you all are missing the most important place that you all are going to be. Where do we learn it? In school. We learn it in school.

S: I do think my question is . . .

T: Okay, go ahead.

S: The area that we're, uh, that we're in, the . . . Gary used to be the number one murder capital of the world. So I think people, especially from this area . . .

T: Yeah, come on.

S: I think it is just a complete, probably distorted view from when I was a young child because people will ask me where I live, and I will say, uh, Portage, and they would be like, "Well, what is that by?" And I would say, "Chicago." "Oh, isn't that by Gary? Well, we lived in Gary, but not any more."

T: See, you just gave me another image—murderers. Right? And I'm alluding to that only because I've been in northwest Indiana long enough to know that Gary is predominantly Black; therefore, the association is that they are murderers. So we ought to put that one up here. And, again, I didn't tell her to say that and it just happens to be negative. We're dealing with perception.

S: [*Everyone is speaking at once*]

T: We are not going to be on this much longer, y'all! We got . . . I only got an hour.

S: I think people are thinking that, okay, now, because of what I said, like I don't think that any White people are murderers. That's not what I'm saying.

S: No, that's not about that. Everybody doesn't get murdered in Gary. People do drop bodies in Gary. [*Everyone laughs*] And the White people, they still call all the people that come from Portage hillbillies. I didn't think that. But when I worked there, oh, I knew what the hell they were talking about! [*Everyone laughs*] So it's just, uh, I mean everywhere. And it's a lot of places that's a whole lot worse than Gary and they will fuck you up! You know what I'm saying?

T: I've got virgin ears and a four-month-old baby. I can't listen to this language because I can't go home saying that kind of stuff around my child.

S: When I lived in . . . when I lived in Chicago, we heard of Gary before, and, you know, it was Black, you know, because the people from Chicago, you know, Gary, when it was back in the day, that was the country. That was where you went to go see your family. Everybody tried to move out the city and moved to Gary. When I lived in Chicago, Hammond was a place like, "Oh, you don't want to go to Hammond! Hammond is bad! Hammond is a lot of murders!" When you come here, it's like, so you know, you hear a different thing and it's not true. Because you going to school in Hammond, then it's not as bad as people make it be in Chicago.

S: 'Cause every area is going to have a bad area regardless. When I think about Gary, I think about Gary as being strong. Because, even if they come up, they don't want to leave Gary because my people are in that area. You know, it's a wonderful place to be.

S: Yes, you can go anywhere. . . .

T: I don't mean to be stepping on any toes. We really got to keep going. We really . . . 'cause we haven't gotten into what it means to be a Black teacher. Okay, one more question and we got to get to female.

S: Okay. I think when you say media, family, history, school is where we get it. But my issue is, all my teachers, they start from the beginning. They where you're starting and they say, "Give me all you got about what you think Black people are all about," and you know, just throw it out there. So it is all out there and everyone is in a tizzy, and everyone is angry, and they leave the class; and we don't know how to get from behind the idea that, yes, that . . . that is awful upon the board. But, we can't get to the part where, you know what, let's take it a step further, and let's get over that because I'm thrown that in every class. I know that stuff! So let's get past that and let's say how we can change the stereotypes to make them more positive, so we're all not leaving the classroom, you know, in heated debate every single class that I have. So how are we going to get out of the stereotypical Black idea or ideology to become better people, to become a more diverse culture, to understand, and welcome, and, you know, not always go to start there, and then you only have an hour. So we can't figure out how to get better. We can't figure out how to step outside of our boxes from what we've been taught.

S: How is it that you know Black people? If you know Black people, you know all Black people aren't ignorant, or murderers, or Ebonics speaking, or loud. If you know a Black person, then you know that stuff because you've never met a Black person. You're in a place where you don't know any Black people. But if you know Black people, you will know that is not true, and she is not ignorant, she is not a murderer, or I'm not loud and I'm not a murderer. You should say . . . you should say smart. I think a Black person is smart. Well [names student] is smart. Or I think of, uh, mature because I know Blacks are, you know [names student] is mature. Or something like that. You don't just start with ignorance.

T: Okay, you are right! We change perceptions through knowing other people, through relationships. But the other thing is, because racism is so indoctrinated within our culture, thirteen weeks is not enough time for you all to . . .

S: No.

T: Any of us to unlearn racism, to unlearn sexism, which is what we're going to next, to unlearn classism. It's not because it's so much a part of our culture. However, it's not a we activity; it is a me activity. If you're really interested in unlearning it, whenever you find yourself faced with these notions, you'll be determined not to agree with them but to question them; and in time . . .

S: Right.

T: It won't become happenstance to see these things as I tried to show you a minute ago as negative because save from a few up until now, the rest of the things for me are not negative.

S: Right.

T: It's a process of unlearning things. And hopefully in classes like this, it is not a resegregation of people that you are forming, that you are getting to know one another, and you can have conversations that refute the stereotypes. I have a Ph.D. So as loud as I am, I don't think that I qualify all the time as ignorant, unless folks don't know that I have a Ph.D. from L.S.U., a Research One institution. That in and of itself can be a vast contradiction in the minds of many people. I haven't got to please anybody but myself so I don't try. That's actually Ebonics too. You see?

S: Right.

T: That complicates things, but that's a me activity. Yes.

S: I mean just to elaborate now. The stuff that I, from my perspective, the stuff is not all bad. Most of it, though, is ideas from uneducated people. You asked what people think.

T: Right.

S: You didn't ask what we personally thought.

T: Yes.

S: So I took it as what . . . what I hear . . . I . . . something I've heard is what I . . . what I say in class. That's not my opinion. I think that's the mostly uneducated people.

T2: Tell me what you mean by uneducated. I have heard people with Ph.D.s make comments like these.

S: I'm thinking about . . .

T2: Well, just think about what you mean by educated. And then if you think about Nazi Germany, think about the people that designed the system that killed people in Germany, they were educated [*Inaudible*].

T: Right.

S: But being educated does not necessarily . . .

S: I didn't say who was educated, though.

S: Yes.

T: Okay. Female, what do we think about when we see this term. Female!

S: I think of a woman sign on the bathroom, you know?

T: The woman sign. I can't draw that little thing, but I think I can do this one. Isn't this the sign for the woman, the skirt?

S: Yes.

T: Something like that.

S: It.

T: It.

S: It's a circle with a little cross at the end.

S: Yeah.

T: With the triangle at the end?

S: Oh, I don't know.

T: Or the cross. Okay. Fine! We got it down! What do you think of females? What does it bring to you?

S: Nurturer.

S: Mama, mostly a mother, nurturer.

T: What else?

S: A great cook.

T: A great cook.

S: Beauty.

T: All women?

S: No.

T: But I'll put it up anyway. We're going to stretch it a little bit.

S: Sex.

T: Sex! Let's talk about sex, baby! [*Everyone is speaking again*] Let me just hear!

S: Like, are you looking for what it means to be female or what is thought of by society?

T: Let me tell y'all something. Y'all, let's put an end to your disclaimers—where I'm not talking about me, but it's me. If it's coming out your mouth, I'm telling you right now, I'm assuming it's you, okay. So, just say what you have to say. That's the reason why I'm saying this. Say what you have to say. And, please, we have to stop attacking each other. That's half the problem why we can't get in a position where we're talking about it because we are afraid to talk. . . .

S: Right.

T: Because we're afraid of being attacked.

S: Right.

T: Now, you can attack me 'cause I don't care. All right. You know, 'cause I'm just saying say whatever; it doesn't matter. Say what you think. Whatever is coming to mind, say it so we can put it on the board, certainly before the professor kicks me out.

S: I don't know, have you ever heard some people say the essence of a woman?

T: What does that mean?

S: Yeah. I don't know what it means. I wanted to say it, but I don't know what it means. I always wanted to know! [*Everyone laughs*]

T: Sounds like a fragrance. All right.

S: I don't know what it means, but that's what I thought of.

T: Well, what . . . what . . . when you say that word, what feeling does it evoke for you?

S: Just something positive, beautiful; a word can't describe it.

T: Oh! A word. We'll just put essence up here. Essence! All right.

S: [*Inaudible*]

S: Words like *delicate* and.

T: Oh, fragile.

S: Yes.

T: Oh, Lord!

S: What about volatile? [*Everyone laughs*]

T: Uhhh! Because I've got to be elegant and fragile all the time, I'm about to snap, right? Okay, because we're angry.

S: I have three brothers and they're always like, anytime I'm mad or something, like, you got PMS or something or another.

T: Let's put PMS up there because we get blamed for that even when we're not PMSing. You know, it is like, uh, there are thirty days in a month, so you're always PMSing.

S: All the time.

T: What else do we think of when we think of females?

S: Strength.

T: Straight?

S: Strength.

T: Strong. Okay.

S: Open-minded.

T: Open-minded. Okay.

S: I have one.

T: But we have to go on to teacher, okay?

S: But we have one—intelligence.

T: Oh! That's so sweet!

S: Yes! Intelligent.

T: He's saying intelligent because he's interested in sex. Okay. [*Everyone laughs*] I hate to disclose the truth. All right.

S: Patience.

T: What do you think of when you think of teacher?

S: I think of a woman.

T: A woman.

S: Yeah.

S: Patient.

T: Patient. What else? Teacher.

S: Kind.

T: Kind.

S: Not all the time.

S: They're mean sometimes. Right?

S: Yeah, mean.

S: A parent.

T: What else? What else? Mean. A parent.

S: Baby-sitter.

T: Oh, Lord! Somebody's been out there teaching already, haven't you? Baby-sitter.

S: Try to be ringmaster.

T: Ringmaster.

S: Lover of children.

T: One who pays a lot anyway. One who loves children?

S: One who has to deal with a lot of drama.

T: All right, what else you all?

S: A communicator.

T: A communicator.

S: You got leader up there?

T: Yes.

S: Leader. Role model.

T: We have role model.

S: Okay.

T: Okay. Now, these are all the images that you see, or that you think of, or that we think of when we think of Black, female, and teacher. Are there any contradictions imbedded in what we've named for each given ideology? If so, let's cancel some things out. All right, you see Black.

S: Murderer.

T: Okay, so if we're a murderer, if I am a murderer, then, therefore, I cannot simultaneously be what?

S: A teacher.

T: No! No! No! See, y'all messing up. Y'all gave me a lot of different adjectives.

S: Once you got caught, then you can't be a teacher.

S: No.

S: But if you were a murderer, you couldn't be a role model.

T: Okay. Thanks! That's right. I'm trying to keep it real simple like that. Where is role model? I can be your role model. What else? Okay. But since murderer is here and you all told me basically that if I'm a murderer, I can't deal with anything else, so then do I strike out all of this because I'm a murderer?

S: Nah.

T: So then what cancels out? And we won't take off murderer; it's not a problem. What cancels out if I'm a murderer from both being a female and being a teacher?

S: The nurturer.

T: A nurturer. I'm not gonna be a murderer if I'm a nurturer. What else? Am I too fragile if I'm going around killing folks?

S: Nope.

T: I'm definitely probably PMSing. [*Everyone laughs*] All right.

S: You're not open-minded.

T: Oh, no! All right. What else?

S: Elegant.

T: Huh?

S: Elegant.

T: Elegant! Have you seen *Madame Butterfly*?

S: Yeah. [*Everyone is speaking at once*]

S: You can be elegant and both a murderer if you want.

S: You can be a great woman and sexy.

T: Yeah, and elegant. And I can be a mom. And definitely strong. Does the essence thing work for a murderer?

S: [*Everyone is speaking at once*]

T: Yes? No?

S: No.

T: No. Okay. We drop essence. What about intelligence. Can I be . . . I can be intelligent and a murderer.

S: Sure.

T: You're exactly right. We haven't gotten to that part yet. You're moving ahead. All right! Now . . . so . . . so forget those little lines. I'm a murderer. Is there any of these things that I can be? What about understanding?

S: No.

S: No.

T: Is that a stretch maybe? I understood that I needed to kill him? I was PMSing and, you know, he stepped on my toe, and I just had to bust! [*Everyone laughs*] What about . . . what else?

S: Kind.

T: Kind, maybe. Uh . . .

S: Patient.

S: No.

T: Am I really patient?

S: What about the people who, like, torture you? You know, they're patient? They're going to kill you.

T: Yeah. I'm going to get that patience.

S: Yeah, that's with murderers.

T: Like, *Silence of the Lambs?*

S: Yeah?

T: Yeah! You take your time in killing them.

S: You're a good communicator if you're a murderer.

T: Yeah!

S: [*Everyone is speaking at once*]

T: You believe in a lot of drama, so we can just keep that.

S: Yeah.

T: So we're going to keep patience?

S: Yeah.

T: So we're often in the images now. So outside of ourselves, do we often-times see women as murderers?

S: No.

T: So can I strike this one out?

S: Yes. [*Collective*]

S: Well . . .

T: And we . . . we did do patience, kind. I need to just be clear. Okay. So what we have left here are . . . is mean, parent, baby-sitter, which you wouldn't keep my children, a ringmaster, one who loves school supplies, and drama. Right. [*Chuckles*] Okay, now going back again to Black, what is the next one shall we tackle that is most negative would be ignorant.

S: Ignorant. [*Collective*]

T: Ignorant. All right. What can cancel out ignorant?

S: Intelligence.

T: Strike that one out quickly. Now . . .

S: Open-minded.

T: We already got that one. That's gone. What else?

S: Patience, tolerant.

T: Wait, we're not over here. Do you see anything else?

S: Communicate.

T: Communicate. Do we have communicate? Got that for teacher and female.

S: Elegant.

T: You can be ignorant and elegant? I know a lot of dizzy people.

S: We're done with essence. We're done with elegance.

T: Okay.

S: Intelligence is with the other one.

T: Now, oh, that is right. All right. We'll take that one. All right. Ignorant in here. What cancels them?

S: Patience.

T: Patience. We already did that one. Which one?

S: Intelligence.

T: Didn't we take that one off already?

S: Communicator.

T: Communicator.

S: You can be ignorant and love school supplies.

T: Yeah, that's true.

S: You cannot be a ringmaster, I don't think.

S: No.

S: Not juggle many tasks if you were ignorant.

T: Oh, that's what you all meant by ringmaster. See, I thought you meant arbitrate a fight, you know?

S: Oh!

S: I thought you meant juggling many things.

T: Oh, that's fine! Whichever, as long as we are on the same page about what we mean. So you mean juggling many things at one time?

S: Yes.

T: Okay. So if you're ignorant, is that possible?

S: Probably not.

S: Ignorant doesn't mean that you can't do things physically.

T: What does it mean to be ignorant? Let's understand that. I think that's one of those expressions we were talking about earlier too in regards to being educated. What does it mean to be ignorant? How do we classify people that are ignorant?

T2: Well, when I think of ignorant, I think of teachers that I've had in grade school and stuff that have said some really insensitive things.

T: Okay.

S: And they are very intolerant in their profession.

T: So, anything else that ignorant cancels out that we still have left? We have mean, parent, and baby-sitter, ringmaster. You said that you couldn't juggle many things. One who loves supplies, although you disagree? So what do you want to do, put a half a line right there?

S: Yes.

S: The ring.

T: We'll keep the ring without the master. All right. What's next?

S: [*Inaudible—she speaks too low and mumbles*]

T: Yes. What you would, yes, let's . . . let's go back to this thing about ignorant. What does it mean to be ignorant? What are y'all talking about?

S: Narrow-minded.

T: Narrow-minded. Because I don't know of anybody, then, that's ignorant.

S: When you're ignorant . . . you are not open to new ideas.

T: Because we all know something.

S: Wait. To say that someone is ignorant, you have to be ignorant of something.

T: Right.

S: Like if you can say you're just stupid. And then I'm not saying that you're stupid, like . . . [*Everyone chuckles*] But you can be stupid, but it doesn't mean that you are ignorant either.

T: No, because I don't know what you mean by ignorant.

S: You can't just be ignorant. You have to be ignorant of something.

T: But you can just be plain stupid?

S: Biology.

S: Correct. [*Everyone is speaking at once*]

T: Okay.

S: So the word *ignorant* . . .

S: Look it up in the dictionary. You have to be ignorant of something.

T: I agree with you. I just said that. What, when you say you have to be ignorant. So everybody, then, will have some ignorance. We're all ignorant.

S: Right! Right!

T: All right.

S: 'Cause no one knows everything.

T: Okay. Exactly. And we won't even go to stupid, but that's what I was trying to understand because the young lady suggested that you could simultaneously be ignorant and be a ringmaster. And given that, you can simultaneously be ignorant and be most of these things that are here.

S: Oh, well then that's true.

T: But I think that we had a particular perception of what it means to be ignorant. One that was associated with being loud and all these other things that we have here. Is that right or wrong?

S: I think a ringmaster. So when you're ignorant, you're missing pieces of something. You're educated to a certain extent, right?

T: Uh-huh.

S: So you're . . . you're dealing with whatever we think. To be a great teacher is a wonderful thing, but you're gonna drop the pieces when you say the wrong thing.

T: So basically, then, no one is a ringmaster. Because it's impossible to juggle everything. I mean, I'll use me again as an example: I'm a mother, I'm a professor, I'm a wife, I'm a daughter, I'm a sister, and I try to do everything at once and try to please everybody at once. But every now and again, somebody will get his or her feelings hurt. So I've dropped it, all right. So, then, I'm ignorant to the fact of realizing that you can't do everything. So is that okay?

S: Sure.

T: Okay, all right. Okay, what do we have left? Loud. And I'm a try to; this is all we have left in regards to being a teacher.

S: And my school supplies.

T: And your school supplies and then the drama, of course. Okay, and then the drama of parents. Right? That's important. 'Cause now it's drama. All right. Loud. Does it cancel anything out?

S: No.

T: No. Okay. So I'm a put an asterisk by this one. That stays.

S: I mean loud in getting your point across.

T: When you say loud, do you mean like loud in regards to the volume of your voice or loud with regards to being animated? What do you mean by this term?

S: Noise like projection of the voice.

T: Okay. You are speaking of projection of voices?

S: Right. So I don't understand why you put that under Black or White.

S: That term, I think it means animated loud.

S: Yeah. [*Collective voices*]

S: To teach, you have to project your voice. Because if you didn't, with a class of thirty to thirty-five students, you have to project your voice to make everyone listen to you.

T: You all didn't put all of that. Y'all added something else to the . . . to the thing. So we can't; we didn't keep loud.

S: I mean but it's two different definitions. I told you!

T: You're right, but we haven't gotten there yet. We have to go; do I have time?

S: Uh.

T: No more time.

T2: Yeah, you've got . . . I'll give you about twelve more minutes.

T: All right. Well, we better do this quickly. We're keeping loud. Uh, Africa. Does Africa cancel any of these things?

S: No.

T: Okay. What about Ebonics?

S: [*Groaning and moaning*] Um.

S: No.

S: No.

T: No.

S: [*Inaudible—students laugh*]

T: So Ebonics is cast out with; I'm fixing to go with . . .

S: When you go to be a teacher, and you're at the interview, and, you know, usually the principal is expecting you to speak . . . It's called uh . . .

T: Standard English.

S: Standard English. And you just come and, you know, saying all that Ebonics and everything, you aren't going to be hired.

S: You can speak; you can speak in two different styles.

T: Have you all read *The Real Ebonics Debate*?

S: Um.

T: Because those of you who may find yourself trying to get a job in an urban area densely populated with African American children, an awareness of Ebonics as well as standard English could work to your advantage. No, I'm not saying go in there with your big breeches hanging down, saying, "Oh, bro! What's up?" [*Everyone laughs*] However, if you can sit there and conjugate the verb to be with a young African American, I as an administrator will be highly impressed with that, of your ability to use the home language of that child as a venue to teach them standard English.

S: Uh-huh.

T: And that is how you do it. See, y'all got to work through this stuff.

S: It's just a time and a place for it.

T: Well, I'm not, right now; I don't care about all of that. It is not about being right or wrong. As Lisa Delpit states: "It just is!" So as a teacher, you have to deal with the fact that it is! And your responsibility is to get that child to understand the mechanics of standard English, which is difficult for most of us anyway. 'Cause we don't understand the mechanics. So in the end, it all comes back here. Yet, we're always ready to point the finger at something or someone else and it becomes a problem; it interferes with the learning experience. All right. Twelve minutes. I know you're checking your watch. Okay, slavery. Does slavery cancel out anything?

S: No.

T: Civil rights, does that cancel out anything?

S: No.

T: All right. Uh, so then, we have a history. I guess that's why we're putting slavery or are we still in slavery?

S: No.

S: There are different forms.

T: How so?

S: Well, you, uh, still experience discrimination.

T: Yes, that is true. Now, what do we have left? Based on what you have shared, what does it mean to be a Black, female, and teacher? Okay, a descendent of Africa whose foreparents were slaves. She is loud, a mother, a great cook, strong, sexy, beautiful. . . .

S: What is your name?

T: Dr. LaVada Taylor Brandon, Ph.D.

S: Well, because you are these things with a Ph.D. aren't you also seen as threat?

T: Am I?

S: No response.

T: Okay, being a Black female teacher back to the board. She is a mean baby-sitter of children that loves school supplies and takes drama from parents. Do you have any more descriptors? [*A lot of speaking in the background*]

S: I would like to start over. [*Everyone laughs*]

S: I do not see a conclusion and I've been looking! I do not see anything.

S: Maybe it's your mission.

T: Um. To draw a conclusion?

S: I don't understand.

T: Are you sure?

S: [*Mumbling*]

T: Come on, please say something! I have nothing to do for the rest of the time.

S: I think okay.

S: Okay. Uh, I feel like . . . this is how I think of, you know, colored is not a word that we use anymore? But I think anybody that is not White is colored. You're colored, I'm colored! He's colored. I deal with it like that. And that's what you actually mean by colored. This goes for, I mean, maybe not slavery, but for the school. I think we're all colored.

S: [*Speaking at the same time*]

S: There is Black and White, and all those things are stereotypes, and everything has been characterized as a stereotype. [*Inaudible*] 'Cause if we could do White, it will be, you know, how much different would it be?

S: [*Everyone is speaking at once*]

S: There are White people who are different too. [*Everyone chuckles*]

S: It's just when you start using stuff like that, you can see, you know . . . [*Inaudible*]

S: I just wonder what it would be like for a classroom full of African Americans and a handful of White people and, then, you say, "What do you think of a White female teacher?" I wonder what they would have to say.

S: They don't have to say things just that would offend you just as it offended me. Because it's how you . . . you are raised and you think things about Black people like they're ignorant and loud, and we sometimes are raised—when I lived in Chicago—we were raised with this. Like how you are raised. Like you are, you know, are raised with?

T: Right.

S: Now, when I think of . . . when I meet [names a student] and she's not like that to me. And when I meet [*Inaudible*], she's not like that to me. Then, I erase that in my mind. I don't even think of that. I don't think of when I was being a racist person. You know?

S: Which goes back to the idea which she said; it is about you.

S: Uh-huh.

S: The conclusion lies within yourself. [*Some yell and clap*]

T: But is that it? Y'all have been a great class! Thank you all! [*Everyone claps*]

Conclusion

This conversation was very enlightening for me. Many of the things students stated I never would have imagined. I guess what was most surprising was the question/statement about embodying notions of being a Black woman teacher and being perceived as a threat because I possess a Ph.D. Through our conversation, what I learned most from the students was the power of perception. Although I had hoped that this exercise would have been a moment to create an understanding for being a Black female teacher, the students informed me that it really did not matter what I thought of myself; they had already come to imagine, realize, and navigate meaning for my being a Black female teacher, and they wanted me to make those images go away. Or, were they simply running from feelings of guilt? Feeling justified and created in the shadows of media, education, and other institutions that frame an ideological knowing for being Black, female, and teacher? Images that informed them that to be a Black female teacher meant to be "a descendant of Africa whose foreparents were slaves, [and to be] loud (animated), a mother, a great cook, strong, sexy, beautiful"? Yet, possessing a Ph.D. complicated these perceptions, causing students not to question their notions of Blackness and womanness but, rather, to see me as a threat, a beast, an oddity created in and through institutions of higher learning. Notions were etched in students' minds through an epistemology that has informed them that to be a Black female teacher means to be uneducated. And, to be an educated Black female teacher means to threaten institutionalized conventions of truth. These are notions created before my birth and, yet, in many ways still define me as I walk the halls and enter classrooms at a PWI ready to teach.

References

Watkins, W. H. (2001). *The white architects of Black education: Ideology and power in America, 1865–1954.* New York: Teachers College Press.

Woodson, C. G. (1933/1998). *The mis-education of the Negro.* Trenton, NJ: Africa World Press.

16

IN THIS PLACE WHERE I DON'T QUITE BELONG

Claiming the Ontoepistemological In-Between

Denise Taliaferro Baszile

The Author

Denise Taliaferro Baszile, Ph.D., is an assistant professor of curriculum theory in the Department of Educational Leadership at Miami University Ohio, Oxford, Ohio. A native of Detroit, Michigan, Dr. Baszile has an M.Ed. in secondary English education and a Ph.D. in curriculum theory, both from Louisiana State University. She has an insatiable passion for teaching, which, as she describes, is the core of her scholarship and service to the academic community. Dr. Baszile's work is centered around curriculum theory, Critical Race Theory, and womanist/feminist theory.

I don't belong here. The thought hits me like a freight train, hard and relentlessly. My eyes flutter open, and as they focus I gaze over my husband's shoulder at the clock on the nightstand. It's 4:00 A.M. I want to go back to sleep. I try to go back to sleep, but the thought, like a freight train rushing over a quiet country road, is still moving through my mind's eye: I don't belong here. "Here where?" I wonder. Then I remember the utterly frustrating day I had at work. It was the kind of day that plunged me into yet another cycle of daunting self-interrogations: Is my work scholarly enough? Did I assign too many books by or about Black folks or women maybe? Am I being unreasonable? Have I overstated the significance of race and gender in curriculum work? Am I too assertive about diversity issues? Are they trying to get one over on me? And so on. These are the questions or perhaps the doubts that seem to outline the essence of my struggle to fit comfortably within this realm of academic abstraction. I take another quick glance at the clock. It's 5:00 A.M. I need to get off this train of thought, so I once again shut my eyes, hoping that I will fall back into some peaceful place. But, no, I awake again with the thought still rumbling in the recesses of my mind: I don't belong here, but I am supposed to be here. It's 7:00 A.M. before I drift off once again in search of that peaceful place.

This up-in-the-middle-of-the-night thing is nothing new or unusual. It happened regularly in graduate school and has continued to wear on me for the five years and counting that I have been a professor. Sometimes I know it is coming; other times I am surprised what creeps through my mind in those moments when I should be resting, recuperating, and recharging my spirit for another day in that place where I don't quite belong. Although I have, over the years, felt welcomed by my colleagues, I have never felt at home in academia. Frankly, as I struggle to carve out and claim a homeplace (hooks, 1994) for myself and my comrades, I feel like what my sistah friend and colleague Yamuna has called "a refugee of the academy." I came to academia seeking refuge from the racist, sensational, and troubled business of television news, filled with fantasies about the freedom I would have to teach, research, reflect, and pontificate on those things that plague education. Much like de la Luz Reyes and Halcon (2000) describe in their work on racism in academia, I was disconcerted to discover otherwise. Although I was not completely naïve about some of the challenges with which I would have to contend, I had certainly underestimated just how profoundly racism, sexism, capitalism, and hypocrisy penetrate the deep structure of U.S. higher education.

There are minimal spaces in the academy where genuine dialogue and revolutionary action are engaged. This point lingers in the subtext of Gordon's (1999) metaphorical use of the 'hood to explain the realities of working in academia. After giving a vivid description of all the things that can possibly happen to you in the 'hood, including robbery, drive-bys, and gang crossfire, Gordon disrupts the reader's assumption that she is speaking about an actual urban dwelling by exclaiming, "The hood I work in is the Academy," where the struggle is dangerous, as it resembles a gang turf war. She goes on to explain: "The hood metaphor is no doubt difficult for some in the Academy, because we see ourselves as a critical helping profession situated in the ivory tower. And yet the struggles we witness and sometimes engage in within our institutions and their consequences, are in many instances no less violent than those on the mean urban streets" (p. 410).

When I first began working in academia, I believed in the illusion of the critical helping profession, but as the weeks, months, and semesters passed on, I became ever more aware of the violence, especially the epistemic violence perpetrated in academia. By epistemic violence I am speaking of the ways in which we profess a commitment to critical thinking and social justice, but at the same time continue to prescribe to standards, traditions, and ways of knowing that are meant to maintain the hegemonic order. More specifically, I am speaking of the rules and codes of power in academia that determine which ideas are the fashionable ones to have, or which ones are scholarly or not, or how ideas should be presented, or who should raise questions and who should just sit down and listen, or what falls under academic freedom and what does not.

Inarguably, these gatekeeping practices are indicative of how knowledge and power create situations of exclusion. Knowledge, which has become part of the currency of academic communities, has gained and maintained its legitimacy to the exclusion of conflicting ideas (Sibley, 1995). Although knowledge in the academy has traditionally been considered objective and universal, it has essentially been defined by and from a White, male, Western positionality. The problem, however, is not the standpoint itself but its tendency to deauthorize itself and claim universality by conflating Whiteness (and maleness) with reason (Kincheloe & Stieinberg, 1998), and creating race and gender hierarchies that exclude the ways of knowing or the epistemologies of other groups of people. In this vein, the production, evaluation, and validation of academic knowledge have been ignorant of and/or abusive to the lived experiences of various groups of people including people of color, homosexuals, and White women. The tyranny and promise of such circumstances lie in their paradoxical nature, which leaves many of us caught in between Adrienne Rich's words—This is the master's language yet I need it to talk to you—and Audre Lorde's powerful affirmation—You cannot use the master's tools to bring down the master's house. Dangling somewhere in between, some scholars, as Ladson-Billings (2000) notes, have attempted to work within the dominant academic paradigm. While I must also, to some extent, recognize and deal with the dominant discourse of academia, I have also decided to work against it, to work in a way that values the pedagogical promise of the space in between, and thus challenges the hegemonic order of things as usual in the academy.

Claiming the Ontoepistemological In-Between

Although there has always been talk here and there about Black women's commitment to racial uplift as being more salient than our interest in our gender oppression, I never quite saw the dilemma that way. When I first read Walker's (1983) definition of *womanist*, I knew immediately I had always been a womanist. Despite the fact that I did not have academic language to describe myself as such, I have always moved through life with every intention of being heard. I suppose such an attitude came from watching my mom, my aunts, and their friends stand up with and against men, other women, and even each other. Listening to their stories around the kitchen table, in the beauty shop, and on the front porch, I certainly got a basic understanding of the ways they felt about the racial and gender oppression they confronted on a daily basis. Although they were not academic women, much of their wisdom has helped me to cope in this place where I don't quite belong.

The notion that Black women do not really care about gender issues was something that never occurred to me until I came to the academy and encountered the "f" word—feminism. Yes, in the beginning I did, like most of the young women I work with today, understand it as a "White thang," but not because I didn't see Black women as facing gender oppression; rather, it was because I never felt my oppression in quite the same ways that many of my White peers did. I more often than not found myself talking racial oppression in feminist circles and gender oppression in Black national-ist circles, and struggling all along to articulate this space in between. Since my early days in academia, I have thought a lot about the construction of this space in between, wondering what has been the relationship between race and gender in the academy.

In her book *The Dark Continent of Our Bodies*, E. Frances White (2001) points to the work of Darwin to elaborate on how race and gender hierar-chies were used discursively in nineteenth-century science:

> To further explain differences between races and to obscure the impact of imperialism, Darwin used gender as an explanatory tool. Here the position of women was used to explain the deficiencies of a race: "The chief causes [of racial inferiority] are, first so-called communal marriages or promiscu-ous intercourse; secondly, the consequences of female infanticide; thirdly, early betrothals, and lastly the low estimation in which women are held as mere slaves." Europeans could relax: Conquest had little to do with degen-eracy; underdeveloped biology and primitive gender relations were at fault. (p. 93)

White builds on her analysis by calling up the memory of Saartije Baartman and the humiliation and exploitation she faced as the infamous Hottentot Venus. Reference to her large behind was used again and again in the "scien-tific" quest to liken Black people to apes; her body became an object of curi-osity, mystery, and disgust as she was paraded for show at carnivals; even after death, her body was dismembered for the sake of science. The memory of Saartije Baartman is indicative of the ways in which race and gender hier-archies established through scientific quest are wed to the production of aca-demic theory and the ways in which the pursuit of absolute truth often comes at the expense of valuing one's humanity, the connection between mind, body, and spirit. The tyranny performed on Baartman's body and no doubt her spirit has forever situated the Black woman's body as abnormal and problematic. So what does it mean to live in this body, to be in the world and to conceive of the world through this body, to teach and write through this body, which without question situates Black women in academia as counterhegemonic texts?

As Black women, we live at the nexus of race and gender hierarchies; we be in the spaces in between, not quite here and not quite there. We are/we be in between Black and White, male and female, and even race and gender as categories that contradict in the defining of Black women's identities. Collins (1990) describes this space in between as our "outsider within" status, which captures the experience of being both a part of and, at the same time, not a part of a group identity. Essentially we are outsiders within the traditional discourse and community of Blackness, femaleness, and intellectualism. Navigating the in-between also speaks to what Min-ha (1995) defines as an "outside in inside out" phenomena in which "differences do not only exist between outsider and insider—two entities—they are also at work within the outsider or insider—one entity" (p. 218). However it is conceptualized, the ontoepistemological in-between allows Black women a "peculiar angle of vision," as we offer a potential element of critique within various communities by challenging the reification of Blackness around maleness, the reification of gender around Whiteness, and the reification of intellectualism around White maleness. Black women in academia who claim the space in between, who theorize and practice from the space in between, are often at odds with the academic establishment, where knowledge is defined in racist and patriarchal ways and grounded as either/ors, top-downs, and theory-practice splits.

In the tradition of Critical Race Theory in general and Critical Race Feminism in particular, one of the ways we have managed to engage our ontoepistemological in-between has been through "The Word." Lawrence (1990) describes The Word as a form of praxis in which pedagogy, scholarship, and struggle are intimately intertwined; a way of teaching and doing scholarship that embraces duality, subjectivity, and narrative in our attempts to authorize our voices. One of the methodological strategies that we use in our praxis is counter-stories. Counterstories are not only a form of resistance and recognition, which disrupt the culture of power; they also depict a kind of complex-ity that is unattainable through traditional academic discourse. Working within a critical race framework, Ladson-Billings (2000) expresses its intertextuality:

> My decision to deploy a critical race theoretical framework in my scholarship is intimately linked to my understanding of the political and personal stake I have in the education of Black children. All of my "selves" are invested in this work—the self that is a researcher, the self that is a parent,

the self that is a community member, the self that is a Black woman. No technical-rational approach to this work would yield the deeply textured, multifaceted work I attempt to do. (p. 272)

Ultimately, our stories are about connections, explicit and implicit, among race, gender, class, sexuality, and so on; between reason and emotion; between experiencing and theorizing; between one issue and another; between what is said and what is silenced. When we use counterstories to express our ontoepistemological in-between, we work toward a form of oppositional scholarship, which brings to bear the "universality of White experience [and male experience] and judgment as the authoritative standard that binds people of color and normatively measures, directs, controls, and regulates the terms of proper thought, expression, presentment and behavior" (Calmore, 1990, p. 318).

Scholarship as a Form of Struggle

There are three moments in my academic career that stick out in my mind as critical to helping me understand my sense of out-of-placeness and, ironically enough, the importance of that out-of-placeness to the survival of academia. One moment was in a class entitled Race, Sex, and Political Style. In this course, we began by reading Edward Said's (1994) *Representations of the Intellectual* along with several biographies of important intellectuals, including Virginia Woolf, Michel Foucault, Pierre Passalini, and Frantz Fanon. Although there was much I liked about this course, I was immediately struck by the fact that Said's book, which has several pictures of such intellectuals as Malcom X, Baldwin, Sartre, Woolf, and Chomsky, did not include one woman of color. I was so bothered by this omission or oversight that I asked the class what Black woman should have, could have, graced the cover of this treatise on representations of intellectuals. They fell silent.

The next moment was in the course of writing my dissertation. I had made a conscious decision not to cite the great White men of education. I wished to make a political statement about the significance of work that is typically not heard or valued in education. I wished to keep, as much as possible, my theorizing about African American education grounded within the African American intellectual tradition. It was a difficult and risky decision, indeed, and a goal which I fell far short of accomplishing. In this process, with the demands of having to think and write both inside and outside of traditional academic discourse, I recognized myself suspended yet again in another facet of my ontoepistemological in-between. This time I was struggling in the space between DuBois's hopes for the "Talented Tenth" and Woodson's warnings about the "miseducated Negro."

The third moment was toward the beginning of my work as an assistant professor. After successfully passing third-year review, the dean recognized my passion for writing but commented that I should always be careful to make sure theory was central to my writing. Although I understood what she meant and where her concerns were coming from, I was still disturbed by the comment. It annoyed me because I felt like everything I had written to that point, and certainly everything I had included in my portfolio, incorporated both theoretical references and a process of theorizing. Thus, the problem seemed to me to be not the lack of theory or theorizing but the way in which I shifted constantly between theory and experience, therefore not positioning traditional theory but, rather, embodying theorizing as the point of my work.

I do not just come to the world from the ontoepistemological in-between. I also conceive of the world through the ontoepistemological in-between. Being and seeing from this space in between race and gender constructions, I have often found the scope and the language of academia limiting, even incapable, at times, of relaying what needs to be communicated. How can I work within a discourse that has historically invisibilized me, berated me, denied my existence, or simply ill prepared me for the work I must do?

Academic origins are rooted mainly in European intellectual traditions, which have been key to establishing the principles of modernity, which, in turn, continues to, even in this postmodern or post postmodern era, define the core of academic work. If we consider all that has been traditional about the concept of theory, what emerges is a connotation that has been, for the most part, abusive to the realities of oppressed peoples. In *Webster's Ninth New Collegiate Dictionary*, theory is defined as a belief, abstract thought, or analysis of a set of facts in relation to one another. By this denotation, everyone engages in theorizing. Yet when we examine theory in terms of its social construction in academia, a process of marginalization manifests and privileges certain beliefs, abstract thought, and analyses over others. Boyce-Davies (1994) makes a similar point when she discusses the "trickle-down approach" whereby some are privileged as theorists, others write about the theories of theorists, and then the teachers use the work of the writers to teach about the theories of the theorists. This hierarchical approach to theory in the academy reifies a theory/practice (theory/experience) split, positing theory as an exclusive practice, and deeming some people knowers and others the known.

hooks (1994) also speaks to how the academic rhetoric of theory works to alienate the public. She insists that any theory that cannot be used in everyday conversation cannot be used to educate the public and is thus not liberating. Her position begs the question: Who/what is theory for anyway? When it is viewed as academically insular, theory is perceived as separate from everyday practice/experience and marginalizes the very people it is supposed to help. How, then, do the marginalized respond to academic theory?

My response has been to write, to communicate in ways that are, in fact, liberating, in ways that not only liberate me from a hegemonic stronghold, but also liberate the voices, the counterstories of numerous Black women who have contributed infinitely to my well-being. For me, claiming counterstories is a way to continue my commitment to the struggle for social justice, by both understanding and celebrating the ontoepistemological in-between of my and other Black women's experiences in academia. This means, of course, that I have to chart a different course, a course that values the discursivity of theory and practice/experience; a course that embraces subjectivity, rather than feigns objectivity; a course that values the voices of those marginalized; a course that values a commitment to the community, to the collective we; a course that is paved with risks, many risks. Yet, as my momma would say, "Nothing will change if you don't take risks!"

Pedagogy Born of Struggle

Just as they have been central to my writing, counterstories have been a critical part of my pedagogy as well. I have spent the last several years teaching prospective and practicing teachers about issues of social justice in curriculum work. When I walk into a new classroom at the beginning of each semester, my first thought is that one of these teachers/students might be teaching my child one day. And, quite frankly, the thought, the possibility, is often a frightening one, especially when I am faced with teachers/students who still cling to "color-blind" ideologies, who are mostly unwilling to explore their own hang-ups, and who speak in dysconscious ways (King, 1991) about what particular children do and do not deserve. The classroom conversation is often rife with the worst kind of racist, sexist, class-dysconscious, and/or homophobic dialogue; it is the kind that disguises itself in benign "can't-we-all-just-get-along" rhetoric. It is the kind of dialogue that cannot be challenged with theory alone, especially traditional educational theory, which has supported ideas of cultural deprivation and biological deficiency

(McCarthy, 1990). These are ideas that work to continue the hegemonic order and are, thus, more likely to feed ignorance, rather than challenge it.

Theories reflect systems, numbers, groups in relationships that need to be supported or perhaps challenged with counterstories, which disrupt the taken-for-granted myths and images by illuminating the struggles in the spaces in between. I choose counterstories strategically, using them to introduce a theory, to put a face on the theory, to point out the discursive relation between theory and experience, to either support or challenge the theory at hand, to reiterate the complexity of educational dilemmas, and to disrupt the tendency of the teachers/students to rest with one answer. In other words, I try to engage them in the space in between. When they are going on and on about proper English, for instance, I tell them about my experiences teaching Spanish-speaking students in Los Angeles when the "English Only" proposition passed. I share the dilemmas this raised not only for Spanish-speaking children but also for African American children who spoke in Black vernacular. When we focus on the devastation of urban school districts, I share the story of "White flight" in my childhood neighborhood. And next semester, when they are telling me they don't have to worry about diversity where they teach, I will invite community folks to talk with them about their experiences with regentrification in their neighborhoods.

Counterstories are powerful teaching tools, especially when the point of the lesson is to disrupt the status quo, to inspire critical thinking, to challenge the culture of power, to critique the nature of knowledge, to encourage students to tell their own stories from critical perspectives, and to capture struggle as a form of praxis. They are, in essence, critical to understanding and practicing teaching as a form of activist intellectual work and as a viable front in the struggle against systemic oppression and for social justice. And, yet, they are, at best, a controversial teaching strategy in higher education. I have sat on several university committees formed to focus on diversity issues in the curriculum; the ways that we talk about our commitment to social justice never fails to amaze and frustrate me, because we convince ourselves that we are making genuine efforts to transform something that we absolutely cannot transform without rethinking some basic aspects of academic life that we have traditionally held in high regard.

For instance, counterstories have been an important pedagogical strategy in areas of study that work mainly within social justice paradigms, such as ethnic studies; peace studies; women's studies; and, in some places, educational studies. Yet, it is no secret that these are often the majors that are viewed as not academically rigorous. Never mind the fact that teaching a course on social justice in traditional academic ways, in banking education style, would be utterly hypocritical and antithetical to the goal of any such class. Nevertheless, trying to convince a committee that we need to rethink what constitutes "academic rigor" or that we need to reevaluate how we decode the student evaluations of social justice courses or that we need to hold all professors accountable for engaging an issue (diversity/social justice) that we say is vital to the life of our institutions is just too much for some to bear. Instead, the discourse of academic freedom and high academic standards, traditions usually desirable, is being used to keep at bay or disengage the necessary changes that would support diversity as both a social and an intellectual priority.

As someone who works for social justice and who uses counterstories as pedagogical strategy, I struggle with others' assumptions about the rigor of my classes. I struggle with how the telling of my stories does not remove me but, in fact, locks me in the gazer's line of vision. I struggle with telling the stories that genuinely challenge the students as to their place in systems of oppression. I also struggle with not telling those stories because of the effect they may have on my course evaluations. I struggle with the way these stories displace the authority I should have earned through my studies for an experiential authority, an authority that is inscribed on my body through race and gender constructions.

Creating Homeplace in the Midst of Struggle

It is now 8:00 A.M., and I awake again to make a note to myself: Reread bell hooks's "Revolutionary Black Women." I suppose that is on my mind because it takes me back to the basic realization that I need to work consciously and critically to make myself subject in this place where I don't quite belong. In this essay, hooks (1992) insists that in order for Black women to make themselves subject in a place/context of racist and sexist domination, they must cultivate their "wild," which she describes as "a metaphoric expression of that inner will to rebel, to move against the grain, to be out of one's place" (p. 49). Yet, cultivating radical Black female subjectivity is not simply a matter of resisting the impositions of domination; it also requires that we engage in a process of self-actualization, a process of making ourselves anew. hooks also warns that "coming to power, to selfhood, to radical subjectivity cannot happen in isolation. Black women need to study the writings, critical and autobiographical, of those women who have developed their potential and chosen to be radical subjects" (p. 56).

Thus, I regularly call on "The Word(s)" of other Black women scholars. Reading the wisdom of Anna Julia Cooper, Angela Davis, bell hooks, Barbara Christian, Ida B. Wells, Mary Church Terrell, Hazel Carby, E. Frances White, Sistah Souljah, Assata Shakur, Elanie Brown, Gerder Lerner, Mari Evans, and many others has been vital to my ability to sustain and even grow in a place that has historically minimized or even rejected Black women's ways of knowing the world. It is these voices that let me know I am not crazy—that I do have a purpose in academia, not the least of which is to make its discourse accountable to me and my community. The counternarratives of these women have helped me to identify and understand my tendency to write in ways that demystify theory, that demystify narrow definitions of intellectual or scholarly work, that transform academic rhetoric into something with which the community can engage.

Another way I have learned to exist, resist, and renew myself in this place where I don't quite belong is to practice what I call radical Black female *inter*subjectivity. In this vein and expanding on hooks's idea, I have also learned to seek out and develop mutually empowering relationships with other Black female colleagues, who have helped me unload, not feel alone, see from another perspective, and continue to challenge myself in significant ways. Consciously and critically cultivating my wild in the company and comfort of other wild women in academia has been absolutely vital to my ability to sustain spiritually and grow infinitely. I call this the praxis of radical Black female intersubjectivity, and I see it not only as crucial for my well-being, but as nurturing the pedagogical promise of Black women, a promise iterated by John (1997):

> The analogy of academe and the plantation is not lost. Both structures reify in content and form, the ideology of power elite, both stand as seemingly self-sufficient entities yet are, in fact, totally dependent on the labor each exploits. So as the black woman in antebellum context facilitated the existence of the planter's family and the survival of her own, so the contemporary black female academic and activist poised between the ideal culture of America's rhetoric and the racial culture of her double jeopardy has a pivotal role. Who has an angel of vision that can view social reality from high and low places in the configuration?

It is in affirmations such as John's and through the praxis of radical Black female intersubjectivity that I have, at last, carved out that place hooks (1994) describes as the site "where one could freely confront the issue of humanization, where one could resist. Black women resisted by making homes where all black people could strive to be subjects, not objects, where we could be affirmed in our minds and hearts . . . where we could restore to ourselves the dignity denied us on the outside in the public world" (p. 448). This is the place I share with LaVada, Tayari, Tonya, Nichole, Thea, Ethel, and Yamuna among others. It's now 9:00 A.M. and time to go out into that place where I don't quite belong.

References

Boyce-Davies, C. (1994). *Black women, writing and identity*. New York: Routledge.

Calmore, J. (1990). Critical race theory. Archie Shepp, and fire music: Securing an authentic intellectual life in a multicultural world. In K. Crenshaw (Ed.), *Critical race theory: Key writings that formed the movement*, (pp. 315–328). New York: New Press.

Collins, P. H. (1991). *Black feminist thought: Knowledge, consciousness, and the politics of empowerment*. New York: Routledge.

de la Luz Reyes, M., & Halcon, J. (2000). Racism in academia: The old wolf revisited. In A. Darder, R. Torres, & H. Gutierrez (Eds.), *Latinos and education: A critical reader* (pp. 423–438). New York: Routledge.

Gordon, B. (1999). Who do you believe—me or your eyes? Perceptions and issues in educational research: Reviews and the journals that validate them. *Review of Educational Research, 69*(4), 407–410.

hooks, b. (1992). *Black looks: Race and representation*. Boston: South End Press.

hooks, b. (1994). Homeplace (a site of resistance). In D. Soyini Madison (Ed.), *The woman that I am* (pp. 448–454). New York: St. Martin's Griffin.

John, B. (1997). The African American female ontology: Implications for academe. In L. Benjamin (Ed.), *Black women in the academy: Promises and perils*. Gainesville, FL: University Press of Florida.

Kincheloe, J., & Steinberg, S. (1998). Addressing the crisis of whiteness: Reconfiguring White identity in a pedagogy of whiteness. In J. Kincheloe, S. Steinberg, N. Rodriguez, & F. Chennault (Eds.), *White reign: Deploying Whiteness in America* (pp. 3–30). New York: St. Martin's Griffin.

King, J. (1991). Dysconscious racism: Ideology, identity and the miseducation of teachers. *Journal of Negro Education, 60*, 133–146.

Ladson-Billings, G. (2000). Racialized discourse and ethnic epistemologies. In N. Denzin & Y. Lincoln (Eds.), *Handbook of qualitative research* (pp. 257–278). Thousand Oaks, CA: Sage.

Lawrence, C. (1990). The word. In K. Crenshaw (Ed.), *Critical race theory: Key writings that formed the movement* (pp. 336–354). New York: New Press.

McCarthy, C. (1990). *Race and curriculum.* New York: Falmer Press.

Min-ha, T. (1995). No master territories. In B. Ashcroft, G. Griffiths, & H. Tiffin (Eds.), *Post-colonial studies reader* (pp. 215–218). New York: Routledge.

Said, E. (1994). *Representations of the intellectual.* New York: Routledge.

Sibley, D. (1995). *Geographies of exclusion.* New York: Routledge.

Walker, A. (1983). *In search of our mothers' garden: Womanist prose.* San Diego: Harcourt, Brace and Jovanovich.

White, E. F. (2001). *The dark continent of our bodies: Black feminism and the politics of respectability.* Philadelphia: Temple University Press.

17

UNA LUCHA DE FRONTERAS (A STRUGGLE OF BORDERS)

Women of Color in the Academy

Maria V. Balderrama, Mary Texeira, and Elsa Valdez

The Authors

Maria V. Balderrama is an associate professor of education in the College of Education at California State University San Bernardino. She is a native of the Mexicali/Calexico Valleys (California), where she attended public schools. She earned scholarships and degrees from Wellesley College and San José State and a doctorate from Stanford University. Professor Balderrama's teaching, research, and writings include the topics of sociology of education focusing on social justice, bilingual and multicultural education, teacher preparation, and resistance to equity and democratic principles.

Mary Texeira is an associate professor of sociology at California State University San Bernardino. She was born in Louisiana and raised in the Watts section of Los Angeles, California, where she attended Catholic schools. Professor Texeira has research and teaching interests in social inequality, especially as it relates to the criminal justice system. Her published and presented research focuses on police personnel, community policing, African Americans and the criminal justice system, the "war on drugs," and drug policy in general. The classes she teaches coincide with her interests, including those on the Black family, the sociology of race and ethnicity, Black women and feminism, and critical criminology.

Elsa Valdez is a professor of sociology at California State University San Bernardino. She was born in Mexico and migrated with her family to the Coachella Valley of California when she was a child. Her teaching and research interests include racial and ethnic relations, the Chicano family, and the sociology of education. She has published three chapters in the following edited books: *Employed Mothers and the Family Context* (1993); *Work, Family and Masculinities* (1993); and *Chicanas and Chicanos in Contemporary Society* (1996). Professor Valdez serves on the board of directors of the University of California Riverside Alumni Association and is the advisor for campus MECHA and the Chicano Coalition. She also serves on the Jessie Bernard Award Committee for the American Sociological Association, which recognizes outstanding scholars in feminist studies.

So many different people saw themselves in this portrait that it became impossible to pretend it was mine alone.

—Albert Memmi (1965)

D iscussions and critiques of stratification and inequity in academe, particularly by faculty women of color, attest to the urgency to provide space for feminist voices of struggle and survival within U.S. institutions. Aisenberg and Harrington (1988) were some of the first women to begin to name the prevalent stratification in White academe and its effects on women, referring to them as "outsiders in the sacred grove." As these "outsiders" began to gain access to the academy, they too joined the chorus naming academe's inequitable treatment of women (hooks, 1984; James & Farmer, 1993; Latina Feminist Group, 2002; Rai & Critzer, 2000; Turner & Myers, 2000).

Here we attempt to extend previous stories of discrimination, resistance, and survival in academe in several ways. First, we provide a conceptual framework that names and binds our shared, lived contradictions. Second, we link our personal stories with a political and structural analysis of the differential treatment we experience in the academic setting. This has not been done previously in testimonials of historically subordinated women scholars. Finally, we suggest that naming the phenomenon that appears to be deeply rooted in the culture of the academy is an important step toward eliminating this existing "alchemy of erasure" (Latina Feminist Group,

2002) that attempts to delegitimize our existence and contributions to the "sacred grove."

We begin this chapter by (re)stating the problem and then follow with a theoretical discussion. Our personal narratives situate the phenomenon at the local level, providing evidence intended to clarify and make it impossible to pretend that our experiences are/were ours alone. We close with recommendations for continued struggle for inclusiveness within academe.

(Re)Statement of the Problem

The literature on faculty in higher education in the United States reveals several trends affecting women faculty of color—African Americans, Asian Americans, Latinas, and Native Americans—and the outcomes related to these patterns of inequity. First, in 1997, historically subordinated women of color accounted for only 2.5 percent of all full professors, compared with 72.1 percent for White men, 17.3 percent for White women, and 8.1 percent for men of color (Harvey, 2001). Second, if we examine gender differences in salaries for full-time faculty, we find that in 1998 full-time male faculty averaged about $61,700 in base salary, compared with $48,400 for full-time female faculty (Bradburn & Sikora, 2002). Moreover, salary advantage among full-time Black males and Latinos is evident: Black males earned $53,640 in base salary compared with $46,870 for Black females, and Latinos earned $58,990 compared with $46,890 for Latinas (Bradburn & Sikora, 2002). Third, in 1998, more male full-time faculty obtained tenure (60 percent) compared with female full-time faculty (42 percent). Furthermore, full-time Black males and Latinos were more likely to have received tenure (51 and 56 percent, respectively), than full-time Black females and Latinas (37 percent for both groups).

What, then, happens to faculty of color who enter academe only to find their numbers small and their treatment different? The dubious distinction of often being the only person of color in the workplace may result in faculty of color having lower levels of job satisfaction (Niemann & Dovidio, 1998). They must often perform more service activities by serving on numerous departmental and university committees (Aguirre, 1993; Rausch, Ortiz, Douthitt, & Reed, 1989) and teach more undergraduate courses with higher enrollments, such as introductory courses, than their White and male colleagues (Menges & Exum, 1983). Hagedorn (1995) argues that wage difference in academe decreases job satisfaction, and increases job-related stress. One study found that unequal salary among faculty has negative effects on work satisfaction and number of publications (Pfeffer & Langton, 1993). Reyes and Halcon (1991) note that research by faculty of color is often "de-legitimized" by their White colleagues, who sometimes regard this research as deviant and thus unworthy. As a result, non-White faculty are given the message that they are not producing legitimate research worthy of merit and are subsequently excluded from participation and membership in a community of scholars.

Aguirre (2000) examined the effects of working in a negative and hostile environment among faculty of color. He notes that

> On the one hand, women and minority faculty find themselves burdened with heavy teaching and service responsibilities that constrain their opportunity to engage in research and publication. On the other hand, women and minority faculty are expected to assume and perform institutional roles that allow higher education institutions to pursue diversity on campus. But those roles are ignored in the faculty reward system, especially the awarding of tenure. The academic workplace is thus chilly and alienating for women and minority faculty because they are ascribed a peripheral role in the academic workplace and are expected to perform roles that are in conflict with expectations. (pp. iv–v)

Other barriers experienced by women faculty of color include having to balance personal obligations and workplace responsibilities (Gmelch, Lovrich, & Wilke, 1984; Gmelch, Wilke, & Lovrich, 1986; McMillen, 1987). Faculty who experience stress and conflict as a result of having to juxtapose work and family are more likely to suffer with respect to their classroom preparation and publications (Smith, Anderson, & Lovrich, 1995). For example, Smith and colleagues (1995) note that many universities have minimal or no family-leave benefits, which more adversely affects all women, especially women of color, because many tend to be the major care providers for their immediate family and/or elderly parents.

Workplace stressors can also emanate from women's subaltern status. Women-of-color faculty are more likely to be ascribed negative stereotypes in the workplace. For example, many White faculty view the presence of women of color as an outcome of affirmative action (Fontaine & Greenlee, 1993; Young, 1984). Consequently, considerations of merit are avoided. Instead, the focus is on their minority status. Montero-Sieburth (1996) notes that Latinas who gain entry into academe are often viewed by White faculty as examples of reverse discrimination or tokenism: "The importance of the preceding studies cannot be overstated especially since: Education is a central site of contests over race, class, gender . . . in the United States both because knowledge is key to resisting oppression and because educational credentials are essential to getting good jobs, salaries, benefits, and better quality of life" (Weber, 2001, p. 54). This research provides ample evidence that faculty of color, especially women of color, find themselves performing conflicting and contradictory roles in the academic workplace. As in the larger society, academe creates barriers for women of color that prevent them from receiving the same benefits and rewards as White male faculty. The culture of the academic workplace must reconstruct its perception and treatment of women-of-color faculty.

Theoretical Framework

The quantitative data we present are useful in establishing that stratification is alive and well in academe, with female scholars of color being relegated to the bottom of the academic hierarchy regarding pay, status, and workload. And while the present picture is very important, it is equally critical to include a brief overview of the history that painted the existing landscape. What follows is a brief history of how historically subordinated people entered the academy.

How Did We Get Here?

The traditional academy was not designed as a place for people of color, White women, or people from working-class origins. As Rich (in Turner & Myers, 2000) suggests, the academy was intended to be occupied by White males and is still designed to serve such a group of men, particularly those with economic power and social status. Placing academe within a historical context thus reminds us that the mission of the academy was consistent with the economic, social, and cultural needs of U.S. capitalist society. The first institutions of higher education in this country (for example, Harvard, William and Mary, and Yale) reflected a society, labor force, and culture legally segregated with pervasive economic inequality. Some colleges were organized for wealthy White women and African Americans for the very purpose of getting around gender and race discrimination. This was not true for individuals of Mexican origin, American Indians, or individuals from the working class.

Executive laws signed by presidents Franklin D. Roosevelt, John F. Kennedy, and Lyndon B. Johnson paved the way for the admission of White women and people of color into White universities, first as students, and later as faculty. The Civil Rights Movement and student activism of the 1960s resulted in federal mandates such as court-ordered Affirmative Action, thus opening the doors of academe for groups historically denied access. Women and scholars of color became visible in the academy in the 1960s and 1970s. Consequently, many of us in academe today are the first generation to cross these color, gender, and class lines and to enter these new academic borderlands. We are newcomers to the sacred grove. Perhaps this is one of the reasons we experience the hardest *chingazos* or "blows" by the institutions. As female faculty of color, we are the first generation in significant numbers to share these spaces previously occupied only by privileged White males. Our presence is often met with resistance. Our numbers remain small and few in proportion to the communities we represent; yet we are still perceived as a threat. Efforts to "academize" us (the socialization process into academic culture) begin as early as undergraduate school and continue into our graduate school experience.

Economic and Colonial Models

What is the basis or rationale for this historical exclusion of oppressed peoples in academe? The seminal work by Bowles and Gintis (1976) examines the U.S. educational system and its relationship to a capitalist economy. It serves to shed some light on this question. Their analysis suggests that education in the United States is reflective of the needs of a capitalist market "dominated by the imperatives of profits and domination" (p. 54) that prepares students for the world of labor. The practices of the educational system are characterized by power relations and are far from the rhetoric of schools being the "great equalizer." The fact that some individuals from historically subordinated groups have attained high levels of education is merely a reflection of the historical times when student activists and the Civil Rights Movement forced social change in societal institutions. Bowles and Gintis also suggest that this phenomenon of inclusion of poor and non-White ethnic groups in the academy is a contradiction of capitalism in that it is touted as the great equalizer, but, as Bowles and Gintis (1976) note, "Education over the years has never been a potent force for economic equality" (p. 8). They add that "despite the vast increase in college enrollments, the probability of a high school graduate attending college is just as dependent on parental socioeconomic status as it was thirty years ago. . . . The substantial equalization of educational attainments over the years has not led measurably to an equalization in income among individuals" (p. 8). Bowles and Gintis's work thus addresses two issues confirmed by the data that we have presented.

First, faculty women of color are societal anomalies and exceptions, relegating their presence to subordinate roles regarding numerical (mis)representation. Second, their unequal pay for the same (or more!) work suggests that similar status as represented by educational attainment does not lead to equal income.

Another resounding theme of this work clarifies the dissonance caused by the differences in ideological perspectives between faculty women of color and academe. One example is academe's continual efforts to delegitimize the scholarly work and other contributions by faculty women of color. Many regard our scholarly work, framed by a consciousness of social responsibility, as "watered-down" scholarship. Indeed, it is not uncommon for us to be questioned about the relevancy of our work, particularly that which is linked to social change and that utilizes multiple perspectives for research analysis and data collection. In short, scholarly work grounded in social-action research is not seen as legitimate, resulting in negative consequences for the researcher (including negative peer reviews in retention/promotion/tenure; ineligibility for sabbaticals and awards; lack of inclusion in academic discussions, events, and journals). Again, Bowles and Gintis (1976) provide useful insights into this phenomenon by suggesting that "it is a mistake to think of the educational system in relation to the economy in simply 'technical terms.'. . . To capture the economic import of education, we must relate its social structure to the forms of consciousness, interpersonal behavior, and personality it fosters and reinforces in students" (p. 9).

Higher education, as a link in the chain of the educational institution, has a social structure grounded in an ideology of unequal power relationships. Framed by a hierarchical social structure and guided by norms of interpersonal behavior traditionally defined by those it is intended to serve, it leaves little room for the contribution of women faculty of color. As suggested earlier, the hegemonic processes of the institution are manifested in the original intent of the academy and rest on exclusion of members of oppressed groups in all aspects of its maintenance—from access to participation to curriculum. This results in ideological clashes. Although the institution of education tends toward rationality and logic in carrying out its social and economic mission, it does have its share of contradictions. The presence of women-of-color faculty and their scholarly work grounded in social-action research crystallizes these ideological clashes between the institution and individuals whose participation was not written in the original treatise. This, we believe, is one of the reasons we three sing the same tune with different lyrics—our experiences begin with personal/individual and local political issues. But as we continue to hear the song, we begin to realize that it is more than local and personal but extends into the institutional and structural as well.

Memmi (1965), in his analysis of colonialism and colonial relationships, also suggests a collective experience of oppression, stating that "all the oppressed are alike in some ways" (p. ix). This shared experience of oppression provides some explanatory power as to why our narratives tend to sing the same tune of lived institutional discrimination. Although some individual Chicanas/Chicanos and African Americans have been allowed access to the academy, these ethnic and racial groups remain oppressed peoples within the larger society, relegated to perform a disproportionately high share of low-paid, unskilled labor, and are politically and economically subjected to control by the majority. Thus, faculty of color represent the contradictions of capitalism discussed earlier by Bowles and Gintis (1976). This may be the reason that, regardless of their legitimate participation in academe, the overall tradition and culture of the academy have not made room for access and inclusion by these individuals (who represent larger social groups), treating them as subordinates and making them victims of discrimination and racist ideology. This is what we as faculty women of color mean when we refer to "being struck by [our] own lived contradiction" (Aleman, quoted in Turner & Myers, 2000, p. 48).

Finally, Memmi (1965) points out that part of the colonial model is not just about resources. He notes that to "observe the life of the colonizer and the colonized is to discover rapidly that the daily humiliation of the colonized, his objective subjugation, are not merely economic" (p. xii). This observation supports the earlier premise made by Bowles and Gintis (1976) that education is not merely a technical endeavor, but an ideological one. We found notable in our analysis and discussions of work by colleagues (including our own) that dominant themes center around daily acts of humiliation ranging from occupational stress to persistent questioning of one's ability to perform, think, teach, talk, and write—*be* a scholar. Our readings and discussions of these lived contradictions point to the fact that it is this pervasive and daily humiliation that is the most apt to break one's spirit, forcing many women faculty of color eventually to leave academe.

In sum, Bowles and Gintis's (1976) analysis of schooling in capitalist America and Memmi's (1965) colonial model conceptualize relevant precepts and put forth theoretical frameworks useful in this chapter. Both sets of theories ground the daily, collective experiences of inequality and discrimination within an economic framework and suggest that understanding

institutional oppression is complex, extending beyond mere economic explanations.

Naming the Contradictions: How We Experience and Survive the Academy

How can we discuss the institutional and political without linking them to
the personal? We live the belief that only by understanding our origins, our
connections to our communities and families, can our reason for pursuing a
scholarly profession be fully understood. In this section, we situate our lived
contradictions and discuss our shared themes of beginnings, motivation, and
survival in academe.

Bootstraps: What Happens When You Got None

Maria: The youngest of three daughters, I grew up in Calexico, California,
a town along the Mexican border. Calexico is in the heart of the Sonoran
Desert and one of the most fertile agricultural areas in the world, the Imperial Valley. My father was a farm worker and my mother a housewife—
both monolingual Spanish speakers and immigrants from the Mexican
state of Sonora, where I was born. After my family's immigration to this
country, I started as a monolingual Spanish speaker in a country school
in the 1960s set up to educate the children of the wealthy farmers.

Growing up on the Calexico/Mexicali border taught me to read the
word and the world in Spanish and English, thus giving me multiple perspectives about life, power, people, politics, social injustice, and compassion. The border also gave me my place within these different spheres.
How can I ignore and forget where I came from and, consequently, who
I am? Where I came from is a big part of who I am and where I am now.
Why would anyone expect me to ignore or erase this? I had the best of
two worlds, in two languages, in two countries, in two cities, in two settings. Literally and figuratively, the academy does not make space for multiple perspectives.

Mary: Like many women of color, I came to the academy, in a manner of
speaking, through the back door, that is, not in the traditional route, directly after high school, that most college students take. I always loved
school. I was one of six children of working-class parents who were the
first generation off of southeastern Louisiana farms. My father was a
"working alcoholic" and my mother was a stay-at-home mom who had
an eighth-grade education. So, my Catholic elementary and high school

experience with African American nuns was my refuge. My teachers gave me the confidence to excel in most subjects. That, coupled with an extended family of courageous and nurturing Southern women, led me to believe that I could be whatever I wanted to be. Despite everything, I continue to feel that way, to be hopeful, but now with some deeper insight.

Elsa: My reasons for going into academe have to do with a series of haphazard and life-altering events. In 1984, I had been married for fourteen years, had three small children, and was working as a clerk typist for a law firm. In an effort to improve my secretarial skills, I started taking classes at a local community college. The small rural-agricultural area where I grew up was ninety percent Mexican, and very few students attended college. My low-income status enabled me to qualify for the Educational Opportunity Program, or EOP. Through EOP I met a Latino counselor who encouraged me to take general education courses as well as secretarial ones. I took his advice, and by the end of the first semester, I had done quite well. This Latino counselor was actually the first educator to tell me that I should think about getting an Associate of Art's degree and transferring to a four-year college. I thought about this for quite a long time but did not share this with my family. I recall thinking here I was thirty-two years old and with three kids. I thought perhaps my family would perceive that putting an education ahead of my husband and children was selfish.

Timing: Beginning to Live the Contradiction

Maria: My middle sister and I were at the right time at the right place. Shortly after immigrating to the United States, Norma and I were enrolled in that rural school for wealthy ranch children. I remember vividly the first day of school; this was probably my introduction to status, wealth, and institutional power. Mrs. M., the wife of my dad's boss, picked up my mom, sister, and me in her new Chevrolet to enroll us in school. Mrs. M. took us into the principal's office and made sure "everything was in place" for our schooling before she and my mom left. Everything did stay in place. My sister and I acquired English quickly and excelled in school, surpassing many of our wealthy peers in academics. Our timing could not have been better! As daughters of a farm worker, we received a top-notch public elementary school education that prepared us well for high school and later college. I continued to excel in high school and was awarded a scholarship to attend Wellesley College.

Mary: After high school I was awarded a four-year scholarship to a Catholic women's college in Los Angeles populated by the daughters of politicians and celebrities, the first "White" institution that I ever set foot in. The racial and class culture shock proved too much, so I left. I held clerical jobs until I reached age twenty-one and heard that police departments were looking for women to fill a "quota." At that time, the term *affirmative action* was not part of the popular lexicon, but policing agencies were coming under fire for not recruiting and hiring women. So, the opportunity arose whereby I could double my clerk's salary. I joined a policing agency as a law enforcement officer, where I remained for eighteen years. When I left I thought I was leaving behind a world where sexism and racism were pervasive. I was dead wrong.

As a first-generation college student, I did not have the benefit of going to my parents or extended family to ask them about the ins and outs of undergraduate or graduate school. So, my experience was truly a baptism of fire. There are things that are never mentioned in recruitment brochures but are nevertheless as real as the admission fees. Things such as the social isolation you feel as the "only one." Or being led to believe that your GRE scores were marginal when later investigation shows that your scores were in the top ten percent of a twenty-five-person cohort. Or sitting in a statistics classroom in which the instructor never makes eye contact with you, is rarely available during office hours, and urges you to "just get your master's and get out" because she does not feel you "get this stuff." Or turning down an offer to work with a White male professor whose anger at being rebuffed led him to tell me that the only place my research would get me was "a spot on *The Oprah Winfrey Show.*" (I could go on, but space does not permit.)

Elsa: By the end of the third semester, I was close to finishing my Associate of Art's degree, and I had also been on the dean's list for three semesters. At this point, I still had not made up my mind about transferring to a four-year institution. My college counselor sister-in-law had a friend who was a counselor/recruiter for the University of California. Her colleague came to my community college with financial aid forms and admissions applications. He conducted a workshop for all of the EOP students and subsequently had us fill out all of the necessary paperwork. About a month later, I received a letter informing me that I had been accepted and was expected to begin my classes that fall.

Duty: You Gotta Do What You Gotta Do

Maria: Part of why I succeeded in schools was that I was taught to figure out schools quickly and thus learned to function within these institutions effectively. After obtaining my B.A., I worked in elementary schools for several years and ended up at Stanford University, where I completed my doctorate in education. While I had accumulated more than twenty-four years of formal schooling, I knew little of the "tacit and informal cultures" within academe. Being a student in educational institutions was a bit different from being a member-player. All I knew was that I wanted to teach others and to help others discover themselves and the world through books, research, learning. I believe *demystifying* is the word used today to describe this phenomenon. Social responsibility became and has remained a priority in my personal and professional life. By social responsibility I mean a sense of altruism, or duty, to do my part in addressing and interrupting inequity, unfairness, injustice, and inhumanity in their various forms, particularly as they have affected members of the Mexican, Chicano community. That is, I attempt to pursue actively ways to undo our (Mexican) history of economic and political subordination. My motivation for entering academia was and has remained constant, clear, and unchanged as I write this. I saw the economic and human exploitation of my father and many other farm workers and quickly learned how knowledge is power and how knowledge and power can be used arbitrarily to rank, dehumanize, oppress, and control people.

For example, my father, like a majority of farm workers, was a monolingual Spanish speaker and had limited literacy skills in both Spanish and English. Because of this he had limited access to knowledge related to his rights as an employee, a taxpayer, and a resident of California. His boss was well aware of this condition of disempowerment that was grounded in my father's economic need to support his family and, thus, took advantage of this situation by exploiting my father (and others) by underpaying him for his labor, having him work eighteen-hour days under terrible working conditions, and providing no sick leave. Seeing my father come home exhausted with only enough time to eat, sleep a few hours, and then return to work began to politicize me. I would see my middle-class friends' parents who did not seem to work as hard, yet were paid more, and I began to ask myself many "why" questions: Why was my father treated differently, and given less respect than the middle-class parents of my friends? Why did he receive less pay for longer hours? Why did people value his work less when it was honest and physically demanding? Why was he treated differently because he did not speak English? I became conscious of the reality that society saw some people as having more of a right to a better quality of life, more respect, and more privilege than others.

I was privileged to see Cesar Chavez many times during his lifetime, but it was his appearance at a conference for migrant parents in San Jose, California, that is memorable because it helped me make a conscious decision about my role in the struggle for social justice. Chavez spoke of how everyone could make a contribution to *la causa* (the struggle). The fight for social justice is not just in the fields, he said. The Mexican community needs teachers, doctors—intellectuals. Our passport to liberation, respect, and power, Chavez said, is through books and knowledge. And we get this from education. As I listened to this powerful speaker, I experienced an epiphany about my role in the cause for social justice. I knew what I had to do: I would use my knowledge and education to interrupt social injustices. I returned to my work in schools with a more clearly defined goal about the "big picture" and shortly thereafter applied to Stanford University's doctoral program in education.

Mary: During my years in policing, I experienced the traumatic and sudden deaths of my mother, sister, and brother, all directly and indirectly caused by social forces beyond their control. In my women's studies and other social inequality courses, I began to understand my parents, my neighborhood, and my place as an African American woman in a White supremacist, patriarchal, and elitist society. It would have been almost impossible for my consciousness *not* to have been raised in these courses and for me *not* to make the obvious connections with my own life. When I read about the indigenous struggle in Guatemala described by Rigoberta Menchu, I saw my grandfather's struggle to sell his crops for the same price as the White farmers in Louisiana and the terror that the Ku Klux Klan instilled in that part of the country. When I read Memmi I began to place my own family within the context of the racial order not only in the South, but also in "desegregated" southern California and, indeed, the world. Gerda Lerner's exploration of African American women made me more fully understand how my mother, who had me at age seventeen, was overcome by so many social forces—her own farm upbringing; the Catholic Church; illiteracy; poverty; my father's abuse, brought about in part because of his frustration over not being able to provide for his family adequately—over which she felt powerless. Du Bois helped me to understand very well the nature of power and how, in the words of the ex-slave and abolitionist Frederick Douglass, "Power concedes nothing without a demand; it never has and it never will." Although I would like to say that, like Maria, I experienced an epiphany in these classes, my intellectual understanding of the nature of power came about gradually. Eventually, however, I resolved to spend the rest of my life through my teaching and research attempting to, as Ginsburg says, "ease the pain of living" for those who, like my mother, do not have the voice to articulate their suffering and sense of despair.

Elsa: I was brought up to keep moving forward no matter what. This is why I continue to do what I do. I also think about what would happen to many of my students if I were not here for them, what would become of them. Had it not been for some of those educators in my own life, I would not have been able to jump the numerous hurdles. Also, I only conduct research that is meaningful to me. My research interests are a reflection of what my grandmother and mother taught me. They taught me the value of collectivism and showed me by example that family and community come first. Whether it was a wedding, a funeral, or other social occasion, my mother and grandmother were the first to offer both instrumental and expressive assistance in the forms of food and money, a space in their homes, or a shoulder on which to cry. I primarily conduct research on issues that pertain to women and the minority community, with a focus on resolving some of these issues. I feel that I have come full circle, without having to compromise my values, heritage, and integrity. I plan to continue along the same tradition that was set so many years ago by women who had the fortitude of an army, the patience of Mother Teresa, and the gentleness of angels.

Interrogating White Academe: Something Is Wrong with This Picture

Maria: Admittedly, I believed in the big academic lie—"life, liberty, and the pursuit of knowledge for the common good"—as academe's purpose. Initially, I did not interrogate academe. I also believed (for a few months, anyway) the academy was a meritocratic institution. After all, I had been given a chance to succeed and I had. It did not take very long for me to experience how academe favored and protected only those intended to be there. It did not take long for me to begin to interrogate academe and its unjust practices.

Mary: My first and, thus far, only job in the academy is at a very diverse (in terms of the students) public university in southern California. Ours is a relatively small department, with four men (three White and one Native American) and six women (three White and one each Latina, Chinese American, and African American). I am compelled to speak about the atmosphere of this or any university that makes life very challenging for someone such as myself.

Elsa: During my first quarter as an undergraduate, I took a course titled "La Chicana" with a Chicana professor. This was the first time I had been able to take a class from a Chicana professor, because during the mid-1980s Chicano studies courses were rarely offered at my local community college. This course forever changed my life. I learned about the history of the Mexican and Chicano communities, and their numerous contributions to U.S. society. I started to realize the importance of getting actively involved in addressing socioeconomic and political issues within the Latino community. Before the quarter was over, the Chicana professor encouraged her students (mostly Latinas) to consider going on to graduate school. The following year I applied to the sociology department. A few months later I received a letter from the graduate advisor informing me that because of my low GRE scores, I was not admitted into the Ph.D. program. So, I enrolled in another graduate program for a year, during which time I took many of the graduate sociology courses. I knew that the sociology faculty rotated and took turns serving on the graduate committee. The year I applied for the graduate program, the committee consisted of several professors who had written letters of recommendation for me. I was accepted into the program, graduated four years later (1991), and received numerous job offers in several different states. Once I started teaching, my goal was to make a difference for minority students and the community.

Cumulative Effects: Living and Surviving the Lived Contradictions—Am I Loca or What?

Maria: I come from a family of survivors, but I never realized it would come to that in academia. Little did I know that teaching and surviving in academe would require more than mere preparation or desire. Little did I know I was entering one of the bastions of conservative ideology and practices—a far cry from a meritocracy working for the common good. Little did I know I was a member of one of the first groups of female non-White scholars with consciousness and social duty to jump these ivy walls of patriarchal, White power. Little did I know that my survival would depend on more than academic, intellectual competency. Little did I know that many of my colleagues (White women and male colleagues of color) would eventually forgo their social responsibility for their personal interest, ego massaging, and go so far as to suggest that "business as usual" is fair. Little did I know that receiving honors, distinctions, and privileges came at a big price—the loss of personal integrity, sanity, self, and community. I think I know a little more than I knew eight years ago. I know that one can survive in academe without having to sell one's soul. I also learned that "being a lived contradiction" is the consequence of these cumulative effects and not necessarily being *loca* (crazy).

Mary: The tenure process is especially grueling for women of color. As in most universities, we are evaluated on our teaching, publishing, and community service. Most of the women of color with whom I am in contact have stellar records for teaching and service. Publishing, over which we have little control, is altogether another matter. In the evaluation process, very few questions seem to be asked about teaching or service, except in my case someone who has much control over the process recently suggested, "Stop all that extraneous stuff [community service] and get more publications under your belt."

As others have noted (Turner & Myers, 2000, p. 26) many faculty of color explore "minority issues" in their research, which is not considered legitimate, especially if that research is qualitative. Oral histories, ethnographies, and case studies, especially if these are done within a feminist framework, are not given validity as quantitative research. Thus, it is difficult to publish in the mainstream, a fact that adds fuel to the denial-of-tenure fire.

Even feminist journals can be disappointing. I once submitted a paper on the racism and sexism experienced by a group of African American women in policing to a well-regarded women's studies journal. Editorial remarks focused solely on the sexism aspects of the paper, ignoring altogether the interaction of sex and race. Was this because the reviewers knew little about race? Or was the journal only interested in the gender discrimination? Conversely, journals whose focus is race rarely wish to publish articles dealing with the intersectionality of gender and class.

Elsa: In reflecting back on my early years as a professor, I do not think I realized how brutal and hostile the academic environment could be. Over a period of time, it became clear that in order for me to survive and succeed I would have to rely on my family/community support networks and on my religiosity/spirituality (just as I had in graduate school) as well as develop some new strategic resistance methods. For the first two years of my career, I was employed at a small liberal arts, private four-year institution. It was an extremely conservative university, and I found it difficult to get to know many of the faculty. Some of the faculty were very uncomfortable around me, and I especially sensed their discomfort in the faculty dining room.

I decided to seek other employment and in 1993 was hired by the CSU system. In the past few years, I have found that working as a woman of color has not gotten any easier. Although I was promoted to full professor in 2002, there have been many times when I have wondered what my life would have been like if I were not a woman of color. The level of stress that women are subjected to in academe is tremendous and has long-term consequences. About two years ago I had major surgery. I attribute my illness to the daily stressors and demands placed on me as a woman in academe. Research and my own personal experiences indicate that women—especially women of color—have several work shifts. Women tend to be responsible for juggling numerous duties such as engaging in intimate relationships, caring for children, caring for extended family (in some cases), teaching, conducting research, providing community and university service, and all of the emotional work that comes with all of these responsibilities. In addition to all of these tasks, women of color have to contend with the interconnected realms of racism, classism, and sexism. When you consider the cumulative effects on the emotional status of women of color, it is amazing that most of us can continue to have a positive outlook on life.

Most of my White colleagues—especially White males—have never had to think about the impact of their actions on their personal and professional life—things such as making insensitive comments while I am standing next to them. There have been many occasions when I have felt that I was invisible. Other examples include having to deal with what I call "toxic" individuals, whose only goal in life is to make it to the top, and to hell with any semblance of civility. I know that if I had behaved in such a hostile and demeaning manner, I would not have been granted tenure.

Wholeness as Humanity: Don't Make Me Over

Maria: As I enter my eighth year in academe, I have resolved that the challenges of my attempts to humanize academe are part of what to expect in the struggle for change. It continues to be a daily struggle—from committee meetings to informal encounters with colleagues who, after eight years, mistake me for the other Chicana colleague in my department. I think of the struggles faced by those before me, and how they faced racism, sexism, and classism and were basically dehumanized and exploited. My ancestors and others before me did not lose hope. I continue to live, interrogate, be hopeful, and practice hope. I continue because oppressed people cannot afford to lose hope and because I realize that the portrait is not mine alone (Memmi, 1965).

Mary: Like so many others, I find myself constantly wondering, as Nelson (1993) does, if I can be simultaneously an African American woman *and* a college professor. Or must I shed who I am at the front door of the university? I find myself constantly tightrope walking, trying to balance who I am with what is expected of me. Am I expected to act, sound, and respond like a White male? It appears so. While I reject this model, I have found that it takes a real sense of equilibrium to maintain that balance and to get to the other side with my sanity intact. I have been able to maintain that balance of who I am with what others want me to be because of my family and friends, a strong sense of social justice, and a spirituality whose roots go way back to the Catholicism I practiced as a child and young adult. That combination has literally saved my life.

Elsa: So why don't I just throw in the towel? Why don't I just decide each day what kind of day it will be? What is very evident to me is that had it not been for my family (especially my mother, who recently passed away), my spirituality, my colleagues, and my students, I might have given up a long time ago. I am propelled forward when I think of the courage it took for my mother to migrate to the United States while leaving behind two small children. She did not know anyone in the United States. But her family was destitute and she had to do something. She came to California and worked picking cotton, lemons, oranges, and grapes; taking care of other people's children and cleaning their houses; sewing; and whatever else she could do to earn money to send back home. I do not ever remember my mother complaining about having to work these menial jobs at odd hours. It is for her, my family, my students, and my community that I remain.

Hope in Academia: The Power of Centeredness

The data presented here clearly illustrate that race and gender have profound consequences for women of color in the academy. We have attempted to embed our voices within the context of a set of social theories that liberates us from traditional ways of doing and thinking. The academy was never meant to accommodate people like us, either as students or as professors. Thus, women of color as outsiders within the academy have not had the same experience as White men, White women, and even men of color. The interactive effects of race and gender have consequences for women on every rung of the economic ladder, even for those of us who have seemingly "made it" and who study these phenomena. Bowles and Gintis, Memmi, hooks, and others allow us to illuminate our experiences and those of our sisters in the academy as we link macrophenomena with our everyday experiences.

What, then, are some of the practical strategies for the institution and the individual for addressing the differential treatment of female scholars of color?

- Genuinely speak to issues related to discrimination of all scholars.
- Use quantitative data to capture the picture of the reality of the university in regard to salaries, promotion, and tenure of university faculty—locally, regionally, and nationally.
- Encourage supportive networks with like-minded colleagues.
- Name traditions of exclusion in academia.
- Do not keep it secret. Dialogue with students and community about practices of discrimination and the treatment of faculty at *their* university.
- Identify and understand sources of power within the institution.
- Learn and name and discuss the tacit, unspoken rules of the academy.
- Choose your battles wisely.
- Do not accept the disempowerment that says, for example, "You do not belong here."
- Remember to laugh!

Ours is a universal story, grounded in our histories and personal narratives as we recount our many border crossings. We survive, and some of us even experience a "bittersweet success' in academia, despite the many obstacles in our paths. Much of our hope for humanizing the academy begins in understanding the ideology grounding its everyday practices. We have used multiple perspectives in painting a picture of the academy as a way to provide multiple hopes for its improvement as well. This can only lead to a better environment for *every entity* at the academy—faculty, students, staff, and administration.

References

Aguirre, A. (2000). *Women and minority faculty in the academic workplace* (ASHE-ERIC Higher Education Report No. 6). Washington, DC: The George Washington University, Graduate School of Education and Human Development.

Aguirre, A., Jr., & Martinez, R. O. (1993). *Chicanos in higher education: Issues and dilemmas for the 21st century* (ASHE-ERIC Higher Education Report No. 3).

Washington, DC: The George Washington University, Graduate School of Education and Human Development.

Aisenberg, N., & Harrington, M. (1988). *Women of academe: Outsiders in the sacred grove.* Amherst: University of Massachusetts Press.

Bowles, S., & Gintis, H. (1976). *Schooling in capitalist America: Educational reform and the contradictions of economic life.* New York: Basic Books.

Bradburn, E. M., & Sikora, A. C. (2002). *Gender and racial/ethnic differences in salary and other characteristics of postsecondary faculty: Fall 1998* (NCES 2002-170). Project Officer: Linda J. Zimbler. Washington, DC: National Center for Education Statistics, U.S. Department of Education.

Gmelch, W., Lovrich, N., & Wilke, P. (1984). Stress in academe: A national perspective. *Research in Higher Education, 20,* 477–490.

Gmelch, W., Wilke, P., & Lovrich, N. (1986). Dimensions of stress among university faculty: Factor-analytic results from a national study. *Research in Higher Education, 24,* 266–286.

Hagedorn, I. (1995, November 2–5). *Wage equity and female faculty job satisfaction: The role of wage differentials in a job satisfaction casual model.* Paper presented at the annual meeting of the Association for the Study of Higher Education, Orlando, FL.

Harvey, W. B. (2001). *Minorities in high education 2000–2001.* Washington, DC: American Council on Education.

hooks, bell. (1984). *Feminist theory: From margin to center.* Boston: South End Press.

James, J., & Farmer, R. (1993). *Spirit, space and survival: African American women in (white) academe.* New York: Routledge.

Latina Feminist Group (2002). *Telling to live: Latina feminist testimonios.* Durham, NC: Duke University Press.

McMillen, I. (1987, February 4). Job-related tension and anxiety taking a toll among employees in academe's stress factories. *Chronicle of Higher Education,* pp. A1, A10–A12.

Memmi, A. (1965). *The colonizer and the colonized.* Boston: Beacon Press.

Menges, R., & Exum, W. (1983). Barriers to the progress of women and minority faculty. *Journal of Higher Education, 54,* 123–144.

Montero-Sieburth, M. (1996). An inquiry into the experience of Latinas in academia. *New England Journal of Public Safety Policy, 11,* 65–97.

Nelson, J. (1993). *Volunteer slavery.* Chicago: The Noble Press.

Niemann, Y., & Dovidio, J. (1998). Relationship of solo status, academic rank, and perceived distinctiveness to job satisfaction of racial/ethnic minorities. *Journal of Applied Psychology, 83,* 55–71.

Pfeffer, J., & Langton, N. (1993). The effect of wage dispersion on satisfaction, productivity, and working collaboratively: Evidence from college and university faculty. *Administrative Science Quarterly, 38,* 382–407.

Rai, K. B., & Critzer, J. W. (2000). *Affirmative action and the university: Race ethnicity and gender in higher education employment.* Lincoln: University of Nebraska Press.

Rausch, D., Ortiz, B., Douthitt, R., & Reed, I. (1989). The academic revolving door: Why do women get caught? *CUPA Journal, 40,* 1–16.

Reyes, M., & Halcon, J. (1991). Practices of the academy: Barriers to access to Chicano academics. In P. Altbach & K. Lomotey (Eds.), *The racial crisis in American higher education* (pp. 167–186). Albany, NY: SUNY Press.

Smith, E., Anderson, J., & Lovrich, N. (1995). The multiple sources of workplace stress among land-grant university faculty. *Research in Higher Education, 36,* 261–282.

Turner, C. S. V., & Myers, S. L., Jr. (2000). *Faculty of color in academe: Bittersweet success.* Needham Heights, MA: Allyn & Bacon.

Weber, L. (2001). *Understanding race, class, gender, and sexuality.* New York: McGraw-Hill.

Young, J. (1984). Black women faculty in academia: Strategies for career leadership development. *Educational and Psychological Research, 4,* 133–145.

Additional Resources

Balderrama, M. V. (2002). *Color, class and consciousness: Women in academia.* Roundtable presentation at Annual Pacific Sociological Association, Vancouver, BC.

Balderrama, M. (in press). Shooting the messenger: The consequences of practicing an ideology of social justice. In L. I. Bartolome (Ed.), *The significance of teacher ideology in urban education: Naming the unnamed in urban education.*

Balderrama, M. V., Texeira, M. T., & Valdez, E. (2003). *I am struck by my lived contradiction.* Paper presented at the National Conference on Race and Ethnicity in American Higher Education (NCORE), New Orleans.

Bartolomé, L. I., & Balderrama, M. V. (2001). The need for educators with political and ideological clarity: Providing our children with the best. In M. L. Reyes & J. J. Halcón (Eds.), *The best for our children: Critical perspectives on literacy for Latin students.* New York: Teachers College Press

Fontaine, D., & Greenlee, S. (1993). Black women: Double solos in the workplace. *Western Journal of Black Studies, 17,* 121–125.

Freire, P. (1994). *Pedagogy of hope.* New York: Continuum Press.

Geok-Lin Lim, S., & Herrera-Sobeka, M. (2000). *Power, race and gender in academe.* New York: The Modern Language Association.

Goldberger, N., Tarule, J., Clinchy, B., & Belenky, M. (Eds.). (1996). *Knowledge, difference and power.* New York: Basic Books.

hooks, bell. (1994). *Teaching to transgress: Education as the practice of freedom.* New York: Routledge.

Martin Roland, J. (2000). *Coming of age in academia. Rekindling women's hopes and reforming the academy.* New York: Routledge.

Smith, D. G., et al. (1996). *Achieving faculty diversity: Debunking the myths.* Washington, DC: Association of American Colleges and Universities.

PART THREE

WORDS OF WOMANHOOD WISDOM: VOICES OF SENIOR FACULTY WHO ARE WOMEN OF COLOR

18

CRITICAL RACE FEMINIST FOREMOTHERING

Multiplicities in the Post 9/11 World

Adrien Katherine Wing

The Author

After graduation from Princeton, Professor Wing earned her Master of Arts degree in African studies from UCLA. While at Stanford Law School, she served as an editor of the *Stanford Journal of International Law*, as an intern with the United Nations Council on Namibia, and as Southern Africa Task Force director of the National Black Law Students Association. At graduation, she was awarded the Stanford African Student Association Prize.

Prior to joining the University of Iowa College of Law faculty in 1987, Professor Wing spent five years in practice in New York City specializing in international law issues regarding Africa, the Middle East, and Latin America. She also served as a representative to the United Nations for the National Conference of Black Lawyers.

Professor Wing has been a consultant to the United Nations, served as a constitutional advisor to the African National Congress for several years, organized an election-observer delegation to South Africa, and taught at the University of Western Cape for six summers. She has also served as an advisor to the Palestinian Legislative Council relative to Palestine's future constitutional options and as an advisor to the Eritrean Ministry of Justice on human rights treaties. Most recently she advised the Rwandan Constitutional Commission on postgenocide constitution.

Professor Wing has held several leadership positions in the American Society of International Law and is a life member of the New York–based Council on Foreign Relations. Additionally, she has served as chair of the International Section of the National Conference of Black Lawyers; as a member of the TransAfrica Forum Scholars Council; and on the board of directors of the Iowa Peace Institute and the

Iowa City Foreign Relations Council, as well as the Stanford Law School Board of Visitors. In 1999, Iowa governor Vilsack appointed Professor Wing to the Commission on the African American Prison Population. In 2002, she was chair of the Association of American Law Schools Minority Section, and during the fall of that year, she was a visiting professor at the University of Michigan Law School.

Professor Wing is director of the Law School's summer abroad program in Arcachon, France. She specializes in both U.S. and international law and has published in such areas as constitutionalism in Namibia, South Africa, and Palestine; Critical Race Feminism; U.S. gangs; legal decision making in the Palestinian *intifada*; rape in Bosnia; and women's rights in Palestine, South Africa, and Black America. Author of more than 70 publications, she is also the editor of *Critical Race Feminism: A Reader,* 2nd ed. (New York University Press, 2003) and *Global Critical Race Feminism: An International Reader* (New York University Press, 2000).

Professor Wing presently teaches constitutional law, Critical Race Theory, human rights, law in the Muslim world, comparative law, and comparative constitutional law and has taught race, racism and American law, law in radically different cultures, and the international and domestic legal aspects of AIDS. She is, in addition, a member of the University of Iowa's interdisciplinary African studies faculty and lectures in the undergraduate African curriculum.

Professor Wing is a member of the New York Bar and currently serves on the board of the U.S. Association of Constitutional Law.

As the editor of two anthologies bearing the name Critical Race Feminism (CRF), I was delighted to be asked to participate in writing this volume. The choice of the term "Critical Race Feminism" to describe an emphasis on women of color was a conscious one, indicating its links to critical legal studies (CLS), Critical Race Theory (CRT), and feminism. Professor Richard Delgado, a CRT founding father then teaching at the University of Colorado Law School, used the term CRF in the first edition of his reader *Critical Race Theory: The Cutting Edge* (Delgado, 1995). I subsequently found an article written in 1993 that also uses the term (Barnard, 1993). CRF has become possible because a token but growing number of women of color became beneficiaries of affirmative action beginning in the late 1960s and managed to trickle up into the legal profession and, ultimately, the legal academy. By the early 1990s, there were several hundred of these women. They currently constitute 6.1 percent of the 9,300 law teachers.[1]

Some of these women began to write about themselves and the plight of their less-well-off sisters, who would never have the benefit of tertiary education, much less join the ranks of the professorate. They were inspired not only by CLS and CRT, but by various kinds of feminism, including feminist jurisprudence and Black feminism, or womanism, developed in the social sciences. It is most gratifying to see this volume being edited and containing the works primarily of women in the social sciences.

My idea for an anthology focusing on women of color stems back to 1991, when the Berkeley *Women's Law Journal* devoted an entire issue to the views of Black female law professors. As a relatively new young academic who contributed to the volume, I was struck by the beauty, strength, and power of the words of my sisters, words that had never been gathered together in a single place. The publication of the issue was especially timely because it coincided with the Clarence Thomas Supreme Court confirmation hearings. I realized that University of Oklahoma law professor Anita Hill, a witness in the hearings, was the first Black female law professor ever thrust into the national spotlight, and the American public, White and Black, did not know what to make of her. She was not a mammy, a welfare queen, a tragic mulatto, a sex siren, an athlete, or any other stereotype of a Black woman. There was no national precedent for dealing with or understanding the worldview of a Black female law scholar and teacher. The intense denigration and vilification of her stellar character wounded many of us deeply. We saw ourselves in her place, regarded as inherently unbelievable and untrustworthy, despite years of hard-won educational and professional accomplishments. David Brock (1993), a conservative White male author who attacked Hill's integrity in *The Real Anita Hill: The Untold Story*, finally admitted the falsity of his work.

University of Pennsylvania law professor Lani Guinier (now at Harvard Law School) was also vilified in the media a few years after Hill when President Bill Clinton, a personal friend, refused to support her nomination for head of the U.S. Justice Department Civil Rights Division. I was overcome with rage and pain as another accomplished Black woman was transmogrified into a "quota queen," her legal theories twisted beyond recognition in the media.

After these two events, I felt compelled to bring together the legal writings of women of color that focused on their plight, so that they could speak for themselves. Additionally, there were men of color and Whites who had also chosen to write on women of color. The views of these scholars are generally unknown to the American reading public, because most of their work appears only in law journals, which are not readily accessible to the non-lawyer. Furthermore, even busy lawyers dealing with the concerns of day-to-day law practice have no time to peruse law journals outside of their areas of specialization. I wanted to expand the topics covered in the Berkeley *Women's Law Journal* and bring together voices ranging from the nationally well-known Anita Hill and Lani Guinier, to women who are prominent within legal academia, such as Anita Allen, Regina Austin, Kimberlé Crenshaw, Angela Harris, Emma Coleman Jordan, Mari Matsuda, Dorothy Roberts, and Patricia Williams. Moreover, I felt it was important to go beyond the existing anthologies on race and gender, which tended to feature a very small group of well-known women, to include promising young voices as well.

The first edition of the CRF anthology came out in 1997, from New York University Press, and was very well received (Wing, 1997). I have met people, literally all over the world, who have used portions or the entire book as a classroom reference. I have met judges as far away as South Africa who have cited it in their opinions. In the years since its publication, the number of CRF articles has grown enormously. Some scholars mainly writing in the CRF area have been granted tenure, and law or graduate students frequently e-mail me wanting advice about articles they are writing on CRF topics. More textbooks may have citations or even a brief section of CRF works. There have even been two national symposia on CRF, one at the University of Iowa and the other at the University of San Diego. A second anthology that I edited, *Global Critical Race Feminism: An International Reader*, published in 2000, also from New York University Press, expanded on issues raised in the last unit of the original collection, embracing strands from international and comparative law, global feminism, and postcolonial theory as well (Wing, 2000). The encouraging responses to both readers led to my editing a second edition of *Critical Race Feminism* in 2003.[2]

When asked to contribute to the present volume as a senior woman in the academy, I was stunned. Where have the years gone? I have been teaching close to 20 years! In this time, I have, among other things, accumulated more than 80 publications; developed several innovative courses; directed a summer-abroad program in France; lectured in a number of countries; advised three nations on their constitutions (South Africa, Palestine, and Rwanda); served on countless committees; made more than 200 panel presentations and speeches; been a board member of local, national, and international organizations; and mentored countless students. In many of these endeavors, I have been one of the very few Blacks and one of the few women. I am even more proud of the fact that I have raised fine sons and currently maintain a personal relationship with an African American man that has lasted for nearly a decade. As any Black woman will tell you, a good Black man is hard to find, especially one willing to deal with a law professor partner!

I have seen the difficulties raised by compounded race and gender discrimination as well as personal situations that prevent some women of color from finishing the terminal degree, getting a full-time tenure-track job, or meeting ever-shifting tenure standards. I have seen how many women and people of color who do get tenure never get promoted to full professor. I have seen how many women in their struggle to achieve professional success have not been able to combine it with having a spouse/partner or family, even though they wished to do so. Through a combination of hard work (often 80–90 hours a week), luck, divine intervention, and the tremendous commitment of my family and supportive colleagues, I am not only a full professor, but a member of that even much more elite category—a chaired professor holding the Bessie Dutton Murray Distinguished Professor of Law at the University of Iowa College of Law. Even though I am not yet 50 years old, I have been the senior Black woman at this university for many years and the only chair holder.

So from this rarified vantage point, what can I contribute to the important scholarly project represented by this anthology? I decided to call this chapter "Critical Race Feminist Foremothering: Multiplicities in the Post 9/11 World." I am reminded of Du Bois's famous prophetic line from more than a century ago, in 1903—that the problem of the twentieth century would be the problem of the color line (Du Bois, 1904). Living to the eve of the Civil Rights March on Washington in 1963, Du Bois saw how right he was. To take his assessment to the next level, I would reprise his refrain for the new century and state that the problems of this century will continue to be race and ethnicity, but also compounded with a heightened awareness of multiple identities such as gender, class, disability, and sexual orientation. These were not categories that the early twentieth-century theorists contemplated in much detail. Moreover, the events of September 11, 2001, have brought the salience of identities such as nationality, religion, language, culture, and political ideology to the forefront as well.[3]

It is important that we in the academy, who represent relatively privileged people who have been multiply discriminated against in the United States on the basis of both our race and our gender, push to expand the boundaries of scholarly discourse to embrace the complexity and multiplicity of discrimination that affects not only us, but other people of color around the world. For example, when my sons and I travel abroad, we are often mistaken nowadays for Arabs or Muslims. My partner, James, who is a dark-brown-skinned Christian African American, often wears a *kufi*, or skull cap, to express his cultural affinity for Africa. He is always taken for a Muslim, although not an Arab. Sadly, I have told my NYU student son, who can phenotypically pass for Arab, that he has to be careful when flying alone so that he will not be mistaken for an Arab. Dressing in the popular ghetto-styled baggy pants, coupled with cornrowing his hair and using an Ebonics dialect, helps ensure that he is not viewed as an Arab. Of course, when he lands in New York, his failure to be able to hail a cab indicates he is clearly seen as a Black and too risky to pick up.

Thus, those who merely look like Arabs or Muslims, like my family, may be racially profiled on that basis. The double group can thus be considered larger than the numbers of actual members. According to one commentator, there may be 7 million Arabs; 8 million Muslims; 1.6 million South Asians, Latinos, and African Americans who could look Arab; and probably at least 10 million people (Kang, 2002), which I think is a vast underestimate of the numbers of the Blacks, Latinos, and some Asians, who could pass as Arab. One African American radio personality stated that French citizen Zacharias Moussaoui, native of Morocco, who may have been the twentieth September 11 hijacker, looks like a brother from around the way (Pitts, 2002).

The two overlapping and socially constructed-as-synonymous groups, Arabs and Muslims, have come to be regarded in some of the negative ways that have historically characterized African Americans. While Arabs and Muslims are often stereotyped as dangerous, evil, sneaky, primitive, and untrustworthy, much as Blacks are, the criminality has a twist—they are considered potential or actual terrorists. They are forever foreign, disloyal, and imminently threatening,[4] whether they are citizens or not.

They are subject to vicious stereotypes in films and television that would not be tolerated if used to characterize other groups (Akram & Johnson, 2002). For example, Jack Shaheen (2001) surveyed a number of movies and found the following characterizations of Arabs and Muslims: assholes, bastards, camel-dicks, pigs, devil-worshipers, jackals, rats, rag-heads, towel-heads, scum-buckets, sons-of-dogs, buzzards of the jungle, sons-of-whores, sons-of-unnamed-goats, and sons-of-she-camels. It is difficult to imagine the movie industry applying these sorts of labels to Blacks or Jews today.

In this post-9/11 world, it is necessary that those who have tenure in countries such as the United States use their bully pulpit to speak out and reach out to address local, national, and global injustice whether it be directed against women of color or African Americans or Arabs or Muslims, whether it be directed against people who look like us or those who do not. CRT and CRF provide a way to do this, because they are concerned not only with theory, but with praxis, the combination of theory and practice.

For me as a law professor, praxis has been as varied as assisting clients, drafting legislation, serving on bar committees, designing innovative legal strategies, joining in practical coalitions, and mentoring a student. I have engaged in praxis that meant serving on a nonprofit board, supporting a candidate, doing op-ed pieces, making a speech, or sponsoring a speaker.

As an extended example of praxis, I became critically interested as a mother and professor in the treatment of Black men in the criminal justice system. In the early 1990s, my interest manifested itself in exploring issues related to gangs. I studied conceptual issues related to gang theory, particularly as affecting ethnic minority males. I determined that I needed to get beyond theories developed predominantly by White male social science academics in ivory towers to understand the reality of Black gang life, and then design culturally appropriate strategies.

My research led me to former gang members of Los Angeles who were dealing directly with preventive and rehabilitative solutions to the gang problem. Through them, I discovered Amer-I-Can, a self-esteem curriculum started by former Hall of Fame football player and current actor and activist Jim Brown. After studying the program's effectiveness, I became involved as a national consultant. I went through facilitator training to teach the curriculum; brought former gang members to interact with law students in Iowa; took law students from Iowa to Los Angeles to meet with gang members there; arranged for Jim Brown to visit Iowa and other states; sold the curriculum for use and supervised programs in Des Moines, Iowa, and New Orleans, Louisiana; wrote congressional testimony on preventive and rehabilitative approaches to the gang problem; drafted a former gang member's autobiography; made numerous speeches; and served on the Iowa gubernatorial commission on African Americans in the prison population. I ended up engaging with various other activists on the gang issue, including scholars; gang members; ex-convicts; congresspersons; state representatives and staffers; executive branch policy makers; cultural and religious community activists; federal and state law enforcement, including then attorney general Janet Reno and then FBI director Louis Freeh; not-for-profit service providers such as the YMCA; potential corporate contributors; professional athletes; and entertainers.

Assessing several years of experiences, I realized that I had not sufficiently explored the roles of women with respect to gangs, whereas my other scholarly interests were examining culturally relevant feminisms. So I did additional research into gang theories related to women, made some speeches and panel presentations, and wrote scholarly articles.[5] Needless to say, these activities were highly educational for my students, as well as personally and professionally transformative for me and even my entire family.[6]

On the global level, I have been very involved with international praxis issues for nearly 30 years. Initially, most of this work involved South Africa under apartheid. In addition to the traditional scholarly research trips and publications, I made numerous speeches, joined demonstrations, organized legal delegations to the region, sponsored children, joined boards, represented a legal organization at the United Nations, assisted with the first post-apartheid constitution, and participated in media interviews. A large part of my work involved trying to explain South Africa to American audiences, especially Black Americans. Linking issues of race discrimination in the United States to South African apartheid was relatively easy for Black and other progressive people to understand. Because I have also been involved in Middle Eastern issues for more than 20 years, I have engaged in the same types of praxis.

On the "personal is political" level, my praxis includes remembering that we as women of color are the nurturers of most children of color. I have chosen to mother several Black young men in addition to my biological sons, and to assist many, many young men and women. In order for these children to have a future, I wish to give them hope—a vision that someone loves them and thinks they are worthy in a world that would rather they vanish. So no matter how depressed I become, I cannot give up hope—for their sake.

I have involved my children in my praxis as well. For example, in 1996, two sons accompanied me for six weeks when I was an independent contractor hired by the United States Agency for International Development to assist the Palestinian Legislative Council with the Basic Law. It was supposed to be a constitution for the autonomy period of the Oslo Accords that would have ended in 1999. Unfortunately, the Basic Law was not signed until 2002 and has remained a dead letter owing to the continued political impasse. Nevertheless, things appeared very hopeful back in 1996 on our trip. My children met high government officials, stayed in physicians' homes and fancy hotels, and attended grand receptions, but they also played in squalid Gaza Strip refugee camps with children whose eyes held only pain. They floated in the Dead Sea as tourists but also felt the fear that comes from going through Israeli military checkpoints. They ate at fancy seafood restaurants but saw malnourished families who lived 12 in one room. Because we all looked as if we could be Palestinians, everyone treated us as members of their families. I told the children that they should be proud African Americans, but that I was also raising them as citizens of the world with global responsibilities. Needless to say, this trip and others enabled them to gain a greater appreciation of their privileged position in life as Americans, even though they were Black ones. They even appeared to be proud of their mom for her role in helping a nation on the road to self-determination.

It was not until many years later that I learned the profound effect of those experiences on one of my sons. Ché-Cabral was applying to college and let me read a college essay. It was about Palestine in 1996, and how much the episode had affected him in deciding to pursue a career in filmmaking and social justice. I was stunned as I remembered how his experiences watching me write law review articles had made him decide that film was a medium that could reach millions of people, rather than a few professors or students. I realized that my meager attempts at praxis on the professional/personal level could result in my child taking his life to a whole new level of contribution.

Juggling the multiplicity of hats that I wear as Black female, chaired law professor, international lawyer, social activist, mother, and partner is exhausting, but ultimately rewarding. Whenever I get especially tired, I draw strength from my foremothers and forefathers, including my father, the late Dr. John Wing, Jr., and my mother, Katherine Pruitt Wing. I keep mementoes of my heroes and sheroes in my home and office, including Paul Robeson, Josephine Baker, Cornell West, Frida Kahlo, Edward Said, Angela Davis, Albie Sachs, Patricia Williams, Derrick Bell, Anita Hill, Ronald Noble, and Lani Guinier. Their auras surround me and nurture me. So when my little grandson calls me Granny Adrien, I am ready to face another day.

References

Akram, S. M., & Johnson, K. R. (2002). Race, civil rights, and immigration law after September 11, 2001: The targeting of Arabs and Muslims, *NYU Annual Survey of American Law, 58*:295, 303–311.

Barnard, A. L. (1993). The application of Critical Race Feminism to the anti-lynching movement: Black women's fight against race and gender ideology, 1892–1920, 3 *UCLA Women's Law Journal, 1.*

Brock, D. (1993). *The real Anita Hill: The untold story.* New York: Free Press.

Delgado, R. (Ed.). (1995). *Critical race theory: The cutting edge.* Philadelphia: Temple University Press.

Du Bois, W. E. B. (1903). *The Souls of Black folk.*

Kang, J. (2002). Thinking through internment, 9. *Asian Law Journal, 195,* 197–198.

Pitts, L., Jr. (2002, July 5). Hassles of airport security worth the inconvenience, *Houston Chronicle.*

Shaheen, J. G. (2001). *Reel bad Arabs: How Hollywood vilifies a people.* New York: Olive Branch Press.

Wing, A. K. (Ed.). (1997). *Critical Race Feminism: A reader.* New York: New York University Press.

Wing, A. K. (Ed.). (2000). *Global Critical Race Feminism: An international reader.* New York: New York University Press.

Endnotes

1. See American Association of Law Schools, Table 1A: All Faculty in the 2000–2001 Directory of Law Teachers at www.aals.org/statistics/T1A.htm (accessed January 31, 2004).

2. A portion of the aforementioned material is drawn from the introduction to *Critical Race Feminism: A Reader,* 2nd ed., ed. Adrien Katherine Wing (New York University, 2003).

3. Most of the paragraph is drawn from the introduction to *Critical Race Feminism: A Reader,* 2nd ed.

4. Natsu Taylor Saito, "Symbolism under Siege: Japanese American Redress and the 'Racing' of Arab Americans as 'Terrorists,'" *Asian Law Journal* (2001), *12* (analyzing treatment of Arabs as a distinctive "race" and stereotyping them as terrorists with negative immigration consequences).

5. See Adrien Katherine Wing and Christine Willis, "Critical Race Feminism: Black Women and Gangs," *Iowa Journal of Gender, Race & Justice, 141* (1997). This article was anthologized in a number of sources: see "Sisters in the Hood: Beyond Bloods and Crips," in *Critical Race Feminism: A Reader,* 1st ed., ed. Adrien Katherine Wing (New York University Press, 1997), 243; "Black Women and Gangs," in *Unfinished Liberation: Policing, Detention & Prisons,* ed. Joy James (St. Martin's Press, 2000), 94; "Critical Race Feminism: Black Women in Gangs," in *Understanding Gangs in America,* ed. Rebecca Peterson (Prentice-Hall, 2003); "Black Women and Gangs," in *States of Confinement: Policing, Detention and Prisons,* ed. Joy James (Palgrave, 2002), 94.

6. Most of the material on gangs is drawn from Adrien Katherine Wing, "Civil Rights in the Post 9-11 World: Critical Race Praxis, Coalition Building, and the War on Terrorism," *Louisiana Law Review* (2003).

19

A NUYORICAN IN THE ACADEMY

Lessons Learned

Sonia Nieto

The Author

Sonia Nieto is professor of language, literacy, and culture in the School of Education, University of Massachusetts, Amherst. For more than 36 years, she has taught students at all levels from elementary grades through graduate school. Her research focuses on multicultural education and on the education of Latinos, immigrants, and students of diverse cultural and linguistic backgrounds. Her books include *Affirming Diversity: The Sociopolitical Context of Multicultural Education,* 4th ed. (2004); *The Light in Their Eyes: Creating Multicultural Learning Communities* (1999); *Puerto Rican Students in U.S. Schools,* an edited volume (2000); and *What Keeps Teachers Going?* (2003). She has also published dozens of book chapters and articles in such journals as *Educational Leadership, The Harvard Educational Review, Multicultural Education,* and *Theory into Practice.*

Professor Nieto serves on several national advisory boards that focus on educational equity and social justice, including Facing History and Ourselves and Educators for Social Responsibility. She has received many awards for her scholarship, advocacy, and activism, including the 1989 Human and Civil Rights Award from the Massachusetts Teachers Association, the 1996 Teacher of the Year Award from the Hispanic Educators of Massachusetts, and the 1997 Multicultural Educator of the Year Award from the National Association for Multicultural Education. From 1998 to 2000, she was an Annenberg Institute senior fellow, and in May 1999, she received an honorary doctorate in humane letters from Lesley College in Cambridge, Massachusetts. In 2000, she was awarded a month-long residency at the Bellagio Center in Italy. More recently, she was named to the *Críticas Journal* Hall of Fame as the 2003 Spanish-Language Community Advocate of the Year.

Professor Nieto is married to Angel Nieto, a former teacher and author of children's books, and they have two daughters and eight grandchildren.

In 1972, at the age of 29, I received my first offer of employment at an institution of higher learning. I was both thrilled and terrified. Little in my background had prepared me for this turn of events. As a Puerto Rican working-class child of parents whose formal education was scant at best, I knew neither the rules of the game in the academy nor how to prepare adequately for a faculty position, and I had to learn quickly. That was more than 30 years ago. As it turns out, I have spent nearly all my professional life in higher education. It has been a fabulous journey, certainly not without its challenges, but exhilarating nevertheless. Higher education has given me the opportunity to learn, to grow, and to find my voice. At times, it has provoked my anger and disappointment. My identities, both personal and professional, have undergone many changes since that day in 1972.

In the past 30 years, I have forged an identity as both a Nuyorican woman and a scholar and academic, a combination some would find improbable. (Needless to say, I have other identities as well, but these are the two on which I focus here.) It is with this lens into the development of identity that I write on the joys and dilemmas of being a Puerto Rican/Nuyorican in the academy. In what follows, I briefly describe the process of each, explaining how they are intertwined. I end with a number of lessons learned and with what I hope will be helpful advice for young women of color in the academy.

Forging a Nuyorican Identity

After having lived in the United States since her early twenties, when the Puerto Rican activist and scholar Antonia Pantoja returned to Puerto Rico some 40 years later, to her surprise, she discovered that she no longer neatly fit into the definition of "Puerto Rican," as she once had. She moved back to the United States about a decade after her return to Puerto Rico, and she lived the last few years of her life in New York City, once again engaged in activism and community work. At the very end of her memoir (Pantoja, 2002), released just days before her death, Antonia revealed that it was only after returning to live in New York City that she was able to answer the question, "Where is my home?"—a question that had plagued her for many years. "I now know," she confided, "that home is New York City. I have returned and resumed my work in my community with old friends and new friends. *I am a Nuyorican!*" (p. 197, emphasis added).

In the past, I have hesitated to define myself as a Nuyorican (somehow it seemed to imply that I wasn't *really* Puerto Rican), but Antonia has nudged me to do so. I begin this essay by drawing on Antonia Pantoja's words, because they are a good reminder that identity is always multiple and shifting, never static nor easy to define. My own shifting and changing identities certainly confirm this truth.

I was born and raised in Brooklyn, New York, the child of working-class Puerto Ricans. My mother did not have the benefit of a high school education, and my father had even less, having had to leave school in fourth grade to help care for his family. I am the second daughter of parents who were in the group now called *pioneros*, those Puerto Ricans who came in the first wave of migration from the island in the early part of the twentieth century. My father's ship docked in New York City in 1929, and my mother's came several years later, in 1934. Papi quickly got a job at a Jewish deli on the Lower East Side, and Mami worked in an ice cream factory. They met shortly after she arrived, married in 1941, and started a family.

My sister and I began school as Spanish monolinguals at a time when English as a second language was little more than a hope and bilingual education little more than a dream. We learned English the hard way—without much help from our teachers. They seemed to be just as perplexed as we were. While our confusion was about the school, the language we heard, and the new cultures we confronted, theirs was undoubtedly the result of dramatic and bewildering changes in the nature of the student body they were teaching. In school, we shared our space with Puerto Ricans and other Caribbeans, African Americans, and assorted European immigrants including Hungarians, Italians, and Irish, among others. I was probably already a Nuyorican then, although I did not know it.

In some ways, I am quintessentially Nuyorican, with all the complexity that the term implies. Born and raised in New York City, I did not see the island of Puerto Rico until I was five years old. I have visited Puerto Rico only a dozen times or so in my life, never for longer than a month. I was not educated in Puerto Rican schools, and although my first language was Spanish, I learned English fairly quickly when I began school at the age of six. I speak English, Spanish, Spanglish, and all variations in between. Ask me to recite numbers and I invariably do so in English—the language in which I learned to add, subtract, multiply, and divide—and, although I have a master's degree in Spanish and Hispanic literature, which I earned at the University of Madrid while living in Spain, I still do most of my reading in English. I speak mainly Spanish at home (in large part because my husband is a native Spanish speaker), and Spanish words are the first to escape my lips when I see a baby or a pet, or when I stub my toe. On the other hand, I speak English almost exclusively with my sister and daughters. I am as likely to eat rice and beans as a hamburger, hummus, or a bagel with lox. I can feel at home in a bodega or in a faculty colloquium, and I can as easily speak with Puerto Rican families in a community meeting as give a major address before 1,500 at a professional conference.

I am, in a word, a Nuyorican, a label I have just recently begun to recognize in myself. Like other Nuyoricans, I am that combination of U.S.-based, U.S.- or Puerto Rican–born or U.S.- or Puerto Rican–reared bilingual, bicultural "border crosser" (Anzaldúa, 1987; Giroux, 1992) whose border crossings occur on a daily basis. One of the most difficult border crossings I have experienced in my life has been as a working-class interloper in higher education, a process helped along by my growing awareness of a Nuyorican identity.

Forging an Identity as a Scholar

I am a minority within a minority: statistics confirm that, despite modest gains in the recent past, faculty of color continue to be severely underrepresented in the nation's colleges and universities (American Council on Education, 2000). For example, Hispanics (the term commonly used) comprise just 2.6 percent of all full-time faculty positions in institutions of higher education. Even more telling, more Hispanics are found at the ranks of *lecturer* and *instructor,* the lowest ranks for full-time faculty, than at any other rank. As a Puerto Rican/Nuyorican woman who is also a full professor, with more than 30 years of experience in higher education, I am an anomaly. Given this context, what does it mean to me to be a member of the academy? In what follows, I pose two persistent questions that epitomize the challenges faced by me and other scholars of color, and I describe how I have attempted to understand and respond to these questions.

Why Am I Here?

Probably the most unrelenting question that people of color in higher education face is: Why are we here at all? The response depends on the context. For instance, when I was hired in the Department of Puerto Rican Studies at Brooklyn College as a 29-year-old, the answer was fairly transparent: I was there because students had taken over buildings and demonstrated in the streets, not just at Brooklyn College but around the country, to demand ethnic and women's studies programs. I was there, in no small part, because students who felt invisible in the curriculum, readings, and even physical presence on campus wanted to make sure that they counted.

My situation is certainly not unique. Because of our very identities, many people of color in higher education contend with questions that faculty of European descent never have to consider: Am I here because I am ____ [Puerto Rican, African American, Native American, and so on]? Am I an "affirmative action hire"? Would I have been given this position if I were not of this background? These questions are based on the assumption that the only reason we are hired is to fill a quota or respond to a community demand. The questions also imply that these are, in fact, bogus or negative reasons to hire faculty. Yet recent research at the K-12 level challenges these notions, making it clear that there are compelling reasons to diversify the faculty (Clewell, Puma, & McKay, 2001; Dee, 2000; Meier, Wrinkle, & Polinard, 1999). The same may be true in higher education.

I was hired to help develop a program, cosponsored by the School of Education, in bilingual education. At the time, there were very few U.S.-based Puerto Ricans (what I have called "homegrown" Puerto Ricans) who held doctoral degrees. As a result, many of the faculty members in Puerto Rican studies programs were imported from the island of Puerto Rico, where the vast majority would soon return. Few had a long-term vested interest in staying in the United States, and certainly none identified as *Nuyorican*, a term viewed with disdain by most. In fact, some viewed U.S. Puerto Ricans—who were quite different from them in that most were from poor and working-class backgrounds and had little formal education—with condescension. Most Nuyoricans, like me, who were hired in Puerto Rican studies programs had neither a doctoral degree nor the privilege of a middle-class upbringing. Although I had a few years of successful public school teaching under my belt, and I had taught in the city's first bilingual school, I did not have the remotest notion of what it meant to be a scholar and researcher.

Using Bordieu's (1977) concept of habitus, I had not been socialized with the dispositions, behaviors, or tastes that would have made the academy a "natural" place for me to be.

Ironically, the literature concerning the education of politically and socially marginalized students of color in the United States also describes quite adequately the situation in which many scholars of color in the academy find themselves. While investigating the experiences of immigrant students in a middle school in the Midwest, Gitlin, Buendía, Crosland, and Doumbia (2003) could just as easily have been referring to scholars of color in the academy when they documented how institutional practices in the school simultaneously welcomed and "unwelcomed" them. For instance, these researchers found that the school's history and its policies and events (discipline, busing, lunch period, school assemblies, and so on) all influenced how immigrant students were viewed and treated in the school. Taken together, these institutional structures positioned immigrant students as "different" and gave them limited access to the school's center. The researchers concluded, "In sum, discursive representations fueled by material conditions encouraged administrators, teachers, White students, and the White community to act in ways that pathologized immigrant students and maintained White privilege" (p. 116).

In higher education, instead of discipline and assembly programs, the "discursive representations fueled by material conditions" might include hiring and tenure policies, as well as school traditions and rituals. Moreover, although scholars of color may be welcomed into the academy with enthusiasm, our interests are frequently viewed as particular and political, whereas those of others are considered "normal" and "apolitical." Even some Whites within the academy who have welcomed our work have done so in the interest of supporting theirs. Thompson (2003), in a critique of critical White studies (CWS), has suggested that this scenario is not unusual: "Most white academics do not read widely across races and, even if we do, we tend to use the writings of scholars of color to bolster rather than interrogate our work" (p. 13). To truly welcome the work of scholars of color in the academy demands more, according to Thompson: "Taking the work of people of color seriously requires studying their projects, not just quoting the occasional point that coincides with what we were going to say anyway" (p. 13).

What Is My Role?

A series of other questions concern our role in the academy. Are we here because we are expected to work primarily with students who share our identities? Is our role to "enlighten" others? Are we expected to be a thorn in the side of other faculty members and the administration? In our teaching, re-search, and writing, are we expected always to focus on issues related to our own identities? In a word, what is our role in the academy? It is almost exclusively faculty of color who face these questions, and others like them, every day.

Kimberly Scott (2003), an African American teacher-educator and scholar, maintains that, given their limited numbers, professors of color in the academy confront "racially unique unanticipated problems." She goes on to say that for teacher-educators specifically the burden is particularly acute because "there is often a commonly held belief in American schools of education that these individuals will single-handedly heighten students' awareness of diversity issues and prepare their students for the increasingly multicultural world" (p. 212). Because of this, Black and other professors of color are often pigeonholed into teaching only courses that focus on diversity, and doing research entirely on topics related to their own identities. The result, according to Scott, is that faculty of color are prevented from "fully developing a self outside of the 'Black Box'" (p. 218). At the same time, she suggests that many White preservice teachers (and probably other students not majoring in education as well) often question the very credentials of faculty of color. As a result, she states, "The Black professor remains marginalized and excluded in the very context that promises academic freedom" (p. 218). The irony of this conundrum is felt by many of us.

In addition, scholars of color are traditionally expected to present the "minority viewpoint" not only in their teaching and research, but also in committee work within the university. And because there are so few scholars of color in most institutions of higher education, they are overcommitted on service-related projects (committees, commissions, advisory groups, and so on) in their departments, in their universities, and in the profession in general. Their research and scholarly work may suffer as a result, confirming in the minds of some of their university colleagues and administrators that they were not qualified as academics in the first place. It is a vicious cycle.

Lessons Learned

I have learned a great deal over the past 30 years as a Nuyorican in the academy. From feeling like an interloper to defining myself as a scholar and academic, I have traveled a long road. I have tried to share these insights with others, particularly my doctoral students of color. Many of them, especially the woman, often feel like frauds (McIntosh, 1985), as if everybody else knows the "dirty little secret": that they do not really belong there. I once felt the same way. Now I know not only that there is a place for me in the academy, but that it is imperative that I be there. I focus next on three major lessons I have learned that may help others in their own process.

Realize That We Bring Unique Gifts to the Academy

In my first few years in higher education, I often sensed that people felt they were doing me a favor by allowing me to be there at all. Although I felt incredibly privileged and fortunate to be a member of the academy, I also felt terribly ill at ease there. I could not easily use sentences in which I identified myself as a "scholar" or a "researcher." For many years, these identities felt out of my reach, unnatural. It took me a long time to figure out that my presence, as well as the presence of other women of color, is an asset to the academy. Women scholars of color bring unique gifts to our jobs.

I often see my doctoral students go through the same struggle as I did, usually in their first year or two of doctoral studies. I try to help them resolve this dilemma *before* they become faculty members, rather than after, as I did. I did not have the privilege of having another woman of color help me negotiate my way in academia. This is one of the unique gifts that women scholars of color bring to higher education: we are able to mentor an entire new generation of faculty who might otherwise go through unnecessary insecurities and self-doubt.

This issue of mentoring is especially pertinent to people of color in the academy because we are often touted simply as "role models" for students of our own backgrounds. Banks (1995) addressed this problem head-on in an essay in which she compared the term *role model* with *mentor*. She argued that *role model* is "soft," unlike the word *mentor*. That is, there is an intellectual side to *mentor* that is missing in the largely ceremonial and superficial *role model*. As women of color in the academy, then, it is our responsibility not just to *inspire* (as if somehow our mere presence would be enough to move our students along), but to *inform, push, critique,* and *demand* from our students.

I wish to make it clear, however, that we are not in higher education just to benefit students who look like us. This would simply reinforce the tendency in colleges and universities to ghettoize the few faculty and students of color into particular departments. *All* students of *all* backgrounds are the responsibility of *all* faculty members. This means that faculty of color also benefit White students, a point made powerfully by Irvine (2003) in her discussion of the advantages of having a diverse teacher pool.

As a young teacher, I often heard the phrase "culturally deprived" applied to the Puerto Rican and African American children I taught in elementary and middle school. I was painfully aware that this term had also no doubt been applied to me and others like me when we were children. Speaking a language other than English as our native language, becoming bilingual, participating in cultural practices different from the mainstream—all of these were viewed as handicaps, rather than as resources. But as scholars of color enter the profession in increasing numbers, this is changing. It is more and more apparent that scholars of color bring what Trueba (2003) calls "a new cultural capital" to our work. Writing specifically about Latinos/Latinas in higher education, Trueba describes the new cultural capital in this way: "The mastery of different languages, the ability to cross racial and ethnic boundaries, and a general resilience associated with the ability to endure hardships and overcome obstacles will clearly be recognized as a new cultural capital, not a handicap" (p. 24).

Women of color bring new insights and contributions to our fields; we help generate new knowledge because of our very identities, a central tenet undergirding Critical Race Theory (CRT) (Delgado & Stefancic, 2001). Theresa Jenoure (1999), for example, an African American woman, a scholar, and a performance artist, developed a distinctive theory of teaching based on the principles of jazz. This kind of theorizing is most apt to happen when we open heretofore-restricted access to higher education to traditionally underrepresented groups. In my own field of education, scholars such as bell hooks, Geneva Gay, Karen Swisher, Isaura Santiago, Jacqueline Jordan Irvine, Michele Foster, Kris Gutiérrez, and many, many others have helped shape a field, a field that without their contributions would be much poorer for the loss. It is time that we all recognize these gifts.

Develop All Your Identities

I am fortunate to have begun my life in academia within a Puerto Rican studies department. Being a faculty member in that particular department made it impossible for me to separate my personal from my professional identities. As a middle school and elementary school teacher before then, I had assumed that *who I was* and *what I did* were supposed to remain separate. This is the message that many new teachers get when they begin to teach. But both ethnic and women's studies departments in higher education have challenged this dichotomy. In contrast to most other disciplines in the academy, these departments have insisted that community issues be linked with scholarly activity. My department, for instance, sponsored a bilingual preschool in the community. We also held a yearly health fair for women with the Women's Center, and we supported community struggles with both our influence and our presence.

Having this experience helped me negotiate and shape my next position in academia several years later. Although I was an assistant professor in the School of Education, I knew I could never again leave behind any of my identities (including my ethnic, cultural, and gendered subjectivities), as I had thought I had to when I was a teacher. What I mean by this is that I did not shy away from discussions in class that focused, for example, on the issues I cared about and had experienced, as long as they were relevant to the theoretical issues addressed in the course. I also felt comfortable in, and committed to, researching those issues I was most passionate about, specifically the education of Latino and other students of color, and poor students in general, in U.S. schools. In my committee work, I realized that I brought a lens that might otherwise be missing in higher education, and I made it my business to advocate for those policies and practices that would support access for students of color at the university.

Telling our "counterstories" (Delgado & Stefancic, 2001) in the academy, based on another central tenet of CRT, is another valuable gift that we bring to the academy. Were it not for our presence, these counterstories, and the experiences upon which they are based, might never be known. At the same time, I have also learned that experience *alone* is not sufficient to create a rigorous climate for learning. I have had colleagues whose classes consisted of little more than recounting their own experiences. As worthy as these might be, they do not by themselves translate into intellectual activity. Developing our identities fully means focusing not simply on our gendered, cultural, and racial identities, but also on our identities as scholars and researchers. This means being free to develop research interests that build on those identities, as well as on others. Otherwise, we are left in the "Black Box" that Scott (2003) warned against.

In line with this, it is important to understand that we all have multiple and shifting identities that take us very far from the static boundaries we understood to be true just a generation ago. Trueba (2003) has defined multiple identities as a new asset that is "crucial for success in a modern diversified society" (p. 24). Using the evolving field of CWS, McCarthy (2003) suggests that in spite of the new insights this field is contributing to our understanding of race and racism, too many of the scholars who focus on the field of CWS "seem to dwell in the Civil Rights era and in a pre-9/11 world in which centers and margins were more clearly demarcated, the forces of good and evil were very clearly marked, and the only available optics on race were within the color spectrum of black and white" (p. 133). In this way, McCarthy (2003) focuses our attention on the new landscape of *multiple identities,* reminding us that faculty of color (and, indeed, all faculty) need to break out of the rigid boundaries that have for too long characterized the issue of difference in U.S. society.

Take Advantage of Your Position in the Academy

I have come to the conclusion that being a member of an elite class of people, such as those in the academy, is of no use unless it can benefit others besides myself. Certainly the advantages of my position are many, and I have received a great deal of affirmation and public support for the work I do. These things are, of course, personally very satisfying. But once the commotion dies down, I always return to Paulo Freire's quintessential question: "In whose benefit am I doing this?" Personal benefit is not enough, it seems to me. This is why I made the decision a long time ago, even before entering academia, that whatever I could accomplish would be in the name of a greater good. As a result, I have spent my professional and personal life attempting to make positive change in whatever context I find myself. For most of my life, this has meant focusing my efforts in higher education.

As faculty members, we are incredibly privileged, and it makes sense to use that privilege for the greater good. Use your influence in admissions, in curriculum decisions, in ordering texts, and in tenure and promotion decisions. Before doing research, think about the impact of your words and your work on your field. Make strategic decisions about where to give your time, energy, and commitment. It is true that other faculty may not need to do these things (although certainly some do), but being a woman of color in the academy carries with it a great responsibility.

Although, like many others, I complain about the workload, the many demands, the subtle and not-so-subtle racism and elitism, and other problems in academia, I also realize every day that I am in a very fortunate situation, a situation that brings with it concurrent obligations to a larger community. I teach, which is something I love to do, and in the process I learn every day. I have the time to read and reflect, to play with fantastic ideas, to theorize and investigate. I have the opportunity to write my ideas down, and to have people actually pay attention to them. I meet interesting students, faculty, and staff, as well as scholars from around the world. I travel a good deal, getting to know places that would have been unimaginable to me when I was a child. I often smile when I think what my father would say if he heard all the complaining that goes on among faculty about their lot in life. His life in the little bodega he bought, when the Jewish deli on Delancey Street where he had worked for many years closed, was no picnic. It was a blur of 16-hour workdays seven days a week (he gave himself the luxury of taking off every other Sunday) on his feet all the time, just to make ends meet and try to give his family a modicum of comfort. As faculty in the academy, we have so much more.

Conclusion

Little did I know when I nervously accepted that first position in higher education so many years ago that it would become my life's work and, even more important, that it would shape who I was to become. Developing identities is never easy, but when those identities seem at such tremendous odds—as in the case with being an intellectual *and* a working-class Nuyorican woman—the process becomes even thornier. The road is often bumpy, and there are numerous obstacles in the way. For women scholars of color, understanding this fact is the first step on a long journey toward both self-fulfillment and community responsibility.

I am now near the end of my time in the academy, although certainly not in the profession. I have never really thought of myself as a trailblazer, but, I suppose, looking back, that I have been among a small group of Nuyorican women scholars who were the first in our departments and even in our institutions. I hope that my experiences and words will be useful to those who follow me. May it be a glorious journey for you as well.

References

American Council on Education. (2000). Faculty of color continue to be underrepresented on the nation's college campuses. *Facts in Brief, 49*(3). Washington, DC: Author.

Anzaldúa, G. (1987). *Borderlands/La frontera: The new mestiza*. San Francisco: Aunt Lute Books.

Banks, T. L. (1995). Two life stories: Reflections of one Black woman law professor. In K. Crenshaw (Ed.), *Critical race theory: The key writings that formed the movement* (pp. 329–336). New York: The New Press.

Bourdieu, P. (1977). *Outline of a theory of practice*. Cambridge: University Press.

Clewell, B. C., Puma, M., & McKay, S. A. (2001). *Does it matter if my teacher looks like me? The impact of teacher race and ethnicity on student academic achievement*. New York: Ford Foundation.

Dee, T. S. (2000). *Teachers, race, and student achievement in a randomized experiment.* Cambridge, MA: National Bureau of Economic Research.

Delgado, R. D., & Stefancic, J. (2001). *Critical race theory: An introduction.* New York: New York University Press.

Giroux, H. (1992). *Border crossings: Cultural workers and the politics of education.* New York: Routledge.

Gitlin, A., Buendía, E., Crosland, K., & Doumbia, F. (2003). The production of margin and center: Welcoming-unwelcoming of immigrant students. *American Educational Research Journal, 40*(1), 91–122.

Irvine, J. J. (2003). *Educating teachers for diversity: Seeing with a cultural eye.* New York: Teachers College Press.

Jenoure, T. (1999). *Navigators: African American musicians, dancers, and visual artists in academe.* Albany: State of New York University Press.

McCarthy, C. (2003). Contradictions of power and identity: Whiteness studies and the call of teacher education. *International Journal of Qualitative Studies in Education, 16*(1), 127–133.

McIntosh, P. (1985). *Feeling like a fraud.* Wellesley, MA: Stone Center for Developmental Services and Studies.

Meier, K. J., Wrinkle, R. D., & Polinard, J. L. (1999). Representative bureaucracy and distributional equity: Addressing the hard question. *Journal of Politics, 61,* 1025–1039.

Pantoja, A. (2002). *Memoir of a visionary: Antonia Pantoja.* Houston: Arte Público Press.

Scott, K. A. (2003). My students think I'm Indian: The presentation of an African-American self to pre-service teachers. *Race Ethnicity and Education, 6*(3), 211–226.

Thompson, A. (2003). Tiffany, friend of people of color: White investments in anti-racism. *International Journal of Qualitative Studies in Education, 16*(1), 7–29.

Trueba, H. T. (2002). Multiple ethnic, racial, and cultural identities in action: From marginality to a new cultural capital in modern society. *Journal of Latinos and Education, 1*(1), 7–28.